Missing from the House

Praise for the Book

'This book will surprise you because in the last seven decades, so many Muslim women have enriched our legislative history but have remained unsung heroines of our plural democracy. For the first time, their stories have been documented in this unputdownable book. While narrating stories of Indian Muslim women MPs in Lok Sabha, this book is breaking stereotypes about Muslim women, too. It is an important milestone because it is an authentic narrative of socio-cultural and socio-political struggles of those who never gave up under the pressures they faced. This book makes us realise how little we know about the lives and times of Indian Muslim women in politics, in Parliament and in our recent history.' – **Sheela Bhatt**

'I saw an amazing statistic which said that since the first General Elections of 1951–52, out of the 690 women MPs we have had till 2024, only 18 have been Muslim women! Which means that the world Rasheed Kidwai and Ambar Ghosh set out to document is most certainly an invisible one. The story of Muslim women's electoral success is a tale of grit, determination and celebration under most difficult conditions, discrimination and odds. As we read about Maimoona Sultan, Zohraben, Mofida Ahmed and others, we discover a story that needed to be told.' – **Sunetra Choudhury**

'This book is an important documentation about representation by women, especially from the Muslim community, in the political sphere. It asks important questions not just about who these women were, what factors aided or hindered them in their careers but also what this representation meant in terms of impact on policy and society.' – **Nistula Hebbar**

'This is a very original, even unique, book as nobody ha[s] analysed the Muslim women who became MP[s] in the Lok Sabha before. They are very few, but their bios are very revealing of the marginalization of their gender and their religious community in post-Independence India. This book [also] revisits interesting facets of dynastic politics, and helps to understand the qualities of the women who were elected on their own merits.' – **Christophe Jaffrelot**

'This is an important book to understand the invisibility of Muslim women from national conversations. Their numbers in Indian Parliament have always been abysmally low. Four out of 18 Lok Sabhas till 2025 had no Muslim women MPs. It shows there are still layers and layers of seen and unseen barriers on their way to public life. As triple talaq, polygamy and hijab become hot-button issues in India, where are the Muslim women representatives? They should be saying: "Nothing about us without us".' – **Rama Lakshmi**

'The book could not have come at a more opportune time, when the long-awaited Women's Reservation Bill has become an act of Parliament but still hangs in limbo because nobody knows when it will be implemented. The most shocking revelations are since Independence, only 18 Muslim women have made it to Parliament and the southern states, that pride themselves on upholding India's plurality and diversity, have not sent a single Muslim woman to the August House. Those that were elected were mainly legatees of political families and not necessarily women who fought societal prejudices entrenched in the structures for centuries. The book documents the life and times of Muslim MPs, some of whom faded away into oblivion. [It is] an extremely well-researched work that deserves a place in political history because it delves into a subject that escaped attention.' – **Radhika Ramaseshan**

'This book by Rasheed Kidwai and Ambar Kumar Ghosh is a very important and much-needed documentation of the role of Muslim women in our parliamentary system. Women in general and Muslim women in particular, being the minority amongst the minorities, have remained at the periphery of the political landscape. The women MPs have been very few and far in the decades after Independence. This book, by way of interesting stories, brings out the personal struggles and success[es] of those women who reached there and left a mark.' – **Naghma Sahar**

'Becoming a woman MP is not easy, but if the woman is a Muslim, the bar of cultural-social prejudice and political-economic marginalization is raised that much higher. With engaging anecdotes backed by sharp analysis, authors Rasheed Kidwai and Ambar Kumar Ghosh tell the stories of the pioneering women who made it. Coming on the eve of the Women Reservations Bill, this book will encourage many more to take the dare.' – **Priya Sahgal**

Missing from the House

Muslim Women in the Lok Sabha

Rasheed Kidwai
and
Ambar Kumar Ghosh

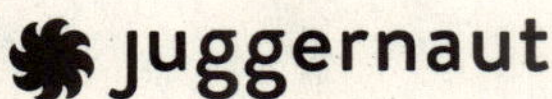

JUGGERNAUT BOOKS
C-I-128, First Floor, Sangam Vihar, Near Holi Chowk,
New Delhi 110080, India

First published by Juggernaut Books 2025

10 9 8 7 6 5 4 3 2 1

P-ISBN: 9789353455842
E-ISBN: 9789353458355

Typeset in Adobe Caslon Pro by R. Ajith Kumar, Noida

Printed at Thomson Press India Ltd

Rasheed Kidwai wishes to dedicate this book in loving memory of Khala Ammi (Begum Hamida Habibullah), Phuphi Ammi (Abida Khatoon), Ammi Jaan (Raffat un Nisa), Phuphi Jaan (Humaira Khatoon), Khala Jaan (Zohaira Khatoon) and Zahida Khatoon (Ammi).

Ambar Kumar Ghosh wishes to dedicate this book to all those who possess the grit for ensuring human empowerment amidst challenges.

Contents

Foreword by Dr Shashi Tharoor ix

Authors' Note xxi

Introduction xxix

1. Setting the Context 1
2. Mofida Ahmed: The Forgotten Begum of Assam 10
3. Zohraben Akbarbhai Chavda: Service Before Self 21
4. Maimoona Sultan: The Life and Times of a Congress Insider 31
5. Begum Akbar Jehan Abdullah: Kashmir's 'Madr-e-Meharban' 43
6. Rashida Haque Choudhury: From Political Prominence to Oblivion 57
7. Mohsina Kidwai: A Life Lived with Dignity 65
8. Abida Ahmed: First Lady as Politician and Parliamentarian 79
9. Noor Bano: Tryst with a Destiny in Politics 89
10. Rubab Sayda: The Revered Daughter-in-Law of Bahraich 98

11. Mehbooba Mufti: Accidental Politician, Able Leader 105

12. Tabassum Hasan: Kairana's Daughter-in-Law, Defender of Her Family Legacy 118

13. Mausam Benazir Noor: Illustrious Political Legacy, Promising Political Future 128

14. Kaisar Jahan: A Political Life Shaped by Circumstances 138

15. Mamtaz Sanghamita: The Good Doctor 146

16. Sajda Ahmed: Navigating Personal Tragedy and Political Trepidation 158

17. Ranee Narah: Bat, Ball and Politics 167

18. Nusrat Jahan Ruhi: Being Her Own Woman 177

19. Iqra Hasan: A Silver Lining for Progressive Politics 190

Epilogue 200

Notes 226

Bibliography 248

Acknowledgements 267

A Note on the Authors 269

Foreword

I

Nearly seventy-eight years have passed since that portentous stroke of midnight on 15 August 1947, when Pandit Jawaharlal Nehru proclaimed a 'tryst with destiny' and India awakened to 'life and freedom.' This was a moment, our first Prime Minister continued, 'which comes but rarely in history, when we step out from the old to the new, when an age ends, and when the soul of a nation, long suppressed, finds utterance.' Yet even after almost eight decades, a shameful reality, which should deflate our self-congratulatory fervour over our democratic track record, still haunts us. Not everyone has found 'utterance' in the world's largest democracy, many of whose towering leaders eulogize it as the 'Mother of Democracy.'

This self-serving description is enabled, in part, by a too-pliant news media, an ineffectual civil society and a menaced academic class, so that no one dares point out the irony inherent in the claim. Although we depict India as a doting mother nurturing and nourishing a clamorous, combative and chaotic republic, corrupt and inefficient, perhaps, but nonetheless flourishing, the truth is that throughout our democratic history, we have consistently failed our women citizens: failed to afford them, in the thoroughfares of our country, a life of dignity and decency. For constantly stalking them is the threat of sexual and gender-based violence, with multiple instances of bone-chilling rapes, having occurred in different parts of India, making headlines every day. And failed to guarantee them, in our corridors of power and in 'the promising realm of democratic politics,' adequate representation. On the second count, however, some of our women citizens have been worse off than others, largely due to our indifference. For we have never paused to ask ourselves why, since the first General Elections of 1951–1952, only *eighteen* Muslim women (otherwise constituting 7.1 percent of the world's most populous nation!) have made it to the Lok Sabha, to that 'embodiment of the freedom and sovereignty of the people of India.' The book you are holding in your hands, a prodigious handiwork of the political analysts and scholars of modern Indian history, Rasheed Kidwai and Ambar Kumar Ghosh, is a searing reminder of this fact, which should shame and shock us in equal measure. At the same time, it is a call to action, beckoning us to do better, especially as we gear up to implement the Women's Reservation Act, 2023.

II

Conscious of the pitiable state of women in Indian society, the foremost architects of modern India made the socio-economic emancipation of women a sturdy and salient plank of the freedom struggle and nation-building endeavour. Banished to the margins of societal consciousness and condemned to the household for rearing children, performing chores and tending to male family members, all without the slightest gratitude in an odiously patriarchal world, women in India bore horrific indignities, regardless of the socio-religious strata to which they belonged. The wheels of history are difficult to turn, especially when they are sunk into a morass of injustice and iniquity. While such women-sovereigns as Razia Sultan, Noor Jahan, Rani Lakshmibai and the Begums of Bhopal blazed a trail down the tracks of Indian history, overcoming terrific odds in the process, they were few and far between, and religious dogma continued sanctioning and sanctifying the suffering of women. Only in the nineteenth century did a faint dawn break, when such visionaries as (to name but a few) Ishwar Chandra Vidyasagar and Raja Ram Mohan Roy in Bengal, and Jyotiba and Savitribai Phule in Maharashtra, began to rail against the horrors to which a woman was subjected throughout her life, whether as a young girl being denied access to education, or as a hapless widow being forced to leap into the pyre of her deceased husband (or, at any rate, being compelled to swathe herself in mourning white, having been expelled from the mainstream of life, not only social but familial too).

The flame of this nineteenth-century crusade for social justice passed into the hands of the luminaries who bestrode India's political firmament in the twentieth. Chief among them, of course, were Dr B.R. Ambedkar and Jawaharlal

Nehru. For Ambedkar, the pursuit of equal rights for women was indispensable to his social mission. He realized that the subjugation of women, particularly Dalit women, was central to the logic of the caste system, which sought control over a woman's body, sexuality and agency to perpetuate the sickening diktats of caste purity, social hierarchy and untouchability. In his writings, he flagged the *Manusmriti* as a stricture that not only legitimized caste oppression and untouchability but also institutionalized the degradation of women, casting them away from social relevance. It was in vehement rejection of this logic that on 25 December 1927, Ambedkar tore the *Manusmriti* page by page and consigned it to the flames. In his view, which he made clear across his immense literary corpus, the subjugation of women was a marker of a society that had lost its moral compass. Therefore, he demanded that the path to liberation, not only from British rule but also from the depredations of religious dogma and social conservatism, be paved with equal rights for everyone, especially women, so that liberty, equality and fraternity may bloom. These, in his view, were the three pillars of modernity and democracy, and only if they held (manifesting in the form of all Indians according to equal respect to one another, regardless of caste, creed or sex) would our experiment with republicanism succeed. Otherwise, he cautioned, democracy would remain merely 'a top-dressing on an … essentially undemocratic soil.'

Nehru concurred and slashed through the thicket of India's socio-religious iniquities with his favoured hatchet of secularism. For Mahatma Gandhi's anointed heir, secularism was not limited to divorcing the political from the religious and creating in a multi-religious society, a neutral, non-religious (not to say irreligious) state. It also extended to wielding political power and mustering political will to rid religion, deeply enmeshed with one's social, religious and economic lives, of its most damning blots, which the political scientist Rajeev Bhargava calls 'intra-religious domination,' and which relegated women and the so-called lower and untouchable castes to a lifetime of indignities. Nehru would bring to bear this conception of secularism on many of his policies after Independence, in concord with Ambedkar as they toiled to pilot the Hindu Code Bill through the provisional Parliament before the first General Election, but as Kidwai and Ghosh argue in the pages that follow, these makers of modern India did not, or could not, go far enough. This, then, is our duty, both as citizens *and* human beings, to discharge.

About the Nehruvian perspective on secularism Bhargava writes:

> Nehru says that 'the word secular conveys something much more to him, although that might not be its dictionary meaning—the idea of social and political equality.' A state that encourages or tolerates such deeply inegalitarian and casteist practices, is not a secular state

This 'social and political equality' has especially eluded Muslim women in post-Independence India. '[T]he first problem that presents itself,' said Nehru in a lecture in 1934, almost as an introduction to this book, 'is how to free India and remove the many burdens of the Indian masses. But the women of India have an additional task that is [to] free themselves from the tyranny of man-made customs and laws.' And then, in a frisson of scorching realism, which should compel us to hang our heads in shame, he added that the women of India will have to carry on this 'struggle by themselves for man is not likely to help them.' After all, not only had he treated 'the woman as a chattel and a plaything to be exploited for his own advantage and amusement,' he had arrested her ability 'to grow and develop her capacities to her fullest ...'

'India's founders,' writes the constitutional scholar and political scientist Madhav Khosla in *India's Founding Moment: The Constitution of a Most Surprising Democracy*, his seminal work on the origins of the Indian Constitution, 'envisioned a country where many religions could thrive, and where one's identity as a political agent was not tied to one's religious affiliation.' But while the drafters of the Constitution rejected the idea of separate electorates, weighted representation and reservations on the basis of religion, seeking to disentangle the newly-minted citizens of India from pre-existing loyalties of religious affiliation, they realized that representation in the political arena was imperative, particularly for the adherents of minority faiths. In my view, therefore, the conduit for community interests was to be the individual, who, by exercising her agency and autonomy in the political fray (either by voting on the principle of 'one person, one vote, one value,' or by contesting elections on a level-playing field), would become a political agent whose civic identity was self-created, and thereby also champion issues of importance to her community. Thus, notes Khosla, '[T]he new logic for political mediation involved a transition from the balancing of communities to the affirmation of the individual. This shift created a political subject whose interests and identity would be forged in the battlefield of politics.' It is from this 'battlefield of politics' that Muslim women have been woefully absent for the past eight decades. While the makers of modern India laboured to create a democratic arena in which individual agency would be the wellspring of political identity and group advocacy, this promise has not translated into equal participation for, and representation of, some of our most vulnerable citizens, foremost among them Muslim women. This also means that causes most crucial to their welfare, such as, among other things, the right to maintenance in the event of divorce (as in the case of Shah Bano), the cruel invocation of triple *talaq* (as in the case of Shayara Bano), and the humiliation and exclusion faced by many Muslim women due to the sanction of polygamy among Muslim men, have had to be raised and fought in law courts and other civil society fora, rather than in the Parliament of India, where the dearth of Muslim women Members of Parliament has, for the most part, precluded such discussions, especially from their point(s) of view.

Kidwai and Ghosh concede precisely this when they write that '[I]n a peculiar contradiction, or rather, a challenge for India's parliamentary politics, although democracy's equitable political landscape promises representation and empowerment of the weak, marginalized and unheard, Muslim women remained at the remote periphery of India's representative politics.' It is time we changed that, and this book is an excellent starting point.

III

Even in a Constituent Assembly of 299 members, a figure arrived at after the proponents of Pakistan had gone their own way, there were just fifteen women members, only one of whom was Muslim: Begum Qudsia Aijaz Rasool, who emerged in the Assembly as an unflagging advocate of the all-inclusive civic nationalism that had fuelled our freedom struggle and sustained it when it split on the question of whether religion should be the determinant of citizenship and nationhood, an idea the architects of modern India vehemently rejected. In the Assembly, Begum Rasool fulminated against the demand for communal representation in legislatures, whether in the form of separate electorates or reservations on the basis of religion. Nominated to the Rajya Sabha a few years thereafter, she tore into the diktats of the clergy, toiling to deliver Muslim women not as privileged as herself from the suffocating grasp of intra-religious domination, all in the face of formidable odds. 'There was,' wrote she in her autobiography, *From Purdah to Parliament*,' much propaganda against me, specially a 'fatwa' by the *ulemas* that it was un-Islamic to vote for a non-purdah Muslim woman.'

It was in recognition of the transformative role these fifteen women of steel and sagacity had played in the Constituent Assembly, helping to afford India a truly emancipatory and egalitarian Constitution that before the first General Elections, on 4 January 1950, Prime Minister Jawaharlal Nehru wrote to his Chief Ministers, noting that:

Even in the Constituent Assembly the women members were very few. Of these some dropped out for various reasons and their places were filled by men. I think it is important that we should keep up and add to the number of women in Parliament. From every point of view this is desirable. I have no doubt that a sufficient number of women, at least as competent and suitable as men, are available.

To realize this aspiration, the Prime Minister urged the Chief Ministers to permit women members of Provincial Assemblies to resign, if they so choose, 'in order to stand for Parliament.' Needless to say, this vision of women MPs participating in the parliamentary process and leading the charge in drafting laws that better the lot of our people, enhance and expand their fundamental rights, and bolster our constitutional promise of liberty, equality, and fraternity has remained largely elusive. The worst symptom of this malaise has been the deplorable absence of Muslim women from our Parliament. All the more depressing is the revelation, made by Kidwai and Ghosh, that '[O]ut of the 18 Lok Sabhas constituted till 2025, five times the Lok Sabha did not have a single Muslim woman member. Equally shocking is the fact that the number of Muslim women elected to Parliament in one tenure never crossed a mark of four in the 543-seat lower house of parliament.' For far too long we have paid lip service in our public and political discourse to the cause of *nari shakti*, women empowerment, harping *ad nauseum* from our highest pulpits on the vitalness of women in positions of power and prestige. It is time we translated this rhetoric into reality, realizing once and for all, no matter how long and hard we may have to work for it, the vision of our Founding Fathers and Mothers. They gave us a Constitution that promised not just recognition but representation, and, hammering away at centuries' worth of savage discrimination, moulded a new identity for all Indians. We were now free and equal citizens of the world's largest and most diverse democracy; as such, we could, regardless of caste, creed, or sex, invent ourselves as we saw fit, forging our destinies with our own toil and sweat. That is the India to which we must recommit ourselves, and the pages that follow illumine our path to it.

What follows are the painstakingly researched and reconstructed, and wonderfully narrated, in prose at once powerful and poignant, lives of the eighteen Muslim women who reached the Lok Sabha. Their paths to becoming MPs were littered with hurdles, each more insurmountable than the one before, but they persevered and pressed on and ultimately, triumphed. Not once did their faith in the foundational promise of India waver, not once did they content themselves with enjoying the loaves and fishes of parliamentary power. Unrelenting always, they soldiered on to better the lives of their fellow citizens and to ensure that, unlike them, other

Muslim women would not have to traverse such tortuous roads to the national legislature. 'Not one out of the 18,' Kidwai and Ghosh, their redoubtable chroniclers, tell us, 'had any major allegations of corruption, criminal charges, or hate speech.' They were, as such, model parliamentarians and set an example that many MPs today, some of whom have spewed extremely hateful and exclusionary venom in the two hallowed Houses, would do well to follow. 'An examination,' write the authors, 'of their [these eighteen MPs'] parliamentary conduct reveals the proactive role that they tried to play as vocal and accountable parliamentarians during their stints in Parliament, however short their tenures might have been. Their active participation in Lok Sabha debates, their questions on a range of diverse policy issues, their deep commitment to secure developmental work for their respective parliamentary constituencies, and their contribution as members in different parliamentary committees battling the conservative confines of their home, community and society makes them extremely inspiring public representatives for future generations.'

All in all, Rasheed Kidwai and Ambar Kumar Ghosh's *Missing from the House: Muslim Women in India's Parliament* is not merely a homage to eighteen unsung trailblazers, but a stirring reminder of what the Parliament of India was always meant to be: a space for earnest service, moral conviction and clarity, and the socio-economic empowerment of the excluded, achieved through the instruments and institutions of democratic politics. In dredging up these lives, vividly and vibrantly, from the forgotten depths of our political past, these scholars do more than chronicle: they challenge. They implore us to confront the silences we have allowed to persist, the apathy we have let ourselves be steeped in for the better part of the last eight decades, the distortions we have come to accept, and the futures we have failed to imagine (and, therefore, secure). This book is timely and urgent, especially because it galvanizes us to ensure, as our Founding Fathers and Mothers wanted us to, that the arc of Indian democracy bends not just towards recognition in principle, but towards representation in practice. An exemplary work of scholarship and political imagination, *Missing from the House: Muslim Women in India's Parliament* forces us to reckon with the cost of our collective indifference and, in doing so, rekindles the hope that our parliamentary democracy can yet live up to its most radical promise: an emancipatory and equal voice, suffused with the cadences of peace, pluralism, and progress, for all our citizens, particularly those who have long languished on the margins of our national consciousness.

Dr Shashi Tharoor

Authors' Note

Refuting prejudiced perceptions of society is as herculean a task as fighting societal prejudices. Muslim women in India have been victims of societal prejudice, cultural marginalization and political-economic alienation. Injustices and discrimination against them have been multi-layered. Muslim women in India have often been projected as exotic, sexual, or adhering to the image of being suppressed by and subordinate to men, of being victims silenced by veils and denied the expression of their feelings and emotions.[1] These stereotypes, ranging from nineteenth-century French Orientalist paintings to Bollywood, books and web series projections, fail to capture the existence of a Muslim woman's independent self. Empirical studies have also revealed that Muslim women in India have remained relatively more socio-economically backward than women of other minority communities, and their participation, for instance, in household economic decision-making is fairly low.[2]

It is no surprise, therefore, that in the political arena, Muslim women have remained far more invisible, historically, than women from other communities. Historians have made sketchy and patchy references to Qudsia Begum,

Sikandar Begum, Shah Jahan Begum and Sultan Jahan Begum, the four illustrious Begums who ruled Bhopal for over a century, and freedom fighters like Abdi Bano Begum aka Bi Amma (mother of the Ali brothers), Bibi Amtus Salam, Begum Anis Kidwai, Begum Nishatunnisa Mohani Baji, Jamalunnisa, Hajara Beebi Ismail, Kulsum Sayani, Syed Fakrul Hajiya Hassan and Begum Qudsia Aijaz Rasool. Also, other illustrious figures like Raiza Sultan, Noor Jahan and Begum Hazrat Mahal also find mention in history. Begum Rasool was incidentally the lone Muslim woman in the Constituent Assembly that framed the Indian Constitution. History bears testimony to the fact that marginalization of Muslim women in leadership and political representation functions is deep-rooted, and predicated upon the patriarchal prejudices prevalent in Indian society and community-driven conservative predilections within the Muslim community.

In the post-Independence period and the promising realm of democratic politics, greater representation of Muslim women in politics continued to be elusive. The Parliament of India is the highest legislative body, and an embodiment of the freedom and sovereignty of the people of India. It occupies a pre-eminent and pivotal position in India's democratic polity. However, only eighteen Muslim women have made it to the Lok Sabha since the first parliamentary polls in 1951–52. It is a shockingly abysmal figure, considering Muslim women are about 7.1 per cent of India's 146 crore population. Out of the 18 Lok Sabhas constituted till 2025, five times the Lok Sabha did not have a single Muslim woman member. Equally shocking is the fact that the number of Muslim women elected to Parliament in one tenure never crossed the mark of four in the 543-seat lower house of Parliament. In a peculiar contradiction, or rather, a challenge to India's parliamentary politics, although democracy's equitable political landscape promises representation and empowerment of the weak, marginalized and unheard, Muslim women remained at the remote periphery of India's representative politics.

This makes *Missing from the House: Muslim Women in India's Parliament* an extremely crucial starting point to begin telling the world about the Muslim women who braved the otherwise inconducive political citadel of electoral politics to make their way through near unsurmountable challenges and succeed and thrive in India's complex political space. However, while documenting the stories of those who could actually make it to the Lok Sabha as Members of Parliament (MPs), we also got a close view of how high the barriers have been for them.

As readers would notice, the majority of elected Muslim women MPs came from dynastic backgrounds. Dynasty has, in fact, been closely linked to women's representation in the Indian Parliament. This made us wonder if, in the absence of a dynastic culture in Indian electoral politics, the representation of women in general and Muslim women in particular might have been more negligible. Though dynastic politics poses its own set of challenges to democratic accountability and a level playing field, political dynasties have played an important role in giving a rare window to women family members to participate in electoral politics.

Two aspects in this regard have been vital revelations. First, though family connections propelled many Muslim women to participate in electoral politics as MPs in the Lok Sabha, them claiming their political identity has rarely been out of their own independent choice. Rather, their presence in electoral politics has been much more about filial responsibility and out of a sense of duty towards their male family members, stepping up to fill their shoes as daughters, wives, daughters-in-law, nieces, and so on. Hence, their political agency, though exercised as leaders, remained trapped in narratives of responsibility towards family rather than their own political calling. Second, the conventional and dominant presumption about dynastic leaders remains that they get a fairly easy path to political authority, electoral success and social legitimacy. A peek into the political lives of the personalities in our book makes the intriguing revelation that, despite family privilege, Muslim women in politics had to confront unenviable challenges, shoulder the real burden of socio-cultural obligations, and face notorious political rivals, social calumny and humiliation in order to establish themselves as 'successful leaders' in their own right.

In the case of some Muslim women leaders in this book, they were propelled into political limelight to support male family members, but were pushed into oblivion after serving one or two tenures in Parliament. The fact that very few could serve as long-term MPs (unlike several male politicians in India) or become ministers reveals the difficulty that even these 'politically successful' women confronted to sustain their political journeys and rise in the field. However, this is not a reflection of their lack of political grit or appetite. Rather, it points to the male-dominated and conservatism-driven world that enabled them to step in when it was required; however, it generally kept their political ambitions at bay.

An examination of their parliamentary conduct reveals the proactive role that they tried to play as vocal and accountable parliamentarians during their stints in Parliament, however short their tenures might have been. Their active participation in Lok Sabha debates, their questions on a range of diverse policy issues, their deep commitment to ensure developmental work for their respective parliamentary constituencies, and their contribution as members in different parliamentary committees – battling the conservative confines of their home, community and society – makes them extremely inspiring public representatives for future generations.

Across the world, including in the Middle East and North Africa (MENA) region, the number of Muslim women participating in political decision-making has been tardy – especially in countries with limited democratic consolidation. While the MENA region has been notorious for having the lowest rates of women's political representation in the world, drastic changes in states dominated by Sharia rule and Islamism, such as Saudi Arabia, Kuwait and Sudan, are seeing women's increased presence in decision-making. However, most of these societies argue for women's participation based on the principle of complementarity, not equality.

In 1973, Sudanese Islamic ideologue Hasan al-Turabi, known for his progressive Islamist ideas about expanding the rights of women in public life, published a pamphlet titled 'Women Between the Teachings of Religion and the Customs of Society', advocating strongly for women's political rights. He noted that during the Prophet's era, too, women were allowed to participate in congregational prayer, and they took an active role in military expeditions. Muslim women participated actively in the community's economic life and acquired education. According to Turabi, 'a woman can be a leader, a head of state, a minister. She can be everything a man can be.'[3] In recent decades, South Asia, in general, and India, in particular, has witnessed the rise of modernist or liberal thought in Islam, where one strand has paved the way for Muslim feminism in India.[4] Personalities like Noorjehan Safia Niaz, founder of the Bharatiya Muslim Mahila Andolan, is, for the first time, organizing Muslim women in India to collectively overcome socio-cultural limitations that prevent them from exercising their citizenship.[5] Another prominent name amongst Muslim women activists in India is Shaista Amber, president of the All India Muslim Women's Personal Law Board (AIMWPLB), and a vocal advocate for women's rights, challenging Muslim orthodoxy.[6]

While writing profiles and contributions of Muslim women MPs, we were struck by certain interesting uniformities. Not one out of the eighteen had any major allegations of corruption, criminal charges or using hate speech. In other words, there were no Enforcement Directorate (ED), Central Bureau of Investigation (CBI), income tax or police cases against them. Those who are familiar with the intricacies of the actual workings of our political system would notice this with a sense of admiration. Many of them, in fact, went back to their daily lives with ease and dignity. Perhaps it is time for all major political parties, including the Bharatiya Janata Party (BJP), to look at Muslim women's role in legislative politics with a greater degree of interest and as having potential, particularly when the Women's Reservation Act of 2023 is set to become a reality in a few years from now.[7]

This was not an easy book to write, even jointly. The contribution of Muslim women MPs has not been documented well. There was an acute dearth of relevant information on their political work. Their stories had to be gathered from Assam to Kashmir, Gujarat to Bengal. It was also surprising that none of the five southern states – Kerala, Tamil Nadu, Karnataka, Andhra Pradesh and Telangana – otherwise known for better political representation than the North and with better literary levels and other socio-economic indicators, have not yet sent a single Muslim woman MP to the Lok Sabha!

As authors, we firmly believe that religion, religious beliefs and practices are personal and a 'no go' area for us. Therefore, the selection of Muslim women Lok Sabha MPs has been conducted in a broader liberal and cultural sense, too. In any case, the framers of the Indian Constitution had envisaged the voters would not accord any importance to politicians' religious beliefs or make faith a crucial part of their decision-making process.

With limited information, researching their political personalities has been a painstaking task, particularly collecting information on MPs who served in the previous century. From looking at secondary sources, news reports, speeches and interviews to interacting with some of the MPs, meeting their acquaintances and party officials, we tried our best to document the necessary details of their political lives. However, we must confess with utmost humility that documenting the lived struggles and experiences of an individual's life in politics, which is often marked by deep complexities, subjectivities, deceits and nuances, is replete with major challenges. Our interpretation of historic events that shaped one's political career, drove their struggles and defined their achievements, though extremely sincere, might suffer from underestimation or exaggerations of certain moments of their political journey. Having said that, this book makes, for the first time, an effort to document the political lives of hitherto lesser-known Muslim women parliamentarians. Despite the limitations, we hope that our endeavour opens a new gateway of research and curiosity in this subject. We hope it heralds a new beginning towards knowing these personalities better. Hence, we took a chance to plunge into this work following William Faulkner's words: 'Get it down. Take chances. It may be bad, but it's the only way you can do anything really good.'

Introduction

Politics is the key to any major social change in societies across the world. And the representation of women in politics is one of the most crucial indicators of women's empowerment. This measure of empowerment has triggered academic interest as well as policy concern across the globe in recent decades.[1] With the consolidation of the process of democratization in diverse regions across the world, concerns regarding individual freedom, gender equality, rule of law and human rights have assumed rightful priority in the idioms of policymaking and governance.[2] In this context, various feminist movements and awareness programmes have shaped modern democratic institutions that facilitated equal opportunities for women to participate in public life as political leaders. A sustained campaign, international consensus and organized pressure to create spaces for women in the structures of power and electoral politics have led to various initiatives,[3] like gender quotas in political positions, and in political parties, parliaments and governmental executive bodies.[4] However, despite such initiatives that have catapulted positive change by encouraging more women to participate in electoral politics, the challenges of adequate inclusion of women in politics remain glaring.[5]

First, the patriarchal norms that dominate the societal structure continue to perpetuate the traditional home-making role for women, which makes their full-time engagement in politics extremely challenging. Even as women have increasingly started to go out to work, they are compelled to balance it with care-giving duties and other household responsibilities.[6] Second, societal prejudices and structural hindrances discourage a large section of women from entering politics and contesting elections.

The patriarchy-aided deep-rooted perception still exists, arguing that women do not have the necessary skills and resilience to participate in public life – especially to thrive in politics that is replete with unforeseen turbulence and threats of violence. The entrenched misogynistic culture also subjects women leaders to humiliation and abuse, further dampening their motivation to pursue politics as a career. Third, and very importantly, in democracies, it is the political parties that wield the absolute power of selecting candidates to contest elections.[7] An overwhelming trend remains that parties are reluctant to nominate an adequate number of women because party functionaries also remain under the dominance of patriarchal prejudice. Such prejudice breeds unfounded apprehensions that women candidates will be less likely to win an election and might struggle in governance.[8] However, data has revealed that women candidates are not only capable of successfully contesting elections but also, once elected to power, perform better than men on many parameters of development and governance.[9]

We must note here that experiences in political participation varies for women across countries, regions and communities. Women belonging to relatively more conservative societies face greater hurdles in entering political and public life. Women belonging to ethnic minority groups or economically marginalized sections face a double discrimination – of belonging to the weaker sections of society and of being women.[10] Also, women in conservative communities, like in many Islamic societies, face unprecedented challenges in participating in public life, let alone participating in politics.[11] Hence, the vulnerability of women stems from an intersectionality of their identity as women, the societal milieu they exist in and their status as members of the majority/minority community within a country.[12]

Battling Double Jeopardy

The last few decades have witnessed an upsurge in academic interest and attention in the political participation of the Muslim community across the globe. The thrust of such discussions has largely remained premised upon the multi-layered dynamics that continue to vitiate the relationship between 'conservative' Islamic values, on the one hand, and political structures and institutions of liberal democracies, on the other.[13] However, such discourse has largely considered 'the Muslim male as the standard model of individual and collective action within and outside Muslim communities', disregarding the situation of women in Muslim communities.[14] More often than not, references to Muslim women have been made predominantly in the context of gender relations, focusing on their perennial plight as subjugated, oppressed and unaware, as being victims of societal malice. Even well-established and authoritative scholarship from the feminist school of thought has not adequately captured the political representation of Muslim women as an independent category deserving scrutiny.[15] The mainstream discourse on the conservative Islamic socio-cultural order has largely addressed the historical vulnerability and acute marginalization of Muslim women in the public and socio-political sphere, and rightly so. However, these grand narratives of marginalization often overshadow the nuanced multi-layered dynamics of the political agency of Muslim women that enables rare instances of political empowerment and amelioration against all societal odds.

This warrants a closer look at the political and social agency of Muslim women, no matter how limited it is, that has, on rare occasions, catapulted them into positions of political power as representatives and decision-makers in various structures of governance.[16] It is crucial and interesting to explore to what extent the democratic political institutions that uphold the principles of individual liberty and egalitarianism facilitate opportunities of empowerment for marginalized sections, like Muslim women.[17]

Muslim Women in Indian Politics

Democracy, as a political system, theoretically envisages a level playing field that guarantees equal political opportunity for all. It aims to overcome the primordial structures of socio-cultural hierarchies and create modern political institutions that can facilitate the representation of all sections of society.[18] However, history bears testimony to the fact that socio-cultural realities have often overshadowed the workings of political institutions, impacting the representative character of democratic polities across the world. India has consolidated itself as the largest as well as one of the most vibrant parliamentary and federal democratic political systems in the world. The country's complex multicultural milieu, with diverse geographical and ethnic landscapes, makes the function of inclusive democratic representation extremely crucial. Amongst a plethora of socio-cultural markers of identity, religion has played a pivotal role in the political history of modern post-colonial states like India within the broader South Asian region.[19] The country's population comprises the majority ethnic Hindus (79.80 per cent) along with a sizeable section of the minority Muslim community (14.23 per cent) and other minority groups like Christians (2.30 per cent) and Sikhs (1.72 per cent) among others.[20] The Indian Constitution, right from the time of its inception in 1950, embraced a secular political fabric in which the State doesn't embrace any particular religion, and accords protection to minority religious and ethnic communities.[21] Therefore, it is worth exploring how a socially vulnerable section, like Muslim women, has fared in the sphere of political empowerment within India's liberal, democratic political and institutional framework.

India has adopted a parliamentary form of government, with a bicameral national legislature. Hence, the directly elected lower house of Parliament, the Lok Sabha, is the powerful legislative chamber to which the Government of India is accountable. The representation of the Lok Sabha is a crucial indicator of the political inclusiveness of Indian democracy. It is true that the social profile of the lower house remained confined to the socio-economic elite in the initial years. However, the composition of the Lok Sabha became increasingly more inclusive and accommodative of all sections, especially the hitherto backward and marginalized communities that were soon represented in large numbers.[22]

As the largest minority community in India, Muslims have relatively increased their representation in Parliament over the years.[23] However, their representation remains considerably below their population size, and therefore, they remain largely under-represented in Parliament.[24] As per the census of 2011, Muslims comprise 14.3 per cent of the population, but only 24 out of 543 MPs – over 4 per cent – in the 18th Lok Sabha are Muslim.[25] This is despite the fact that there are a total of 101 Lok Sabha seats where Muslims make up more than 20 per cent of the population.[26] Sizeable sections of the Muslim population also remain one of the most socio-economically backward sections in the country along with other sections like Dalits and tribal communities.[27] Another social category that has remained historically marginalized and under-represented in the Indian Parliament, as well as state legislatures, are women leaders.[28] The total percentage of women MPs in each Lok Sabha till date has not exceeded 15 per cent and their presence in even worse in state legislatures – though women comprise 50 per cent of the country's population.[29] The recently passed Women's Reservation Act, 2023 aims to bridge this gap by providing one-third of reserved seats for women in national and state legislatures; however, its implementation will take a few more years.

Doubly marginalized as part of the minority and conservative Muslim community and as women, Muslim women, have remained extremely under-represented, with a total of barely eighteen representatives in the Lok Sabha in the last seven decades.[30] It reveals a telling yet largely glossed over fact that out of nearly 7,500 MPs voted to power since 1951, only 0.6 per cent have been Muslim women.[31] Out of the eighteen Lok Sabhas constituted till June 2024, in four Lok Sabhas, there was not a *single* Muslim woman! Equally shocking is the fact that out of the 543 seats in the lower house, more than four Muslim women have never been voted to power at one time.[32] Such glaring under-representation of Muslim women can be clearly attributed to the socio-cultural and politico-institutional factors that have impeded their participation and success in India's parliamentary politics.[33] According to noted French scholar Christophe Jaffrelot, Muslim women face a double bind – discriminated against as women and as Muslims. His sentiments echo political scientist Gilles Verniers, when he observed, 'In terms of cumulative discrimination—being a Muslim and being a woman—there is a compounding effect for sure. The usual barriers to entry that apply to all women, apply even more strongly to Muslims.'[34]

About the Book

The minuscule number of Muslim women leaders in the Lok Sabha, along with other representative institutions like the upper house – Rajya Sabha – state legislative assemblies, and Union and state governments reveals the monumental challenge faced by them to enter and thrive in India's electoral politics.[35] Thus, it is imperative to pay attention to the political journey of these Muslim women politicians who have battled multi-layered discrimination stemming from patriarchy, religious orthodoxy and minority status to contribute to India's legislative institutional deliberations. A peek into the literature reveals that a sincere and detailed documentation of their stories of political struggle, resilience, their achievements and limitations is long overdue. In this context, this book intends to capture and account for the multiple factors and catalysing conditions that have enabled Muslim women parliamentarians to breach the socio-political hurdles to carve a political ecosystem in which they could successfully represent their constituency in the Lok Sabha, despite heavy odds.

This book aims to provide a political account of individual Muslim women leaders who have made it to the Lok Sabha as members since Independence (from the 1st Lok Sabha) to the 18th Lok Sabha. The objective of this book is to map the personal, political, socio-economic and geographic conditions in which these Muslim women entered and succeeded in the electoral competition in India's parliamentary politics.

It aims to offer an analytical account of their political journeys, along with a theoretical framework to draw broader inferences on the nature of India's electoral politics and how accommodative institutions are by understanding the conditions under which these leaders succeeded. This study will also briefly assess the performance of these leaders as parliamentarians and representatives of their respective constituencies to underline the political agency of Muslim women parliamentarians in India. Even a cursory assessment of the social profiles of the eighteen elected Muslim women parliamentarians reveals interesting insights. For instance, a sizeable number of these leaders come from dynastic backgrounds and specific regions in India, like Bengal, Assam and Uttar Pradesh. The book delves into some of these trends in order to analyse the nature of the parliamentary representation of Muslim women leaders.

The book comprises 19 brief chapters, along with an introduction and an epilogue. The first chapter delves into the theoretical framework of the book, premised on contextualizing Muslim women and democratic politics in general, as well as the Indian democracy's impact on the discourse of political empowerment and the leadership of Muslim women in the country's parliamentary politics. Chapters 2 to 19 briefly map the political journeys of 18 Muslim woman MPs. We study the political, familial, geographical and socio-cultural circumstances of these parliamentarians. The chapters touch upon multi-dimensional attributes, like the personal background, parliamentary constituency, party affiliation, electoral competition and socio-economic heft of these leaders, in order to understand the ecosystem in which they either used to function or continue to function. Finally, in the epilogue of the book, we have analysed conceptual trends and thrown light on the enabling conditions that facilitated the entry of these leaders despite high structural barriers. This work aims to provide a revealing yet brief and focused account of the struggle and achievements of these Muslim women MPs, and how they thrived in India's electoral political landscape.

We hope this book can help encourage and develop a larger discussion on the nature of inclusivity in India's democratic institutions and electoral architecture.

1

Setting the Context

The introduction explained the broad contours of this book. This chapter discusses a key aspect that we would like to address – the political agency of Muslim women in India. A credible measure of the representation and participation of any group or community in any sphere comes from the level of agency, or the ability, that the group can develop to utilize such an opportunity. However, human agency is not a linear or monolithic attribute. Apart from individual personality traits, it is shaped – to a large extent – by overlapping and diverse situational conditions. It is the same with women's representation in politics, which predominantly depends upon two major factors. The first factor is structural – the ecosystem within which women's political participation is ensured. The second is the political agency of the women themselves; that is to say, their interest in pursuing politics, which is shaped by and, in turn, shapes the personality and conduct of women in politics. In other words, the structural dynamics of the societal ecosystem and the building of political agency of women are inextricably linked.

Where Is the Political Agency?

As we saw in the introduction, there are some major impediments that deter women from participating in politics, thereby eroding their political agency. These are, broadly speaking, rigid patriarchal norms that restrict their avenues of socialization and thus hamper their scope to acquire the skills necessary for a successful career in politics; voter scepticism; financial dependence; and the verbal – and sometimes physical – antagonism that women have to contend with in public life. The last one is a global phenomenon that often takes the form of slander or vilification to deter women from joining politics.

Therefore, women, because of societal prejudices and related issues, remain at a disadvantage when it comes to pursuing a career in politics. The more rigid the social framework, the tougher it becomes to navigate. Needless to say, the challenges multiply in 'difficult settings' such as war zones, conflict-stricken environments and authoritarian political systems.

For Muslim women in India, it is a double whammy. First, as women in a conservative socio-religious setting; and second, as members of a religious minority group. Let's look at available statistics. Figures reveal that there are approximately 70 million Muslim women in India, but an abysmally low percentage of these women are part of the total workforce – government or private.[1]

As already discussed earlier, their participation in electoral and parliamentary politics since Independence has remained glaringly low because of overlapping social, cultural and political hindrances. Only eighteen Muslim women leaders have been elected to the Lok Sabha, the people's house of India's bicameral legislature, since 1951–52, when the country voted for the first time since gaining freedom. This is the intriguing premise on which our study is contextualized. It is about these women leaders – who they are or were – and under what conditions they were introduced to and succeeded in India's turbulent space of electoral politics, despite overwhelming odds. The individual profiles of these leaders also provide an account of their conduct in office and discuss their political legacy.

Who Are They?

It is both important and interesting to ponder over the two above-mentioned dimensions of political participation of Muslim women MPs in India – firstly, who they are/were, and secondly, how they entered and shaped the country's politics. Political scientist Kanchan Chandra's work on dynastic politics in India and a cursory glance at the profiles of these Muslim women MPs reveals that quite a few of them belonged to well-established political dynasties. Such a pattern has often triggered dismissive claims that these women leaders owe their position and achievements more to family connections than to their own political struggles, merit or agency. Our attempt to tell their stories is, therefore, an endeavour to delve deeper into each of their unique paths of political ascendancy. In the process, such sweeping allegations – that women from political dynasties do not have political agency of their own and work predominantly as a proxy for male members of their families – might get tempered and nuanced, if not entirely refuted.

Second, feminist studies on gender, politics and development have often focused on exploring the impact women have on governance and development. There is an emerging body of research that suggests that the presence of women in politics has had a positive impact on welfare parameters.[2] Studies on women's representation in panchayats in India have shown that women in governance often differ from men in their policy preferences. It has also been found that women-led villages saw improved delivery of services with lower levels of corruption, while greater investments were made in water infrastructure, sanitation, education and roads.[3]

Taking a cue from these studies, we felt that the political legacy of these Muslim women MPs in their respective domains of influence needed to be documented. We wanted to assess whether their entry into the high-walled world of politics actually impacted the political and developmental parameters for women, especially those belonging to their community.

Third, at the level of self-identification, it is important to know how these women have perceived their role as politicians within an ecosystem largely dominated by men. Interestingly, history bears testimony to the fact that notable women leaders in the 20th century, such as Indira Gandhi, Margaret Thatcher and Golda Meir, not only did not explicitly identify themselves as feminists, but also hardly used the feminist idiom in their politics. This is what Indira Gandhi had written to a friend, 'I am in no sense a feminist, but I believe in women being able to do everything. Given the opportunity to develop, capable Indian women have come to the top at once.'[4]

Golda Meir, Israel's fourth prime minister and West Asia's first female head of government, didn't think much of the women's liberation movement. 'Do you mean those crazy women who burn their bras, go around dishevelled and hate men?' she told an interviewer. 'They are crazy. But how can one accept such crazy women who think it is a misfortune to get pregnant and a disaster to bring children into the world? And when it is the greatest privilege we women have over men! I got into politics at the time of the First World War; I was sixteen, and had never belonged to a women's organization. The fact of being a woman has never been an obstacle.'[5]

Margaret Thatcher, Britain's first woman prime minister, was essentially anti-feminist and even declared herself as one. 'I think they have become too strident. I think they have done great damage to the cause of women by making us out to be something we are not,' she said, speaking about the particularly militant ones within the feminist movement. 'Each person is different. Each has their own talents and abilities, and these are things that you want to draw and bring out. You don't say, I must get on because I am a woman. You should say – You should get on because you have a combination of talents that are right for the job. The moment you exaggerate the question, you defeat your case.'[6]

The crux of the matter, then, is identifying the challenges and responding accordingly, irrespective of gender. That applies to Muslim women leaders, too, and hence, it is important to understand how they have identified and perceived their role and position in Indian politics as women.

Women MPs in the Lok Sabha

The authors of this book feel that documenting the role of these women leaders will be crucial in understanding aspects of not only their political lives but also of India's electoral-political landscape, trends in the country's deep-rooted dynastic politics as well as feminist political discourse. The three dimensions of their political journeys – their motivation, access and entry into politics; their ability to achieve electoral success despite heavy odds; and lastly, their legacy in politics and governance both as politicians and as women – will be touched upon. Through the mixed methods of storytelling, juxtaposed with attempts at a broader theorization on women and politics in India, this book, we feel, would cater to both biographical and academic interests.

However, we are mindful of the fact that the individual profiles will not be exhaustive. Also, the narratives offered here are based on secondary published sources available in the public domain, and on interviews and interactions with women leaders who are still active in public life and whom we could access. Hence, like any other biographical account, the narratives on their political lives and careers are entirely based on how we could comprehend and perceive them. Therefore, no claims of this work being an authoritative account of the politics and political legacy of these women leaders are being made.

We are also aware of the fact that history is replete with biases and politics is pregnant with contradictions. Thus, the pursuit of innocuous history and pristine politics is not only factually erroneous but also intellectually untenable. So, there is no attempt at making any overt moral claims about the political achievements (or failures) of these leaders. However, this work can be a helpful starting point to understand and delve into when, where and how these handful of extraordinary Muslim women politicians left their mark on India's diverse and vibrant electoral landscape. This would also help to propel a broader debate on locating the political agency of women in 'difficult settings' within democratic conditions, and how that might, in turn, shape the feminist understanding of politics and public life in general. But it remains entirely the prerogative of readers to decide how they would like to perceive and assess these accounts, some of which have, till now, remained underexplored.

Table 1: List of Muslim Women MPs in the Lok Sabha from 1952 to 2024, Covered in this Book

SN	Name	Party	Constituency	Year
1.	Mofida Ahmed	Indian National Congress	Jorhat	Lok Sabha, 1957
2.	Zohraben Akbarbhai Chavda	Indian National Congress	Banaskantha	Lok Sabha, 1962–67
3.	Maimoona Sultan	Indian National Congress	Bhopal	Lok Sabha, 1957–67
4.	Begum Akbar Jehan Abdullah	National Congress	Srinagar, Anantnag	Lok Sabha, 1977–79, 1984–89
5.	Rashida Haque Choudhury	Indian National Congress	Silchar	Lok Sabha, 1977–79
6.	Mohsina Kidwai	Indian National Congress	Meerut	Lok Sabha, 1977–89 Rajya Sabha, 2004–16
7.	Abida Ahmed	Indian National Congress	Bareilly	Lok Sabha, 1980–89
8.	Noor Bano	Indian National Congress	Rampur	Lok Sabha 1996, 1999–2004
9.	Rubab Sayda	Samajwadi Party	Bahraich	Lok Sabha, 2004–09
10.	Mehbooba Mufti	People's Democratic Party	Anantnag	Lok Sabha, 2004–09, 2014–19
11.	Tabassum Hasan	Samajwadi Party, Lok Dal, Bahujan Samaj Party	Kairana	Lok Sabha, 2009–14
12.	Mausam Noor	Trinamool Congress	Maldaha Uttar	Lok Sabha, 2009–19

SN	Name	Party	Constituency	Year
13.	Kaisar Jahan	Bahujan Samaj Party, Indian National Congress	Sitapur	Lok Sabha, 2009–14
14.	Mamtaz Sanghamita	All India Trinamool Congress	Durgapur	Lok Sabha, 2014–19
15.	Sajda Ahmed	All India Trinamool Congress	Uluberia	Lok Sabha, 2014–24
16.	Ranee Narah	Indian National Congress	Lakhimpur	Lok Sabha, 1998–2004, 2009–14
17.	Nusrat Jahan Ruhi	All India Trinamool Congress	Basirhat	Lok Sabha, 2019–24
18.	Iqra Hasan	Samajwadi Party	Kairana	Lok Sabha, 2024-Present

2

Mofida Ahmed: The Forgotten Begum of Assam

Most Indians today have probably forgotten that the national flag was designed by a Muslim woman named Surayya Tyabji. Jawaharlal Nehru had assigned this task to Tyabji, who was an active member of the Indian National Congress (INC). It was her idea to replace the symbol of the charkha with that of the Ashoka Chakra at the centre of the flag. Tyabji felt that the charkha, a symbol of the INC, might appear partisan.

As contemporary Indians normalize a partisan gaze towards their surroundings and history, more and more such anecdotes are consigned to oblivion. Such an approach introduces filters, often linear and illogical, that condition us to identify friends as enemies and partners as adversaries. They also often lead to identification based on language, religion, food habits and even attire. But the fact of the matter remains that India's political and social evolution has never been linear. It has always been a process of constant churning, in which communities and individuals emerge and disappear.

One such remarkable – yet largely forgotten – figure in India's political history is Begum Mofida Ahmed (1921–2008). She was not only one of the first female MPs from Assam but also among the earliest Muslim women to enter Indian politics at the national level. Her election in 1957, during India's second parliamentary elections, marked a significant moment for women's representation in governance, particularly for Muslim women in independent India.

Mofida Ahmed contested from the Jorhat constituency in Assam, an area known for its diverse demographic composition, with a significant mix of tribal, Assamese and Bengali populations. Despite the presence of strong contenders from established parties – including the undivided Communist Party of India (CPI), the Praja Socialist Party (PSP), led by Jayaprakash Narayan, and the regional Sarbadal party – she emerged victorious. Securing 80,028 votes, amounting to 45.36 per cent of the total votes polled, Ahmed's win was a decisive one, as her opponents each garnered less than 20 per cent of the vote share on average.[1]

Her electoral success was more than just a political milestone; it was testament to the progressive shift taking place in Assam's socio-political landscape. At a time when women in politics were a rarity, especially in states like Assam, Mofida Ahmed broke barriers, proving that leadership was not confined to gender or community-based expectations. Her victory also symbolized the trust she had garnered among a broad spectrum of voters, cutting across religious and ethnic lines.[2]

Beyond electoral politics, Ahmed played a crucial role in advocating for women's education, social upliftment and minority rights in Assam. Her tenure in Parliament saw her raise critical issues related to rural development, women's empowerment and the socio-economic condition of marginalized communities. Yet, despite her significant contributions, her name has faded from public memory, overshadowed by more dominant political narratives.

A Long and Storied Career

Ahmed was not a one-shot politician; rather, she had a long political and public life. She joined the INC in 1943. In 1962, she contested from the same constituency as a sitting member, but was defeated by the PSP candidate, Rajendranath Barua, by 907 votes. After Nehru's passing in 1964, a leadership issue rattled the INC. Factions appeared, and the party went into a mode of self-destruction. As Indira Gandhi tried to consolidate her position with Congress (I), regional satraps like K. Kamaraj, Devaraj Urs, Morarji Desai and Jagjivan Ram started to break away from the Congress stable. Each of them formed their own version or faction of the Congress party, usually by adding a suffix (such as their own name or an identifier) to the 'Congress' name, in order to distinguish their group from Indira Gandhi's Congress (I). India went into a political tailspin, leading to frequent elections. Ahmed contested the 1971 by-election as a Congress (N) candidate for the Jorhat seat against Tarun Gogoi, who was representing

Congress (J).[3] She polled only 1.86 per cent of the votes and forfeited her deposit. It also marked the end of her political journey. Tarun Gogoi played his cards well, returned to the mainstream Congress and became Assam's chief minister in 2001, five years after the end of the Hiteswar Saikia era.[4]

Parliamentary Career

Mofida Ahmed's legacy is a reminder that the fight for gender equality in India is far from over. Her story deserves to be revisited, retold and reclaimed, so that she is not just a footnote in history but a symbol of what is possible when courage meets conviction. By no means was Ahmed a Parliament backbencher.

Mofida asked several questions in the Lok Sabha, ranging from the attack on the wife of an Indian diplomat in Congo, the arrest of Kashmiri Muslims in Tibet, steps taken by the Government of India to meet the danger arising out of a 'jihad' campaign by Pakistan against India, the illegal entry of Pakistanis into Assam, the United Kingdom associating itself with the European Common Market, to the British citizenship granted to Phizo, a Naga revolutionary and Naga Nationalist Council (NNC) chief who dreamed of making a free state for Nagas but died in exile.

She also brought forward issues like the services of sea mail delivery delayed by several months, offering a suggestion to the Roads and Transport Development Association on how to handle the movement of coal from the collieries, proposing the construction of the ship *The State of Andaman* in Hindustan Shipyard Limited (HSL), and discussing the utilization of forest produce in the north Andaman Islands by a firm in 1951. She focused on Assam-specific problems, such as the tea industry reeling under a drought and many gardens facing a massive crisis, the excise duty placed on Assam tea, the price hike on petrol and kerosene by Burmah Oil Company, the killing of two civilian drivers when several Naga hostiles ambushed two petrol tankers between Mao and Kohima on 20 September 1961, and the underground fire in the Pure Jharia Colliery endangering the safety of three adjoining mines. According to the records maintained by Parliament, she also led an enquiry on the Siliguri rail mishap of 11 August 1961, in which 30 people died on the spot and 91 were injured; she also led an enquiry on the fire at Alexandra Docks, Bombay – an unfortunate incident that took place on 8 August 1961.[5]

A run through the archives reveals that she raised 650 questions during her five-year term. Among the most important ones were those on the naming of Saraighat Bridge over the Brahmaputra, on the Regional Research Laboratory in Jorhat, the rapid industrialization India was seeing then, railway lines in Assam and the Naga Bill (regarding the establishment of a centrally administered Naga Hill district, now known as Nagaland).

Ahmed was a member of the State Social Welfare Advisory Board, the Zonal Railway Users' Consultation Council and on the Small Savings Advisory Board, among others. She was also on parliamentary committees such as the Direct

Taxes Advisory Committee, the Central Advisory Board of Education, the P&T Advisory Committee (Eastern Division), the National Railway Users' Consultation Council, the Central Waqf Board, the National Savings Advisory Board, the Assam Language Disturbances Enquiry Committee, the All-India Congress Committee (AICC), the Composition of the Joint Committee (Lok Sabha and Rajya Sabha) on the Prevention of Cruelty to Animals Bill, 1959, the Programme Advisory Committee (PAC) at the All India Radio (AIR) and the Site Selection Committee for Oil Refinery in Assam.

Ahmed was not only a trailblazing politician but also a dedicated social activist and philanthropist. Her deep commitment to national service was evident when, during the Chinese aggression of 1962, she donated her personal jewellery to the National Defence Fund – an act that underscored her unwavering patriotism. She was a firm believer in education as a means of empowerment, particularly for women, and took active steps to support academic excellence. To this end, she established the Nurbahar Begum Memorial Award, named after her mother, which has been awarded annually to the top-performing student in the BA examination at D.C. Barua Girls' College, Jorhat.

Retreat from Public Life

Despite her early prominence, Ahmed's political career came to an abrupt halt following her defeat in the 1971 Lok Sabha elections. This loss, coupled with the death of her husband,

Mohammed Ahsonuddin Ahmed, in 1975, led her to withdraw from public life. Once a vibrant figure in Assam's political and social landscape, Ahmed now chose a life of solitude, retreating from the world she had once played an active role in shaping. The couple had no children, and after her husband's passing, she gradually distanced herself from political and social engagements.

In 1976, Ahmed undertook the sacred pilgrimage of Hajj, marking a significant spiritual shift in her life. Following her return, she embraced a life of quiet devotion and self-reliance, even choosing to live without any domestic help. Despite her withdrawal from public affairs, her commitment to social causes never waned. In her later years, she made the extraordinary decision to donate all her property to the Assam Falah Society, a Guwahati-based organization dedicated to promoting women's education.

Struggle and Humility in Political Life

There are reasons why we know so little about Ahmed. To begin with, she was a 'low-profile' politician; she kept such a low profile that it is now impossible to locate her statue, or bust, while walking down the bustling streets and squares of Jorhat, where she was born and brought up. Ahmed was born to a prominent Muslim family. Her father was Mohammad Barua Ali; not much is known about her mother. As Axomiya Musalmans, the family was well regarded in Assam's social hierarchy – not only because they were well-assimilated within the Assamese socio-cultural milieu, but also because the members were mostly educated and worked as professionals, which explained their affluence when compared with other Muslim groups in Assam.

Ahmed received institutional education only up to Class VI, but her family ensured adequate homeschooling for her. Later in life, she became a regular contributor to Assamese journals. Her works include *Biswadip-Bapuji* and *Bharatar-Nehru*, along with six other books containing short stories. By the time Ahmed grew up, Gopinath Bordoloi had emerged as the Congress strongman from Assam. He was also the first chief minister (1946–50) of Assam. Bordoloi's national stature inspired many young men and women to join the Congress in the state, and Ahmed was no exception. Bordoloi died in office in 1950. By the time Ahmed earned her spurs in the state's politics, Assam's INC leadership saw the emergence of leaders like Bishnuram Medhi, followed by B.P. Chaliha. It was also the Nehru era at the national level.

Ahmed's induction into public life happened through the Jorhat unit of the Indian Red Cross Society, where she served as a joint secretary (1946–49). In the Congress, she rose through the ranks. She was the assistant secretary of the party's Tezpur District Women's Cell (October 1951–January 1953), working on issues like maternity welfare and the rescue of women in distress. She was also the convenor of the Women's Cell of the Congress in Golaghat from its inception in 1953 till 1956. Between 1955 and 1957, Ahmed worked for the National Savings Scheme in an honorary capacity.

Challenging Notions

Why do we conveniently forget women like Mofida Ahmed or brand them as 'low profile' – of little consequence? Is it because they hold the mirror up to the beliefs we regard as sacred? Do they challenge the dominant stereotype of modern India, which describes Muslim women as a monolithic group of hijab-clad, oppressed, orthodox and backward creatures to be pitied, and who need a Messiah to protect them? Do we approach critical issues like triple talaq, halala and purdah from a do-gooder angle?

Begum Mofida Ahmed's life and work challenge the reductive stereotype that Muslim women are a monolithic and homogeneous entity. Like women from any other socio-cultural background, they come from diverse communities, hold a range of beliefs and pursue varied paths. Ahmed's life is a powerful testament to the fact that gendered oppression is not inherent to any one religion but is, instead, a consequence of deep-seated patriarchal structures. She proved that a Muslim woman can be much more than just a symbol of tradition – she can be a writer, teacher, scientist, lawyer, political leader and a social reformer.

Growing up in the India of the 1930s and 1940s, Ahmed defied societal norms that sought to limit her. She abandoned the purdah, asserted her independence, and embraced Islam in its most progressive and liberal spirit. In an era when women, particularly from conservative backgrounds, were often relegated to the domestic sphere, she stepped out with remarkable confidence. She not only pursued an education but also carved a space for herself in politics at a time when very few women were visible in the public domain.

Her trajectory also highlights a larger and more uncomfortable truth about Indian politics – the systemic reluctance of political parties to groom women for leadership positions. Across all levels, from local governance in panchayats to Parliament, women struggle to even secure nominations, let alone rising to influential positions. When they do gain power, it is often because of family connections – either as placeholders for male relatives or as political matriarchs in dynastic set-ups. The fate of the Women's Reservation Bill, which has faced decades of political inertia, is a stark reminder of how all major parties – regardless of ideology – remain reluctant to genuinely empower women in politics.

Ahmed's story should have been one of continued relevance, but instead, it became one that faded into obscurity. As mentioned earlier, after her electoral defeat in 1971 and the loss of her husband in 1975, she retreated from public life. Her decision to withdraw was not just personal – it also reflected a larger pattern that continues to date, where women leaders, especially those without strong dynastic ties, often find themselves sidelined once they are out of office. Despite her formidable achievements, there was no concerted effort to keep her legacy alive, no institutional recognition of her contributions and no attempt by political circles to bring her back into public discourse.

Yet, her life's story continues to be a crucial narrative of resistance, agency and political participation. By breaking barriers, and demonstrating that faith and feminism are not mutually exclusive, she paved the way for future generations of women, particularly from minority communities, to dream beyond the constraints imposed on them. Her final act of philanthropy – donating her entire estate to the Assam Falah Society to promote women's education – was a fitting culmination of a life dedicated to service.

3

Zohraben Akbarbhai Chavda: Service Before Self

When Zohraben Akbarbhai Chavda won the Banaskantha Lok Sabha seat in February 1962, she not only secured a place in India's parliamentary history but also became part of a distinguished group of husband–wife political duos, including Fakhruddin Ali Ahmed and Begum Abida Ahmed, Chaudhary Munawwar Hasan and Begum Tabassum Hasan, and Nawab Zulfiqar 'Micky Mian' Ali Khan and Begum Noor Bano. However, unlike Abida Ahmed, Noor Bano and Tabassum Hasan, whose political prominence largely followed their husbands' careers, Zohraben had firmly established herself as a committed public servant, Gandhian and freedom fighter long before her marriage to Akbarbhai.

Her journey in politics was deeply intertwined with the Indian independence movement and the principles of Mahatma Gandhi. A dedicated social worker, she was actively involved in grassroots activism, advocating for women's rights, rural upliftment and community welfare. Zohraben's political career was, therefore, not a mere extension of her husband's influence, but rather, a continuation of her own independent work in public service. Even before entering electoral politics, she had been engaging in mobilizing people for national causes, spreading Gandhian ideals of self-reliance and working extensively for the betterment of underprivileged communities in Gujarat.

Life of Ideals

Zohraben's marriage to Akbarbhai was not a conventional one and was born out of a larger purpose. It was Mahatma Gandhi himself who suggested that she move to Banaskantha to carry out social work, leading to her eventual marriage with Akbarbhai. This decision was not just a personal one but also a reflection of her commitment to Gandhian ideals and nation-building. Her work in Banaskantha encompassed education, healthcare and rural development, addressing some of the most pressing issues of her time.

By the time she entered the Lok Sabha in 1962, she was already a seasoned public figure with a legacy of activism. Unlike many women of her era who entered politics through dynastic ties, Zohraben was a leader in her own right, driven by a strong sense of duty and a vision for a better India. Her election was a testament to her deep-rooted connect with the people of Banaskantha, her commitment to public welfare and her ability to command respect beyond her marital identity.

Early Life

Zohraben was born on 2 September 1923, in Prantij village of Sabarkantha district, Gujarat. Her father, Jamiatkhan Umarkhan Pathan, was a respected member of the community and ensured that his daughter received an education – an uncommon priority for girls at the time. Zohraben completed her primary education in Prantij and displayed an early interest in social work, which would go on to define her life and career. Recognizing her passion for serving others, her father sent her to Wardha, Maharashtra, to pursue a course in nursing – a decision that would shape her lifelong commitment to healthcare and grassroots activism.

It was during her time in Wardha that Zohraben came under the profound influence of Mahatma Gandhi. She spent more than seven years in close association with him, imbibing his principles of non-violence, selfless service and grassroots mobilization. Inspired by his teachings, she dedicated herself to the upliftment of marginalized communities, particularly in the areas of women's health and rural welfare.

According to Ahmedabad-based journalist Binit Modi, Zohraben later worked at Gujarat Vidyapith in Ahmedabad, an institution founded by Gandhi to promote nationalist education. It was here that she met Akbarbhai Chavda, a fellow Gandhian and social worker. Their shared ideals and commitment to public service brought them together and, at Gandhi's suggestion, they entered into matrimony. However, their marriage was more than just a personal union – it was a partnership built on a common mission to serve society.

Following Gandhi's directive once again, the newly-weds moved to Sanali village near Danta in Banaskantha district, where Zohraben took on the role of a full-time midwife with the local health department. In an era when maternal and child healthcare was severely neglected in rural India, she worked tirelessly to improve conditions, providing medical assistance to expecting mothers, raising awareness about hygiene and advocating for better healthcare facilities.

Zohraben's deep-rooted dedication to social work eventually transitioned into a political career, but her entry into politics was never a pursuit of power. Rather, it was an extension of her lifelong commitment to community service. Her early experiences in Wardha, her association with Gandhi and her hands-on work in healthcare laid the foundation for her political journey.

Sarvodaya Ashram

She and Akbarbhai painstakingly set up Sarvodaya Ashram in 1948 to serve the Bhil Adivasi community. The ashram was completely destroyed by floods in 1965, but was reconstructed later. Gandhi's Sarvodaya Movement was a non-violent method to improve the social, economic and moral condition of India. The word 'sarvodaya' implies progress for all, and the movement's stated goals were to:

- Create a society based on love and non-violence.
- Develop India's socio-economic and moral independence.

- Establish a classless society where no one is privileged based on birth, wealth or talent.
- Ensure that the benefits of national progress reach the most disadvantaged sections of society.
- Ensure dignity of labour and that everyone should engage in some productive physical work to earn their daily bread.
- Create a decentralized socio-political and economic structure.
- Elect empathetic, kind and helpful panchayat heads to solve matters at the grassroots level.

While Zohraben was a trained nurse, Akbarbhai landed a job with the police department. But very soon, he left the job to become a full-time freedom fighter and social activist. Akbarbhai was deeply pained to see the utter lack of development in the region – there was nearly zero literacy, the predominance of a hunter-gatherer lifestyle and the apparent exploitation of the region by a local prince. He took it upon himself to help and started a small school in a hut with five children attending it. Zohraben was his steadfast partner in these endeavours.

In the first General Elections, Akbarbhai got elected to the Lok Sabha from Banaskantha. Despite his duties as a lawmaker and his frequent visits to Delhi, he maintained a close relationship with Sarvodaya Ashram, opening an Ayurvedic clinic to tend to the health and welfare of the local tribes. This was soon followed by the expansion of the hut school into a formally established primary school in Danta taluka.

Both Akbarbhai and Zohraben led spartan lives. Mahant Rajendranand Giri, a journalist-cum-activist who eventually turned into a spiritual guru, knows the couple and recalls meeting them at their spartan residence. It was like a hermit's hut. Giri, who had eventually taken sanyas and become a Mahamandaleshwar,[1] said, 'I was amazed to see the near absence of furniture, consumer durables or cookware. Everything present were bare essentials – even beds and sofas were absent. But they were content and happy. Virtually anyone or everyone could walk in and they were greeted with warmth and affection. There were no trappings of power. He [Akbarbhai] was addressed as "bapji" by everyone.'

Giri also noted that while the couple was deeply spiritual, he did not see them following many Islamic practices. 'They were totally immersed in social work, working for the downtrodden, particularly Adivasis. There was no concept of a religious identity in Gujarat then.' He added that Akbarbhai's prized possession was a pocket watch gifted to him by Mahatma Gandhi. It is also worth noting that the couple remained childless.

Political Journey

Chavdas in Gujarat are Rajputs who trace their lineage to the Chavda dynasty that ruled parts of the state between 690 and 942 CE. The dynasty is also known by names like Chawda, Chavada, Chapa, Chapotkat and Chapotkata. Akbarbhai's great-grandfather is said to have converted to Islam, but the family continued to proudly retain their Chavda surname.

By 1962, Akbarbhai Chavda, a seasoned politician with two Lok Sabha victories under his belt, saw the rise of Zohraben as a formidable political leader in her own right. She had already made a name for herself as the district Congress president, earning the respect of both party members and the people of Banaskantha. Recognizing her growing influence, many stalwarts of the Congress, including the influential Morarji Desai, rallied behind her candidature. In what was seen as a passing of the political baton, Akbarbhai stepped into the background, allowing Zohraben to take centre stage in electoral politics.

Her resounding victory in the 1962 Lok Sabha elections cemented her position as a political heavyweight. She secured a landslide win, garnering 1,15,931 votes, while her nearest rival, from the Swatantra Party, managed only 60,975 votes. This emphatic triumph not only reinforced her credibility as a leader but also underscored the faith the people of Banaskantha had placed in her.

A Devoted Parliamentarian

Once in Parliament, Zohraben distinguished herself as an active and vocal legislator. Parliamentary records from her tenure between 1962 and 1967 reveal her relentless pursuit of diverse issues – reflecting both her deep engagement with local concerns, and her awareness of national and international affairs. She raised pressing questions about trade and infrastructure, such as the regulation of the cement industry in India, the plight of hospitals in Delhi and the delays in the construction of a railway station in Bhopal. Her concerns extended to economic development, including enquiries into the potential of diamond mining and the rehabilitation of goldsmiths.

Zohraben also displayed a keen interest in issues related to governance and security. She sought clarity on matters as varied as the visit of the union health minister to the USSR, reports of a Pakistani spy ring in Kashmir and even thefts occurring within Parliament House itself.

Her attention to education and welfare was equally evident. She questioned the non-availability of affordable British textbooks for Indian students, advocated for better training facilities for Royal Nepal Airlines personnel and emphasized the need for a mental health hospital in Delhi. She also took a stand on social issues, voicing concerns about the increasing incidents of girl kidnappings in the capital and calling for pension schemes for traditional craftsmen.

One question of interest was how the English daily *National Herald* was owned by Associated Journals Ltd, a company registered under the Indian Companies Act. Her research revealed that out of a total of 9,990 non-cumulative preference shares of Rs 1,001 each and 1,05,607 equity shares of Rs 101 each, one single share of Rs 101 was registered in the name of a member of the Dalmia Jain Group, while another 250 equity shares of Rs 101 each were registered in the name of an employee of this group. There was no indication that any of the remaining registered holders of the shares belonged to Associated Journals Ltd. *National Herald* was founded by Jawaharlal Nehru and, in the 1960s, it was considered to be a mouthpiece of the ruling Congress Party. Archives reveal that Minister B.R. Bhagat gave a curt reply: 'We cannot give an opinion about the working of the press.'[2]

As a Lok Sabha member, Zohraben Akbarbhai Chavda was not only an active parliamentarian but also a vocal participant in key policy discussions. One of her most significant contributions came as a member of the 1966 parliamentary committee that investigated the use of chemical pesticides in India. At a time when the nation was grappling with severe food shortages and the urgent need to modernize agriculture, the committee's work held immense significance.

Pragmatic reformer

A committed Gandhian, Zohraben understood the ethos of self-sufficiency and minimalism championed by Mahatma Gandhi. However, as a pragmatic leader, she could also sense the winds of change sweeping through India's political economy. The country, still reeling from centuries of colonial exploitation and resource drain, was on the brink of a transformative era. The traditional Gandhian model of subsistence farming and cottage industries, while morally appealing, was proving inadequate for a rapidly growing population desperate for food security, employment and economic growth.

Zohraben recognized that new solutions were necessary. The introduction of chemical pesticides and fertilizers – part of the early steps towards the Green Revolution – presented a stark dilemma. On the one hand, these pesticides and fertilizers promised to boost agricultural productivity and help India move towards self-sufficiency in food production. On the other, there were concerns about their long-term impact on health, environment and rural livelihoods. Unlike many of her contemporaries, who either resisted change or embraced it blindly, Zohraben took a balanced approach. She engaged critically with the issue, advocating for policies that would modernize agriculture without compromising human and ecological well-being.

Her work in the committee reflected her ability to evolve beyond rigid ideological boundaries. While she deeply respected Gandhian values, she understood that a new India required new strategies. Her foresight in identifying this transition was a testament to her intellectual depth and commitment to pragmatic governance. This makes her political legacy unique with admirable idealism and commitment to public life.

4

Maimoona Sultan: The Life and Times of a Congress Insider

Bhopal's story has been one of the most extraordinary accounts of eighteenth- and nineteenth-century India. In February–March 1818, Bhopal became a princely state in British India as a result of the Anglo-Bhopal treaty between the East India Company (EIC) and Nazar Muhammad Khan (the nawab of Bhopal during 1816–19). Between 1819 and 1926, the state had the unique distinction of being ruled by four women, or Begums. Unfortunately, however, the Begums of Bhopal and their contribution in the field of education, women's literacy and emancipation has escaped serious academic research.

In *Outlook Traveller*, Gustasp and Jeroo Irani wrote:

> It was a pistol shot that went wrong and had far-reaching consequences…across the centuries. Fired playfully by an eight-year-old at a royal picnic, it tore through 28-year-old Nawab Nazar Muhammad Khan, who had ruled the

former princely state of Bhopal for three years. His wife, the formidable Qudsia Begum, whipped off her veil at her husband's funeral and declared herself regent. In a resounding voice, she made it clear to restless male claimants gathered there that her 15-month-old daughter would be his heir. That single act of courage foreshadowed the chutzpah of her female successors who would rule the city-state with panache for 107 years.[1]

In Bhopal's folklore, Begums Qudsia, Sikandar, Shah Jahan and Sultan Jahan were no ordinary names. Together, they ruled over the princely state for more than a century. Their matrilineal reign, which began in 1819, would have continued to flourish had the reorganization of Indian states, and the merger and abolition of princely states had not taken place. The Begums' rule in Bhopal saw justice, gender sensitivity, peace and reforms, even as faith and traditions remained intact.

Archival records are filled with the Begums exhibiting their commitment to Islam by building mosques in London and Basra, along with funding the Aligarh Muslim University (AMU) and setting up modern schools in various Indian cities. These gestures were extremely significant. Such initiatives were put in place at a time when women's education – or, for that matter, women taking a lead in community affairs – was frowned upon. Even a progressive of that era like Sir Syed Ahmad Khan wanted to focus on elite Muslim men getting the benefit of Western education. This was a period when women were supposed to remain inside the zenana and obey the existing line of authority established in the family. The maximum concession extended to 'educated women' was them being allowed to focus on the morality and grooming of children.

Family Legacy

Maimoona Sultan thus belonged to a city where women had ruled for more than a hundred years. Such was their impact that, for many decades, most women of aristocracy did not attach their fathers' or husbands' surnames to their own. Most of them simply used 'Sultan' as their surname, just as Maimoona did. In an interview, Maimoona's younger sister Salma, a known Doordarshan news anchor, had explained, 'I belong to a city [Bhopal] where women ruled for 100 years. So much is the pride in that place that till date most women don't attach their father['s] or husband's surname. Most girls still use "Sultan", just like I do.'

Born into a family that valued both tradition and education, Maimoona's early years were shaped by a blend of scholarly influence and conservative upbringing. Her father, Mohammed Asghar Ansari, was a distinguished scholar who served as a secretary in the Ministry of Agriculture, while her mother, a Pathan homemaker, ensured that the family adhered to cultural and religious values. Despite the constraints often placed on women's education in conservative households, Maimoona was encouraged to pursue her studies, reflecting the family's progressive outlook on learning.

She completed her graduation in English literature from the prestigious AMU, a bastion of academic excellence and intellectual discourse. Her passion for language and literature led her to pursue another degree – a postgraduate diploma in teaching – further refining her skills in communication and pedagogy. It was not long before her command over the English language became widely recognized, earning her admiration from colleagues and even instilling a sense of competition in political circles.

An Eloquent Leader

During her tenure in the Lok Sabha between 1957 and 1967, her eloquence and articulate speeches often set her apart. It was said that even the formidable Rajmata Vijaya Raje Scindia – one of the most influential women in Indian politics – felt a certain degree of unease when engaging with Maimoona in parliamentary debates. This linguistic prowess not only helped her carve a niche in Indian politics but also played a pivotal role in expanding her influence beyond domestic affairs.

It was Maimoona's flair for language and diplomacy that caught the attention of Jawaharlal Nehru, India's first prime minister. Known for his appreciation of intellectualism and eloquence, Nehru found in Maimoona a capable interlocutor who could effectively navigate discussions on politics and foreign relations. Their interactions opened up new avenues for her, allowing her to play an active role in shaping diplomatic discourse and representing India on various international platforms.

She headed the Congress's Department of Foreign Affairs, greeted visiting dignitaries from Josip Broz Tito, the president of Yugoslavia, who was the first European leader (head of a state) to visit India after the country's independence, to Leonid Brezhnev, the former general secretary of the Communist Party of the Soviet Union, in 1980. When Nehru heard Maimoona greet Tito, he instantly decided that she should be a member of the Indian Parliament instead of a member of the legislative assembly (MLA). Maimoona was, at that time (1952–57), serving as an MLA from Kotri (in Sehore district of Madhya Pradesh). V.K. Krishna Menon who was the country's defence minister, and a diplomat and statesman, admired Maimoona's understanding of world affairs. Sultan had even addressed the UN General Assembly (UNGA) in 1958 where Krishna Menon had led a delegation.

According to Alim Bazmi, a senior editor with *Dainik Bhaskar*, old-timers had told him how Maimoona had taken Tito to Chiklod Estate spread over 748 acres that boasted of farms, lakes, a polo ground and even an airstrip, among other things. Tito, whose charisma and concentration of power helped bind former Yugoslavia's diverse peoples together, reportedly told Maimoona about how the journey reminded him of a villa in Bugojno, where he was fond of hunting for bears among the fir trees. At Chiklod, Tito was said to have hunted two Hard-ground Barasinghas, a type of deer. Apparently, these hunted deer were eventually consumed after being cooked over a slow fire.

Maimoona Sultan's political career was marked by groundbreaking achievements, making her a pioneering figure in Indian politics. Having first established herself as a state legislator, she made history in 1957 by becoming one of the first two Muslim women elected to the Lok Sabha, along with Mofida Ahmed of Assam. This milestone was particularly significant at a time when women's representation in Indian politics was minimal, and Muslim women faced even greater societal constraints.

Maimoona went on to serve two consecutive terms in the Lok Sabha, from 1957 to 1967, firmly establishing her presence in national politics. Her electoral victory in 1957 was decisive – she defeated the Hindu Mahasabha's Hardayal Deogun by a margin of 25,184 votes. She secured 81,134 votes against Deogun's 55,950, a commanding lead that signified not only her political acumen but also the trust she had built among her constituents. Her ability to connect with voters across religious and social lines was a testament to her inclusive and progressive approach to governance.

A Unique Lineage

Maimoona's entry into politics was as dramatic as it was significant. She hailed from a distinguished lineage, with deep historical and cultural roots. Her father, Mohammed Asghar Ansari, was a respected bureaucrat who served in the Bhopal state services before taking up key administrative roles in the Indian government. He was a highly educated man, having completed his BSc and LLB degrees from AMU, an institution known for producing some of India's most influential leaders and intellectuals.

Ansari's career saw him hold important positions, including serving as a secretary of a government department in Bhopal, registrar of cooperative societies and later as a senior officer in the Ministry of Agriculture. However, his identity was not merely limited to his administrative achievements. His ancestry traced back to the Durrani dynasty of Afghanistan, and he was a direct descendant of Shah Shuja, who ruled Afghanistan from 1803 to 1809. This lent Maimoona a unique heritage – blending aristocratic traditions with the intellectual and administrative rigour of her father's professional background.

As an AMU alumnus, Asghar Ansari was deeply impressed by the quality of education imparted there, particularly to women. As luck would have it, his daughter was in touch with two sisters of Maulana Abul Kalam Azad, namely Abru Begum and Fatima Arzu Begum. Both Abru and Arzu were early feminists and educationists who had played an important role in establishing the Aligarh Women's College, the Women's Conference, and a number of schools, hospitals and colleges. Maulana Azad and Nehru met Maimoona at the residence of Abru Begum and Arzu Begum.

Maimoona was married to Mohammad Mujtaba Khan who was from the Fatehgarh locality of Bhopal downtown. For most of his career, Mujtaba remained in the Bhopal Municipal Corporation (BMC) and rose to head it as its chief executive. Mujtaba's involvement with BMC meant constant social and professional interaction with city planners, politicians, elites and virtually everyone who mattered in the state capital. As a hostess, Maimoona had a wide-ranging interaction with a cross-section of society, giving her a profile and status in Bhopal's social ladder.

When the first general and state assembly elections were announced, Nehru sent a communication to Dr Shankar Dayal Sharma, a towering Congress leader of central India, recommending young Maimoona as a Congress nominee from Sehore. Sharma was thinking of fielding Begum Sajida Sultan, daughter of Nawab Hamidullah Khan of Bhopal. Sajida was married to Nawab Iftikhar Ali Khan Pataudi and was busy raising ten-year-old Mansoor Ali Khan, who would go on to be remembered as the cricket legend 'Tiger' Pataudi.

Maimoona had an illustrious sister, Salma Sultan, who was a well-known newsreader with the state-run Doordarshan. Salma once recalled, 'I was an unplanned child but a blessing to my lonely sister [Maimoona] who would protect me from the wrath of my disciplined father who would make sure that I offer all my prayers (*namaz*) and read the Quran on time. But he has a great contribution in the making of my personality. My father used to emphasize education and extracurricular activities in school. He would prepare my debate and make me rehearse in front of him.'[2]

Salma did her graduation from Bhopal. 'I did my post-graduation in English from Delhi's Indraprastha College and simultaneously auditioned for an announcer on Doordarshan.'

Active Parliamentarian

As an active MP, Maimoona asked many questions in the Lok Sabha, from the country making progress on a treaty on non-proliferation of nuclear weapons, to Chinese intrusions into Sikkim and Bhutan; about the outcome of the recent correspondence between India and Pakistan regarding holding the next round of talks in accordance with the terms of the Tashkent Agreement; from the dumps of arms bearing Pakistani markings found in Kashmir, to the exchange of impounded ships between India and Pakistan, and the rehabilitation of displaced persons from East Pakistan.

According to records maintained in Parliament, her questions ranged from treaties on the exploration of outer space and the moon, to the installation of electronic computers in Delhi to locate water-trouble spots. She also enquired about the setting up of a one-person commission to go into the boundary disputes between Mysore and Maharashtra as well as between Mysore and Kerala. She also raised questions on varied policy issues which gained traction at that time, such as the follow-up measures taken after the currency devaluation to reinvigorate the country's economy; inclusion of education in the fourth plan; the lockout in Hindustan Aeronautics Ltd, Kanpur; the outcome of the US collaboration for the Madras Fertiliser Project, and the completion of the enquiry into the affairs of Bennett Coleman and Company Ltd. Her parliamentary interventions also embraced outstanding issues which included the refusal of the Indian Airlines Corporation's

(IAC's) pilots to take a test flight at Bombay (now Mumbai); the number of proposed buses to be added to the Delhi Transport Corporation (DTC); the fleet of buses required to alleviate transport difficulties in Delhi during the years 1966–87, and also the commissioning of the Gujarat Refinery.

In one of the debates, Maimoona had raised concerns about the Union of India's response to UN's resolutions on the subject of the illegal, racist regime in southern Rhodesia, steps taken by the government to solve the Vietnam problem and rection the USA,[3] trade with Russia and East European countries, and an Indian correspondent from the Press Trust of India being physically assaulted by United States Secret Service (USSS) agents in the UN's international territory.

Mark of Political Resilience

In 1967, Maimoona Sultan lost her third Lok Sabha elections from Bhopal to J.R. Joshi of the Bharatiya Jan Sangh. A section of the local Congress unit had reportedly opposed her by fielding a poet named Abdul Ahad Khan, who went by the name 'Takkhalus Bhopali', as an independent candidate. While Bhopali received a paltry 8,807 votes, the presence of CPI nominee M.D. Srivastava proved costly for her. Maimoona reportedly felt disillusioned by this defeat.

Scholar and Congress historian Shashi Kumar Singh felt that in the 1967 elections, people did not vote for or against Indira Gandhi, even as the Congress returned to power with a reduced margin in the Lok Sabha. This was the post-Nehru era, when Congress was besieged with internal contradictions led by regional strongmen. 'People gave their public opinion against the frustrated politics of some big leaders. In fact, Indira Gandhi could not secure tickets for the people she wanted, Krishna Menon being one of them,' he said. The truth was that in every state, a large number of Congress leaders had left the party. These were the same people who formed regional parties and came together as the Opposition. 'Due to this, the strength of the Congress decreased at the Centre and the party lost power in Kerala, West Bengal and even Punjab,' Singh pointed out.[4]

Soon, Indira Gandhi stepped in. She appointed Maimoona as the head of the AICC's foreign affairs department, an important office in the ruling party hierarchy. She travelled to more than a dozen countries and addressed press conferences in support of Indira Gandhi's Emergency that had curtailed civil and political rights.

In 1974, recognizing her political acumen and unwavering dedication, Indira Gandhi nominated Maimoona Sultan to the Rajya Sabha, giving her a new platform to contribute to national policymaking. Her tenure in the upper house of Parliament was marked by active participation in debates on governance, social justice and minority rights. When Indira Gandhi returned to power in 1980, she reappointed Maimoona for another term, extending her tenure until 1986. This reaffirmation of trust underscored Maimoona's stature as a seasoned parliamentarian and a respected voice within the Congress Party. She served as a member of the Rajya Sabha from April 1974 to April 1980 and from June 1980 to June 1986.

However, by the early 1980s, Maimoona's health began to decline, even though she was only in her mid-fifties. The physical toll of years spent in rigorous political engagements and public service began to show. Despite her failing health, she remained committed to her principles and continued to influence political discourse.

Eventually, she withdrew from active political life, marking the end of an era in Indian politics where she had played a crucial role in shaping legislative discussions. Her passing in 2006 drew the curtains on a remarkable life that had straddled different phases of India's socio-political transformation.

A Lasting Commitment to Public Service

Maimoona Sultan's life story is emblematic of the generational shifts in India's political landscape. She belonged to a time when power was transitioning from an exclusive, elite club – rooted in aristocratic privilege and colonial-era Western education – to a more democratic and inclusive political order. While this old guard had its flaws, often being hierarchical and exclusionary, it was also shaped by a sense of justice and civic responsibility. Maimoona stood at the crossroads of this evolution, navigating both privilege and progressivism to carve out a legacy of her own – one defined by intellect, resilience and an enduring commitment to public service.

5

Begum Akbar Jehan Abdullah: Kashmir's 'Madr-e-Meharban'

As Dr Myra Jehlen, professor of English at Rutgers University, observes, a woman's selfhood is contingent on her 'ability to act in the public domain'.[1] It is challenging to reconstruct women's lives, even of those who have been visible in the public arena, because women are conditioned to wipe away their footprints and end up leaving very few traces of the kind that historical exploration would accept as legitimate. Hence, it is imperative to reiterate the rich political legacy of Begum Akbar Jehan.

On her demise in July 2000, the incumbent prime minister of the country, Atal Bihari Vajpayee, flanked by then Union Home Minister L.K. Advani, rushed to Kashmir to attend her funeral.[2] The cabinet of the Government of India also condoled her death. This itself is indicative of the political heft of Begum Akbar Jehan, fondly remembered as Kashmir's 'Madr-e-Meharban', which can be roughly translated as 'the epitome (mother) of kindness'. Such a title can be attributed to her distinctive career in social work and her politics which built an illustrious public life. Begum Sahiba was a freedom fighter, social reformer and politician, who left a significant mark on the socio-political landscape of Jammu and Kashmir. What makes her journey remarkable is her ascent in Kashmir's corridors of power and influence, in a social structure that is weighed down by the heavy, conservative shackles of patriarchy.

Love, Companionship and the Turbulence of Politics

Begum Akbar Jehan first rose to prominence due to her marriage to Sheikh Abdullah (known as 'Sher-e-Kashmir'), the former prime minister and chief minister of Jammu and Kashmir, and the founder of Kashmir's most prominent political party, National Conference (NC). The party is now headed by his son, Farooq Abdullah, and grandson, Omar Abdullah – both of whom have also served as chief ministers (CMs) of Kashmir during different periods of time.[3]

Sheikh Abdullah's immense popularity as the undisputed leader of the Valley stems from how vehemently he fought against Kashmir's erstwhile monarchical regime by spearheading a pro-democracy movement. He is widely regarded as a key figure who facilitated Kashmir's merger with India at the time of Independence. However, in the early 1950s, he fell from grace in the eyes of the Indian government, and remained in a long incarceration and exile from Kashmir till 1972. It is at this time of immense turbulence, both political and personal, that Begum Akbar Jehan rose to prominence to spearhead the party and keep Abdullah's legacy unblemished.

However, her actual baptism by fire had happened a long time ago. Born in 1916 to a European father, Michael Harry Nedou, and Kashmiri mother, Mirjan (also known as Ranijee), Akbar Jehan was brought up in a household of immense affluence. Her family owned an Indian hotel chain that included the Nedous Hotel in Srinagar, once a rare and appealing tourist destination with a well-known bakery, which is now in a dilapidated condition. Apart from being a hotelier, Michael was known for his altruistic work, an attribute that Akbar Jehan would inherit from her father. Her mother, Ranijee, was known to be an indomitable Gujjar woman whose family lineage can be traced back to the martial, patrilineal and rigidly traditional Rajputs of Rajasthan, who once owned vast tracts of land in Gulmarg.

Before Akbar Jehan's birth, a saintly figure from Amritsar, Maulvi Mohi-ud-Din, assured Akbar's parents that the child 'would be his spiritual child who would embody high ideals and piety'. He told them to name the girl 'Akbar Jehan'. Akbar Jehan, born on 24 March 1907, was not particularly tall, but she had a regal demeanour, resembling a statue in dignity, grace and proportion.[4]

Begum Akbar Jehan's granddaughter, Nyla Ali Khan, an academician, wrote an in-depth and revealing biography of the Begum a few years ago, titled as *The Life of a Kashmiri Woman*. In her book, she wrote about Akbar's interesting choice to marry Sheikh Abdullah. 'Akbar Jehan, born and raised in the lap of luxury, who made the exacting choice of marrying a young Kashmiri Muslim greenhorn, Sheikh Mohammad Abdullah. The wedding took place on 5 Jamadi-us-Sani 1352 A.H., which would translate as 1933.'[5]

Nyla was reportedly told by her mother that Maulvi Mohi-ud-Din, whom Akbar Jehan greatly revered, influenced her decision to marry the Sheikh, which, metaphorically, entailed swimming against the tide. Later in life, whenever she encountered an unyielding situation, she would pay obeisance at her mentor's tomb in Pattan, now in Pakistan, and submit to God's will.

Her strong resolve can be seen as a legacy passed down from her mother, who 'had clearly made a success of her interracial and intercultural marriage [with a European], a union which can be difficult to navigate even in today's global and cosmopolitan age'.[6] Ranijee was a forthright and courageous woman, who persevered against all odds. Years later, in 1953, it was Ranijee who financially supported her daughter during her most difficult time of indignity and alienation, when Sheikh Abdullah was imprisoned by the Indian government.

In his autobiography, Sheikh Abdullah writes that Ranijee was a virtuous, religious and 'good-natured lady'. He credits her with having infused the value of religious teachings and traditions in Akbar Jehan.[7] Raised in a religious environment under the guidance of her mother, she developed an interest in religious studies even while attending the Convent of Jesus and

Mary, Murree (now in Pakistan). She also took lessons in the Quran and Hadith at home. Visits to shrines and tombs were an integral part of her religious life. In her final commentary on Akbar's religiosity, Nyla writes, 'The wise say that "faith can move mountains", and I believe that Grandmother's faith gave her the pugnacity and resoluteness to face the many whirlwinds in her immediate as well as distant world.'[8]

Akbar Jehan completed her Senior Cambridge in 1933. It was time for her marriage and, against all odds, she chose to marry Sheikh Abdullah, a freedom fighter busy challenging the autocratic rule of the Dogras in the Valley while also fighting for India's independence. Akbar Jehan remained unfazed by the uncertainties that a life with a freedom fighter could entail.

Writer Tariq Ali made a controversial claim that Akbar Jehan was earlier married to an Arab man named Karam Shah, who had vanished after a Calcutta newspaper, *Liberty*, reported that he was actually T.E. Lawrence (or better known as Lawrence of Arabia), a British intelligence officer. It was also claimed that she divorced Lawrence in 1929. This claim has been strongly dismissed by Nyla in her book and has also been refuted by Lawrence's biographers.

Transcending from Private to Public

Akbar Jehan demonstrated her inherent knack for public service quite early. Her talent for rallying people became evident during the Quit Kashmir Movement, and later, when her husband was imprisoned. In 1946–47, she stepped out of her home and travelled to villages, inspiring hope in the hearts of the oppressed and standing by the families of martyrs. During the time her husband was imprisoned under the Maharaja's regime, she welcomed Mahatma Gandhi to Soura, Srinagar, during his visit to Kashmir in 1947. Mahatma Gandhi's prayer meeting in Srinagar began with the recitation of the Quran by Akbar Jehan. Her contributions in social service were commendable: During the traumatic period in the Valley in 1947–48, when the pro-democracy movement clashed against the Dogra rule and an attack by Pakistani militants rocked the region, Begum Akbar worked hard to provide comfort and aid to victims, demonstrating her compassion and resoluteness in public service. She organized the Red Cross, offering crucial support to those in need, and played a vital role in rescuing and rehabilitating abducted women.

Akbar Jehan strongly advocated for women's education, believing it would empower girls, especially from disadvantaged backgrounds. She worked alongside Lady Mountbatten to repatriate women separated from their families during Partition, restoring their dignity and offering vocational training for their financial independence. In 1948, she helped form a relief committee to aid those affected by the tourism collapse after Partition. Being cognizant of the work that Akbar Jehan and her colleagues could undertake to help refugees, the Sheikh asked her to join him in the task of managing relief camps. The Sheikh later wrote in his autobiography, 'When I asked my wife about it, she agreed at once to help me in relief work. She gave up the purdah and did commendable work in organizing relief camps.'[9] His appreciation of Akbar Jehan's espousal of public life by jettisoning conservative values bears credence because, at that time, the purdah reinforced a powerful cultural ideal and was a pivotal element in the reproduction of familial status. As we've established earlier, Akbar Jehan's parents were part of the aristocratic and wealthy strata of society, in which women's seclusion from the public realm and the donning of the purdah were, in fact, status markers. Therefore, her relinquishment of the security, privilege and dependence that the institution of the purdah bestowed on women was a courageous move. The Sheikh believed that Akbar Jehan had the backbone and grit to 'turn her veil into a banner'.[10]

In the wake of the Quit Kashmir Movement against the Dogra regime in the Valley, Akbar Jehan started diligently engaging in activism. Nyla observes in her book that Akbar Jehan 'invested herself in inspiring the desire for a dignified existence in the despondent, the fires of whose hearths had been cruelly quenched. She stepped into the stream of public consequence by choice, not through "divine intervention"'.[11] Nyla further observed in her book that similar to nineteenth-century French feminist leaders, Akbar Jehan came together with other Kashmiri women to form the Women's Self-Defence Corps. According to Nyla, they 'used the concept of motherhood figuratively to refer to women's spiritual qualities and social mission'.[12] Akbar Jehan's political and social activism for the empowerment of women vocalized the desire for freedom and liberation as 'a historically situated desire whose motivational force cannot be assumed a priori, but needs to be reconsidered in light of other desires, aspirations, and capacities that inhere in a culturally and historically located subject'.[13]

Another major legacy of Akbar Jehan is the Markaz Behbudi Khawateen, an institute which continues to exist and impart literacy, providing training in the fields of arts, crafts and healthcare to enable empowerment and social security. She diligently garnered funds to build schools for indigent children and championed adult education in a state where a significant part of the population was illiterate. According to the current vice chairperson, Suraiya Ali Matto, the youngest daughter of Akbar Jehan, this institute was the first non-governmental organization (NGO) in the Valley to help destitute women, indigent Gujjar and Bakarwal tribes of Jammu and Kashmir who are officially regarded as socio-economically disadvantaged, and orphaned boys belonging to those tribes.

Amidst Politics and its Trepidations

Akbar Jehan represented the Srinagar and Anantnag constituencies of Jammu and Kashmir in the Indian Parliament from 1977 to 1979 and from 1984 to 1989, respectively. She was also the first president of the Jammu and Kashmir Red Cross Society from 1947 to 1951. Nyla, in her book, observes that 'during her husband Sheikh Mohammad Abdullah's incarceration, [Begum Akbar Jehan] had been burdened with the arduous task of raising five children in a politically repressive environment that sought to undo her husband's mammoth political, cultural, legal attempts to restore the faith of Kashmiri society in itself.'[14] Sheikh Abdullah deeply appreciated Akbar Jehan's moral courage during these challenging times, affectionately addressing her as 'Begum Sahiba' or 'Buboo' in family circles. He often reminded his children of her devout adherence to Islam, which strengthened their bond. Akbar Jehan stood strong against government pressure, offering support and advice to the Sheikh, even warning him against compromising his position by succumbing to Prime Minister Nehru's charm.

After his arrest, when their home in Srinagar was sealed and the family evicted, Akbar Jehan's pride was hurt, but she refused government assistance. Though her brothers were unable or unwilling to help for fear of political repercussions, Akbar Jehan's mother supported her financially. Despite mounting hardships, she remained resolute, managing her husband's political organization and continuing the resistance against the Sheikh's opponent Bakshi Ghulam Mohammad's regime. Even in the face of physical threats, like an attack on the Hazratbal Shrine, she stood her ground, driven by unwavering faith. Throughout the Sheikh's imprisonment, Akbar Jehan endured isolation but remained determined. She played a key role in the Jammu and Kashmir Plebiscite Front, working tirelessly behind the scenes to empower people, especially women, to participate in public discourse and activism.

Nyla recalls in her work that Akbar Jehan's appearance, as her photographs showcase, was as resplendent as her will was resolute. Begum Akbar Jehan skilfully straddled the linguistic paradigms of English, Urdu, Gojri and Kashmiri and just as dexterously straddled three cultural paradigms – European, Gujjar and Kashmiri.

Despite being implicated in the Kashmir Conspiracy Case, the Sheikh remained committed to his political beliefs, with Akbar Jehan steadfastly by his side, never wavering. As the Sheikh remained in jail, Akbar Jehan ably supervised their daughter's wedding. She fulfilled her role as the matriarch with grace and determination, ensuring that her daughter's transition to her in-laws' home was carried out with traditional care and respect. Mustafa Kamal, the Sheikh's youngest son, recalls how Akbar Jehan spent two years with the Sheikh during his exile in Kodaikanal as his shadow, providing him rock-solid support.

Seasoned journalist Ajit Bhattacharjea also observes, 'When freed of her domestic chores, Akbar Jahan [sic] developed the personality latent in her ... She was regarded as being even more committed to securing Kashmir's autonomy than her husband.'[15] Akbar Jehan was accused of being the conduit through whom the Sheikh purportedly received 'illegal funding' for 'espionage activities', but she remained unfazed by such allegations.

Electoral Politics

Akbar Jehan's political sagacity became evident in 1971 when she campaigned for independent candidate Shamim Ahmad

Shamim, challenging the former prime minister of Kashmir, Bakshi Ghulam Mohammad, in the prestigious Srinagar parliamentary constituency. After successfully campaigning in the 1971 parliamentary elections for a political newcomer supported by the Plebiscite Front, Akbar Jehan's political influence was noticed. Following the election, she was exiled for three and a half years by the central government. When the ban was lifted in 1974, her return, along with the Sheikh and others, was met with widespread celebration, notes Nyla. The 1977 assembly elections in Jammu and Kashmir saw an unprecedented voter turnout, with Akbar Jehan taking the lead in campaigning while her husband, who had suffered a heart attack, was forced to rest. Despite the physical strain, Akbar Jehan travelled the length and breadth of the entire Valley, tirelessly supporting her husband's vision, while he recuperated. As he later reflected, her perseverance and political insight helped navigate the shifting political landscape.

Having been raised in a milieu that enabled Akbar Jehan to blossom not just academically but also socially and culturally, she was as much at ease campaigning at a political rally for the Sheikh's political organization as she was in conversing with career diplomats and statesmen. Nyla emphatically argues that Akbar Jehan was one of the harbingers of feminism in Jammu and Kashmir, which she defines as 'the inclusion of women in political citizenship and top-down reforms initiated by the State, without the notable participation of women, for the improvement of the legal, social and economic status of women'.[16]

Her political acumen was evident during her election campaigns, including the 1984 polls, where she campaigned tirelessly, winning a seat in the Lok Sabha. Pakistani writer Bilqis Taseer had witnessed her skill and proficiency as a speaker at the Urs (religious festival celebrated by Muslims) of Pir Zaman Shah of Malamkam village near Wulur Lake. 'Begum sahiba,' Taseer respectfully narrates, 'spoke for more than an hour, first in Kashmiri, then at murmurs from the Jammu-ites she switched to Urdu, then at murmurs from the Gujjars and Bakarwals to Gujri, all with equal ease ... The amount of effort she put in for those 20 days would have broken a younger woman, but for one who has now reached her seventies the achievement was phenomenal.'[17]

Nyla reported that she accompanied Akbar Jehan during campaigns and saw her vigour in the electoral battlefield in 1984 as her car was halted at every step by enthusiastic supporters stopping Akbar to kiss her hand or her forehead.[18] Her hard work paid off and she won the election.

Despite her wealthy background, Akbar Jehan's home was always simply furnished, with her personal space often in disarray. She lived a life of humility, having sold her family's valuable jewellery during tough times. She remained unwavering in her support for her husband and son, Farooq Abdullah, even as internal political conflicts arose within the NC after the Sheikh's death, with her elder daughter, Khalida, and her husband, Ghulam Mohammad Shah, orchestrating a putsch in cahoots with the Indira Gandhi–led Congress, much to Akbar Jehan's chagrin. She steadfastly supported Farooq, on which Nyla reflects in her book:

> She considered it incumbent upon her to make obvious her predilection for her older son at the expense of her motherly solicitude for her older daughter, Khalida. This is where I realized that, although Akbar Jehan hadn't lived in an environment in which she had been told that women were incapable of significant achievement, she considered it her bounden duty to reinforce the culturally supported attitude toward mothers, which was the expectation of their unquestioning constancy and devotedness to sons, especially first-born sons.[19]

Despite the challenges, she remained a key figure in Kashmiri politics, defending her son's leadership. However, by the late 1990s, she became more of a symbolic figure, as the NC weakened progressively, and the Valley descended into turmoil. Even as her health declined and the political landscape shifted, Akbar Jehan refused to leave Kashmir, remaining a rallying point for loyalists who valued conviction over pragmatism. She passed away, deeply saddened at the disintegration of her husband's political legacy and the decline of the National Conference (NC).

A Formidable Yet Lesser-known Legacy

Nyla, in the opening pages of her grandmother's biography, points out that she tried to write about 'a woman of iron-clad determination, persevering, articulate, politically savvy; a vulnerable mother and grandmother, who, at times, turned a blind eye to the faults of her children; a believer in traditional kinship structures; a dedicated social activist, fiercely proud of her heritage, and just as fiercely keen on preserving it; an independent woman whose life redefined the stereotypical feminist notion of "emancipation," because her desire for emancipation was mediated by a sense of responsibility to her community.'[20] Nyla also observes that 'Akbar Jehan Abdullah was a benign, affectionate, slightly detached, and much lauded presence in Sheikh sahab's lifetime.'

Her death anniversary is observed by her party every year and has been declared as Women's Day by the Jammu and Kashmir National Conference (JKNC) since 2007. Rattan Lal Gupta, senior vice president of JKNC, noted while paying obeisance on her death anniversary that it was under 'Akbar's inspiration that National Conference Government had provided 33% reservation to women in all spheres. She even ensured that State Government start maximum schemes for the welfare of the women folk for empowerment.'[21] Akbar Jehan's appearance on the political scene in a male-dominated society speaks about her grit and competence.

It is paradoxical that although Begum Akbar Jehan was a determined political and social activist, 'according to biographical genealogical conventions, the [lives of the] fathers are known and largely accounted for, while the [lives of the] mothers are unknown, unrecorded, and, until relatively recently, little explored.'[22] This was our attempt at correcting this and recording her political legacy – a benefaction which echoes not just in Jammu and Kashmir but across India, to date.

6

Rashida Haque Choudhury: From Political Prominence to Oblivion

In the historic 1977 Lok Sabha elections, the only Muslim woman leader who could make it to the Congress party's list of candidates was Rashida Haque Choudhury, widow of late Union Minister Moinul Haque Choudhury. Rashida also went on to become the first female central minister of independent India from the Barak Valley of Assam, when she joined the Chaudhary Charan Singh government at the Centre as the minister of state of social welfare from 1979 to 1980. Rashida got the party ticket in 1977 when her husband, Moinul Haque Choudhury, a Congress stalwart, passed away suddenly at the age of fifty-three. She contested from Silchar, considered her husband's fiefdom, and won easily, thus entering politics.

Early Life

Rashida, who was born in April 1926, hailed from Silchar and had an elite family background.[1] She was the daughter of a former magistrate of British India, Nasib Ali Mazumdar. She studied at Misson School, Silchar, and later completed her bachelor's degree from Lady Brabourne College in Calcutta. Rashida got married to Moinul, a rising political star and the son of a well-off family, in December 1948, and the couple had three daughters and one son.

Influence of Moinul's Politics

Moinul's father, Montajir Ali, was an educated man himself and understood the value of providing a good education to his son. After his primary education at Middle English (ME) school at Sonabarighat, Moinul completed his matriculation from Silchar Government High Secondary School, and was later sent to Cotton University in Guwahati and Murari Chand College in Sylhet. He graduated from the historic Presidency College in Kolkata, and went on to pursue his master's degree in history from AMU, where he came first in his batch.

Moinul had an early encounter with student politics when he defeated Bangladesh's founder Sheikh Mujibur Rahman in the college election at Presidency. Moinul, in his early days in politics, joined the All-India Muslim League (AIML) and served as a secretary in its youth front. His representation of the Barak Valley during a meeting with Muhammad Ali Jinnah became well-known. Later, Moinul was influenced by Netaji Subhas Chandra Bose and Maulana Azad, and joined the Indian freedom movement. After Independence, he was inducted into the Congress Party by the then Congress leader and future President of India, Fakhruddin Ali Ahmed.

After completing his LLB from AMU, Moinul joined the Bar Association of Silchar in 1948. He was soon involved in active politics when he joined the local board in 1950 and he was nominated to the Silchar municipality. Moinul became an MLA for the first time from the East Sonai constituency in 1952 and his political graph rose spectacularly after that. He became agriculture minister in 1957 in Assam and became the leader of the Congress legislative party in 1962. Despite his fourth consecutive win in assembly polls in 1967, Moinul was deprived of a ministerial berth over his growing differences with the sitting chief minister of Assam and senior Congress leader Bimala Prasad Chaliha. Moinul then decided to enter national politics and he was elected from the Dhubri Lok Sabha seat in 1971, and went on to become minister of commerce and industrial development – a capacity in which he served from 18 March 1971 to 22 July 1972.

Moinul is regarded as one of the chief architects of the Barak Valley region in Assam as he ushered in crucial industrial reforms in the region during his stint as central minister. The establishment of the Silchar Medical College, the Hindustan Paper Mill at Panchgram, the sugar mill at Anipur and the Regional Engineering College in Silchar – now upgraded as

NIT – are all credited to him.[2] He is still remembered in the region for his early proposal for the construction of the Barak Dam and attempts to initiate a green revolution in the valley. His younger brother Nurul Hoque Choudhury also became an MLA from Sonai in 1972 when Moinul vacated his MLA seat to move to the Centre.

As a tribute to his legacy, the Moinul Haque Choudhury Memorial Science College was established in 1997 in Algapur district in Assam.[3] Haque's death anniversary is commemorated by clubs and institutions located in Hailakandi district (in southern Assam). The functionaries during one such event hailed him as one of the modern architects of the Barak Valley. They said that every developmental activity in the valley was actually planned by him, and these activities were finally taking shape. They further said that Haque was a symbol of communal harmony and national integration, and that and he fought against corruption at all levels of society.[4]

Life in Politics

It was in the backdrop of her husband's illustrious political career that Rashida was exposed to a public life. She joined the Congress party in 1950, soon after her marriage to Moinul, and worked as a member of the Bhartiya Gramin Mahila Samiti and the Committee of Social Work for Bangladesh Refugees.[5] When Rashida got the party ticket from the Congress to contest the Lok Sabha elections after Moinul's death, she demonstrated exceptional political calibre by defeating her opponent, a senior CPI(M) leader from Assam, Nurul Huda, by a sizeable margin of 28,000 votes. Rashida had to face major obstacles not only from her rival parties but also from her own party colleagues who left no stone unturned to weaken her hold over her husband's political bastion in the Barak region.

A resident of the area and dean of the Indian Institute of Management, Kashipur, Professor K.M. Baharul Islam describes one incident, underlining the odds Rashida had to face. To wrest Silchar from his own party MP, Rashida Haque Choudhury, the Congress's Santosh Mohan Dev enabled the migration of Hindu refugees from Bangladesh to Silchar in the 1970s, he says.[6] It didn't stop Rashida from winning the 1977 election, which was a tough poll for her party as Indira Gandhi lost power at the Centre after imposing her contentious Emergency. Though the party only fielded Rashida as the lone Muslim woman candidate that year, she didn't disappoint when she handed over a notable victory to the Congress in its difficult time. Interestingly, though Congress didn't have any other Muslim women in the electoral fray that year, the party had a sizeable number of illustrious Muslim women leaders who worked very hard in Indira Gandhi's campaign, such as Mohsina Kidwai (Congress committee president, Uttar Pradesh), Maimoona Sultana (MP, Madhya Pradesh), Aziza Imam (MP, Uttar Pradesh) and Ushi Khan (Hindu widow of the late Barkatullah Khan, chief minister of Rajasthan). Indira also lost the most visible Muslim face of the party that year with the death of President Fakhruddin Ali Ahmed.[7]

MP and Minister

Rashida, as a parliamentarian, participated in Lok Sabha debates and routinely asked relevant questions regarding the developmental concerns of Assam, the state she represented. She posted a detailed question about whether the State Bank of India would establish a branch in Assam. She questioned the government's delay in setting up the Cachar paper mill there. On another occasion, she demanded an explanation from the Central minister of petroleum, chemicals and fertilizers regarding ONGC's plan for oil-bearing areas in Cachar district. She also raised important questions regarding developmental issues such as inadequate facilities at the Silchar Airport, challenges faced by passengers to reserve train tickets, and the need to provide compensation to the families of those who lost their lives in public tragedies. A glimpse of her nuanced parliamentary interventions involving larger industrial prospects as well as everyday hardships faced by common people reveals the deep involvement and commitment that Rashida demonstrated as an elected representative of Silchar and Assam.

Despite her spectacular entry into electoral politics, Rashida's relations with Indira's Congress (I) were severed very soon. In the aftermath of the shocking defeat of the Congress Party, riding on the negative public sentiment regarding the alleged excesses committed during the Emergency, a section of Congress leaders became wary of the return of Indira's younger son, Sanjay Gandhi, into party affairs. Sanjay was widely considered as a key figure who called the shots in the government during the Emergency. His presence at the party helm created resentment amongst a host of senior Congress leaders. Finally, a rebellion was initiated by the then chief minister of Karnataka, D. Devaraj Urs, and the Congress, led by Indira, witnessed a split that led to the creation of a new splinter group called Congress (Urs). Rashida also switched sides to the faction led by Urs. Devaraj Urs eventually joined the ruling Janata Party at the Centre. As a result, Rashida was appointed as the minister of state of social welfare at the Centre at the age of 53 in the government of the then prime minister, Chaudhary Charan Singh.[8] During this time, Rashida also served as chairperson of the National Bal Bhavan from September 1979 to December 1979.[9]

The Descent Downhill

However, the political tide turned rapidly against Rashida as Indira's Congress (I) made a spectacular political comeback in the 1980 Lok Sabha elections. Rashida contested from her Lok Sabha seat, Silchar. Though she garnered a sizeable vote share of 46.98 per cent, she lost to the Congress (I) candidate, Santosh Mohan Dev, who won 52 per cent of votes.[10] Along with Rashida, several other leaders of the ruling regime lost their seat in the 1980 elections. A news report on the 1980 election results in *The Hindustan Times* reveals Rashida's political heft as a sitting Central minister at that time and also suggests how the media captured her electoral loss from Silchar as a major political development. According to the report, 'Notable among those who were defeated were: External Affairs Minister Shyam Nandan Mishra and Mrs Rashida Haque Choudhury (Congress), Union Minister of State for Education and Social Welfare.'[11]

Rashida's party, Congress (Urs), eventually disintegrated as the party leader joined the Janata Party. Several leaders who had broken away from Congress (I) swiftly returned to its fold when it swept the elections. Strongman A.K. Antony moved out of Congress (Urs) to float his own political faction, Congress (A), in Kerala, and Sharad Pawar took over the presidentship of the party under the banner of Indian Congress (Socialist) in 1981.

Rashida, following her defeat in the 1980 elections as well as the disintegration of her political outfit and her distance from Congress (I), ended her political career as she went into political oblivion. She reportedly died on 23 October 1994.[12]

7

Mohsina Kidwai: A Life Lived with Dignity

It was 20 December 1978. Mohsina Kidwai was in Uttar Pradesh, where sugarcane farmers were in the middle of a protest against the predetermined low price of their produce when news of a plane hijack reached her.

When she heard the details, she was horrified. Apparently, the hijackers had said they would release the plane if she asked them to – thereby dragging her name into a controversy that could potentially embroil her in a long and messy legal tangle. The situation was already grim for the Congress. The party had been routed in the recent polls – voters had been unequivocal in their condemnation of the excesses of the Emergency – and Indira Gandhi was in jail, charged with offences related to the twenty-one-month-long muzzling of the Opposition and media.

Mohsina's personal career graph had seen a steady rise until then – she was president of the Congress's Uttar Pradesh unit

– but there was little to cheer about. And now, out of the blue, two hijackers had plunged not only her but also the party into another crisis.

Two young men, Bhola Nath Pandey and Devendra Pandey, had reportedly hijacked the Lucknow–Delhi–Kolkata Indian Airlines Flight 410. The Boeing 737 had 126 passengers on board, among them two former ministers of Indira Gandhi's cabinet, Ashoke Kumar Sen and Dharam Bir Sinha. Barely 15 minutes before the plane was to touch down in Delhi, the hijackers had got up and moved towards the cockpit. Captain M.N. Battiwala was forced to abort the landing in Delhi and had to head for Varanasi instead. The Pandeys were not related but their hijacking bid was driven by their mutual admiration for Indira Gandhi. They spoke about the 'vindictiveness' of the Janata Party–led government, and demanded the former prime minister's immediate and unconditional release from jail. Both said they were Youth Congress members, a claim the Congress and Mohsina would deny vehemently.

The hijack drama had ended by the evening, after the aircraft landed at Varanasi, where the father of one of the hijackers spoke to his son over the wireless set in the cockpit. The father's voice reportedly shattered the bubble of heroism. The two men, who were not carrying any firearms or explosives, emerged from the aircraft shouting pro-Indira slogans and surrendered to the police.

While the hijack drama was still going on, a senior government official informed Mohsina that the two hijackers had told the authorities they would release the plane only if she asked them to. Mohsina told the official she didn't know the hijackers. Since her name had come up, some legal luminaries advised her to apply for anticipatory bail at once. Mohsina would later say she did not have a law degree, but common sense came to her rescue. She told her lawyers that an anticipatory bail plea might be seen as an admission of guilt and association with the hijackers. She remained firm in her decision, which saved her from endless rounds of court visits.

This was Mohsina's only brush with any major controversy in her six-decade-long political career, which otherwise remained calm and dignified. At 93, like Dr Manmohan Singh, she is considered one of the Congress's most respected leaders. Sonia Gandhi, while writing a special note in Kidwai's 2022 memoir, *My Life in Indian Politics*, observed:

> Mohsina ji has a remarkable ability to establish a warm rapport with people from across the political spectrum as well as from all walks of life. These qualities, together with her integrity and gentle candour, her deep concern for the more vulnerable sections of society, her personal charm, and her abiding belief in the principles of democracy, pluralism, and social justice, are reflected in her memoirs. No wonder she is a much loved and respected figure in our national life. She is a cherished member of the Congress Party, whose rich experience and wise counsel we value greatly, and also a cherished personal friend.[1]

Manifold Identities

Mohsina's political career began in 1960 when she won a seat in the Uttar Pradesh Legislative Council. She was just 28 years old then – a young, idealistic homemaker, ready to dedicate her life to politics and public service. In 1974, she became a member of the state assembly and, by the time she won an election to Parliament in 1978, she had already been a minister in the Uttar Pradesh government for about five years. It wouldn't be long before Indira, by then back as prime minister, would appoint her a member to her council of ministers. For Mohsina, that would be the beginning of a series of key assignments in the central government – holding several portfolios, including labour, health and family welfare, rural development, transport and urban development – first under Indira and then under Rajiv Gandhi, as she gained the trust of both mother and son through her tireless work at every level of the party. After several stints in the Lok Sabha, Mohsina entered the Rajya Sabha, in 2004. She continued to hold her seat in the upper house of Parliament well into her eighties.

In her memoir, Mohsina has recounted fascinating incidents from her personal life and her career, from her early years in Barabanki, Uttar Pradesh, to the scrappy battles of local politics and, finally, to the corridors of power in New Delhi. Author-politician Shashi Tharoor says that all through her memoir, he was struck by the themes that seemed to consistently characterize her work: '... humility, dedication, integrity and a fierce determination to do the right thing. Her identities are manifold: a staunch Congress loyalist, a loving mother of three daughters, a proud Muslim and, above all, an Indian, dedicated to the well-being of her country.'[2]

Remarkably, Mohsina did not use her memories of her years at the highest level of government as a political weapon. Instead, she stuck to telling inside stories linked to the Congress from the standpoint of a person to whom truth and civility meant much more than material wealth.

In 1957, Mohsina, who was yet to join politics, had got a glimpse of what civility meant. It happened that Lal Bahadur Shastri, then a senior minister in Jawaharlal Nehru's cabinet, had come to visit her home in Barabanki in connection with the upcoming assembly elections, where her father-in-law, Jameel ur Rahman Kidwai, was contesting. Shastri was a simple man and the family's domestic help, who did not recognize him, asked where he had come from. When Shastri, a future prime minister, replied that he wished to meet Jameel ur Rahman, he was told that Jameel ur Rahman had gone out to campaign and would return only in the evening. So, Shastri sat down and waited. After a while, the domestic help served him tea, but it never occurred to him to inform the other members of the household that someone was waiting for Jameel ur Rahman. In the evening, when Jameel ur Rahman returned, he saw Shastri waiting for him. Deeply embarrassed, he scolded the domestic help and apologized to his guest.

It was Jameel ur Rahman who had a few years earlier introduced Mohsina to Nehru when he took his new daughter-in-law to meet the prime minister in Delhi. While they waited in the living room of Teen Murti Bhavan, the prime minister's daughter, Indira, walked up to them. 'Is this pretty young woman your daughter?' she had asked. 'Daughter-in-law,' Jameel ur Rahman had replied. 'My eldest son's wife. They got married just two months ago.' Indira congratulated them and then sat down beside Mohsina.[3]

Indira Anecdotes

Over the next thirty years, before Indira's assassination by her own bodyguards in 1984, Mohsina would get to know the leader in a way few other Congress politicians would. Naturally, therefore, her recollections of the time she spent with Indira offer fascinating glimpses into the character of the former prime minister, both as a person and as a politician.

For instance, while travelling, Indira had the habit of carrying some snacks with her in a basket. Once, on a long and tiring journey, Mohsina recalls, she saw the leader taking out some biscuits from the basket kept beneath her seat. She then broke the biscuits into four pieces and asked the driver to pick the pieces one by one from her hand while driving. This was a facet of Indira that only a few like Mohsina were familiar with.

Another incident Mohsina remembers shows the support Indira enjoyed even when she was voted out of power. While travelling to a famous gurdwara in Haridwar, Indira's convoy was suddenly stopped by a group of Sikh devotees. Indira was in the Opposition then and, therefore, without much security detail. But that didn't seem to bother her. The former prime minister got out of the car to greet the devotees. Suddenly, a Sikh woman took out her kirpan, slit a part of her hand and drew a tilak of blood on Indira's forehead, saying, '*Indiraji, aap ki haar ka badla hum lenge* [Indiraji, we shall avenge your electoral defeat].'

Mohsina would also be privy to another side of Indira that was totally different from her tough, strong-woman image. In her memoir, she talks about Indira's meeting with Anandamayi Ma at her ashram in Kankhal (in Haridwar). It was after Indira's younger son, Sanjay Gandhi, had died in a plane crash and she was in an emotional turmoil. From a distance, Mohsina, who had accompanied the Prime Minister to the ashram, saw Indira place her head on Anandamayi Ma's lap and the mystic gently stroking her hair, trying to comfort a grieving mother.

Lok Sabha Success

Born into an aristocratic Muslim family in Avadh, Mohsina made her debut in the Lok Sabha in 1978 and followed up that success with two more victories – in 1980 and 1984. But more remarkable than her three victories are the constituencies she won from. The first was from Azamgarh in eastern Uttar Pradesh (the by-election would set the stage for Indira's post-Emergency comeback) and then from Meerut in the west. Those aware of the socio-economic fundamentals of Uttar Pradesh and the state's caste matrix would know how difficult it is to garner acceptance from both of these diverse regions.

As an elected representative, Mohsina is remembered for her simplicity in public life, her probity and her ability to act judiciously. So, in May 2016, when she was no longer an MP at the age of 84, there was a sense of quiet fulfilment. But there was also an element of worry. The former housing minister of India did not have a house she could call her own, except for an ancestral, jointly owned property in Badagaon, Barabanki. In the national capital of Delhi, in many prime properties – from Jor Bagh, Golf Links to Vasant Vihar and Vasant Kunj – politicians, particularly those who enjoyed the fruits of power during the Indira and Rajiv Gandhi era, have palatial bungalows and kothis without having known sources of income to purchase such expensive houses.

On the political front, what distinguished Mohsina from many others in the Congress was that she never shied away from speaking her mind but also never crossed the line of party discipline. A lot has been written about the Shah Bano judgement and the Rajiv Gandhi government's move to overturn the verdict; the Ayodhya imbroglio; the Congress's ties with the Samajwadi Party and Bahujan Samaj Party (BSP); communal riots and tackling issues of probity. Had the political leadership of the Congress heeded Mohsina's sound advice in all of these issues, the course of the country's s politics and contemporary history might have looked very different.

Turbulent Decade

But even irreproachable careers can come under a shadow because of factors beyond one's control. Long before the

Godhra carnage of 2002, Meerut would witness two ugly riots, in 1982 and 1987, when Mohsina represented the constituency in Parliament. In her memoir, she writes:

> While I would win from the city again in 1984, Meerut's tradition of peace had shattered in September 1982, a little more than two years and a half into my stint as MP from the constituency. By the time elections were held again in 1989, frequent riots had vitiated the atmosphere. My defeat in the Lok Sabha elections in 1989 had a lot to do with these incidents of violence that I tried to quell, while criminal elements and Right-wing Hindutva parties had a field day.[4]

She goes on:

> Communalism, majoritarianism, riots, arrest of innocent people on the charge of sedition and selective use of law have been blots on our otherwise vibrant and participatory democracy. Dissecting communal violence is always tricky, although most people blame district authorities for ignoring signs of an impending explosion. Meerut was no exception. The district administration failed to win the confidence of the two communities and was afraid to take unpopular measures.[5]

Mohsina had her reasons to feel let down. As a politician, she had won maintaining a pan-Indian identity. She was never seen as a 'Muslim face', and her voters in Azamgarh and Meerut cut across communities and sects.

The 1982 violence had broken out over a minor disagreement – a 200 square foot property claimed by two communities. But the impact was huge. There were dozens of deaths and property worth crores of rupees was damaged. A report published by *India Today* then had said:

> As always in such conflicts, it was the poor and the underprivileged who had to bear the brunt of the violence. The conflict started as a religious one. It turned quickly into a confrontation with the Muslims on one side and the Scheduled Castes and Scheduled Tribes on the other. Then it developed beyond that into a stand-off between the district administration and the minority community.[6]

About five years later, between March and June 1987, Meerut would again be rocked by a series of communal disturbances that resulted in the death of more than 350 people and leave behind – as their searing legacy – memories of two massacres: at Hashimpura and Maliana.

The role of the Congress and the inaction of its leaders in Uttar Pradesh finally led to Muslims severing their long link with the party. In her book, Mohsina writes:

> The biggest problem for the district administration turned out to be the Provincial Armed Constabulary (PAC) that was pressed into service in different parts of the city. The PAC did not have the confidence of the people. More than 20 companies of PAC men were stationed around the town and as the riots

> progressed, there were allegations that they were terrorising Muslim localities by resorting to unprovoked firing.[7]

Within the Muslim community, there was a feeling that Mohsina could have done much more after these incidents of violence broke out. In her defence, she has said that in a constitutional democracy, the rule of law must prevail and institutions – the police, judiciary, executive, civil society and the media – should all act swiftly and decisively. A Muslim championing the cause of Muslims may be good optics but what Mohsina sought to convey by stressing on an appropriate institutional response was that a secular polity needed to do more to address the concerns and expectations of the people. In Mohsina's case, she did try to intervene but without rushing to the media.

In her autobiography, Mohsina would also raise some thought-provoking questions:

> It is worth remembering that Meerut, throughout the 1980s, was one of the richest districts of Uttar Pradesh. One-third of the sugar produced in the state comes from the district and it was famous for its steel goods, too. Meerut is also known for its handloom industry that employs over 70,000 Muslim artisans. What the repeated incidents of violence also did was explode the myth that economic prosperity and education reduce communal tensions in a society. Or, was there something more sinister that kept unfolding in the years to come?[8]

One criticism that Mohsina had to face in the Urdu media was that she did not open any major educational institutions in Uttar Pradesh even though she was close to top leaders of the Congress. Mohsina's counter to such criticism is that institution-building is a major task that requires cooperation between the government, the intelligentsia, the industry and the community as a whole. But she did try in her own way. There are many educational institutions in Barabanki, apart from the behind-the-scenes roles she played in starting educational institutions in states like Maharashtra, Karnataka and Andhra Pradesh as a union minister. It would, of course, be unfair to compare her to Zakir Husain, educationist and the first Muslim to hold the post of the President of India, but Mohsina, too, has been part of the nation's story of growth and the strides it made in education.

Personal Views

Mohsina's career in politics coincided with the evolution of a more liberalized society. That leads to the inevitable question on the position of women, especially within her own community. This is what she says, citing a commentary on the Quran by Maulana Abdul Majid Daryabadi, who was one of India's most influential Muslim scholars:

> I firmly believe that the basic teachings of Islam do not discriminate much between men and women. It is largely due to the cultural and social ethos of Muslim societies and

> their human failings that such perceptions of inequalities have evolved. The rights of women granted by Islam are many. They are, however, often denied what Allah and His Messenger have granted them. In the blessed era of Prophet Muhammad … and the rightly guided caliphs, Muslim women enjoyed an equal standing in society and were entrusted with public duties. They had their say in policy-making and market trends and ensured supply of provisions to the battlefield, apart from taking care of wounded soldiers. As far as the Holy Quran is concerned, it describes women and men as complementary to each other and as 'soul mates'.[9]

It may not be wrong to say that Mohsina herself is an example of the 'equal standing' she talks about – in her transformation from a demure homemaker into a public person. Mohsina also talks about the blending of 'Muslimness' with 'Indianness' and the tradition of pluralism where Islam too played a role in shaping the country's future:

> We need to also remember that the contemporary ethnic India is an accumulation of several cultures, religions, languages and evolutionary histories and Muslims are an inalienable part of this matrix. Since its introduction into the Indian subcontinent, Islam has had significant religious, artistic, philosophical, cultural, social and political influences on Indian history. Muslim traders, mystics, preachers and invaders have shaped and influenced the Indian subcontinent for thirteen centuries, ensuring a significant cultural diffusion

of Muslim traditions among the ethnic Indian population till date.[10]

Politics may have taken up a big part of her life, but Mohsina has also been a keen student of the subcontinent's history and India's evolution as a nation, especially how it has assimilated such diverse influences guided by the wisdom of the ages.

Now in her nineties, Mohsina is in the twilight of her life. But it's a contented twilight of a life lived with dignity.

8

Abida Ahmed: First Lady as Politician and Parliamentarian

In 1974, Indira Gandhi was at the height of her popularity. Under her leadership, India had conducted its first successful nuclear weapons' test and had stunned the world. But she wasn't the only female leader steering the country. Visiting heads of state and other dignitaries, such as Mohammad Reza Shah Pahlavi of Iran, President Omar Bongo of Gabon, and Nancy and Henry Kissinger, were surprised to see another elegant lady playing the official hostess at the 104-foot-long banquet hall at Rashtrapati Bhavan.

The lady in question was Begum Abida Ahmed, wife of the country's fifth president, Fakhruddin Ali Ahmed. Fifty-one years old when he took over presidentship in August 1974, Abida was the first visible and socially active First Lady in the then 24-year history of the republic.

Every single one of her predecessors had stayed away from the limelight. Rajvanshi Devi, wife of the first President,

Dr Rajendra Prasad, had trouble with her health and preferred to dine in her private chambers. The second President, Dr Sarvepalli Radhakrishnan, was a widower. Shahjahan Begum, wife of the third President, Dr Zakir Husain, was a devout Muslim who observed the purdah. Saraswati Bai, wife of V.V. Giri, India's fourth President, had frail health and preferred to write devotional poetry in Telugu to the clamour of Delhi's diplomatic and hectic social life.

Abida was different. While food and cuisine were her forte, she was also a sportswoman who led Assam in the 1958 National Badminton Championships. She played billiards and tennis, too. Among her other interests were flower arrangement, bamboo design, ceramics and painting. In December 1975, she organized the International Art Exhibition of Women Artists with the help of her social welfare enthusiasts on the Mahila Imdad Committee. As writer and critic Uma Vasudev put it, Abida 'had the definite objective of providing another feminist boost to the closing phases of the International Women's Year', as the United Nations had designated in 1975.[1]

'She is not a militant feminist,' Vasudev wrote in *India Today*. 'In fact, she [is] not a feminist of the kind who believes that any fundamental restructuring of the social pattern is necessary to provide [a] woman the ideal circumstances for her fulfilment. But she is a believer, in the powerful capacity of [a] woman to create those circumstances for her fulfilment within the existing limitations, or, basically, to transcend those limitations.'[2]

Abida was born in Badaun, Uttar Pradesh, where her father, Mohammad Sultan Hyder 'Josh', served as a civil servant. He was also an Urdu writer of repute and he made sure that his daughter got a good education too. Abida graduated from Women's College, AMU. Her marriage to Fakhruddin Ali Ahmed – a freedom fighter and full-time politician 18 years older than her – was arranged when she was still in college and, significantly, both partners insisted upon meeting each other before their wedding. At one point, when negotiations for the marriage were under way, Abida's family wanted to know what the prospective bridegroom was doing. The answer came from one of Ahmed's relatives: '*Filhal toh jail mein hai* [At present, he is in jail].' Ahmed was then serving a jail term in Jorhat as a political prisoner.

Decades later, in an interview given at the Rashtrapati Bhavan, Abida recalled, 'My husband was in prison when our marriage was arranged. Of course, we all thought we knew the British time was ending, but we had no idea of what was really to come. But even then, I was prepared – there was no certainty of not going to prison again.'

Fakhruddin Ali Ahmed

Ahmed, whose father, Colonel Zalnur Ali, was an army doctor, studied history at St Catharine's College, Cambridge University, and obtained a law degree from the Inner Temple. While in England, Ahmed had met and befriended Jawaharlal Nehru in 1925. Impressed by his friend's progressive ideas, he eventually joined the INC in 1931 after his return to India, choosing to become a freedom fighter instead of appearing for the Indian Civil Service examination. Ahmed soon became an ardent follower of Nehru and Mahatma Gandhi, and participated in individual satyagraha, a platform to express dissent against British policies at a personal level, and the Quit India Movement, for which he was arrested in 1942. After Independence, Ahmed held several important political positions. He was elected to the Rajya Sabha in 1954 and later to the Lok Sabha in 1967, holding portfolios such as food and agriculture, industrial development, company affairs and education.

Although born in Old Delhi, Ahmed shared a bond with Assam, where his father had served extensively. Before Independence, he had been elected to the Assam assembly for the first time in 1937 and became the minister of finance, revenue and labour in the Congress-led coalition government formed by Gopinath Bordoloi. As minister, Ahmed introduced the Assam Agricultural Income Tax Bill, a-first-of-its-kind legislation in India that levied taxes on tea gardens. His pro-labour policy during the labour strike in the British-owned Assam Oil Company Ltd won public support for the Bordoloi government.

Ahmed is credited with rehabilitating a large number of immigrants in Assam. The continuing atrocities in what was then East Pakistan (modern-day Bangladesh) in the 1960s and early 1970s led to the unchecked entry of refugees into India. The Indira Gandhi–Mujibur Rahman agreement in

1972 redefined the status of these refugees as it ratified Indian citizenship for all those who had arrived before 25 March 1971, provided they fulfilled certain conditions.

Behind the scenes, Ahmed was seen as the architect of this agreement. This led to an agitation by a section of the Assamese population and the then chief election commissioner, S.L. Shakdher, publicly attributed the 35 per cent increase in the state's population between 1961 and 1971 to 'the influx from the neighbouring country'.

The Emergency

Although Abida stayed away from politics, she was privy to Indira Gandhi's efforts to persuade Ahmed to sign the declaration of the Emergency in 1975. The President reportedly had reservations about the 'draconian' provisions of the Emergency that sought to drastically curtail press freedom and civil rights. Then, on the night of 25–26 June 1975, Indira Gandhi imposed a countrywide Emergency after Ahmed, in a nocturnal bout of supplication, signed a crisp three-line proclamation that read: 'In exercise of the powers conferred by clause (1) of Article 352 of the Constitution, I, Fakhruddin Ali Ahmed, President of India, by this Proclamation declare that a grave emergency exists whereby the security of India is threatened by internal disturbances.' Subsequently, hundreds and thousands of political activists, including Atal Bihari Vajpayee, Chandra Shekhar, L.K. Advani and Mulayam Singh Yadav, were arrested.

In his book, *Emergency Chronicles: Indira Gandhi and Democracy's Turning Point*, historian Gyan Prakash claims that Ahmed had several reservations about the order and had taken a tranquillizer after signing the proclamation.[3]

The declaration of the Emergency, however, did not affect Abida's ties with the prime minister. In Abida, Indira Gandhi not only saw a modern Muslim woman but also someone who was on the same page when it came to food, culture and gender issues. Indira herself was a light eater but she loved fine dining, particularly in the French tradition. Together, she and Abida overhauled the high table at the Rashtrapati Bhavan and Hyderabad House, where many state banquets were held. Indira and Abida would often personally proofread menus before all state banquets so that the French dishes were not misspelt.

This was a time when President Fakhruddin Ali Ahmed was often lampooned for giving his assent to the Emergency. For instance, one cartoon by noted cartoonist Abu Abraham depicted Ahmed, semi-naked in a bathtub filled to the brim, handing over a paper he had signed to a person who is partly visible. Only the outstretched hand of the person can be seen, but it's clear he is dressed in a formal suit. The caption read, 'If there are any more ordinances, just ask them to wait.'[4]

As President, Ahmed publicly spoke in favour of the Emergency. In his address to the nation on 15 August 1975, he assured citizens that the Emergency was a 'passing phase', and its imposition was necessary to save India from chaos and disruption. He also cautioned that liberty should not 'degenerate into licence' and exhorted the nation to focus on increasing production.

In private, however, Ahmed appeared to have misgivings about the Emergency. This was revealed in a cable sent from the US embassy in Delhi in August 1976, which suggested an estrangement between the President and prime minister of the country. The cable noted Ahmed's growing concern that Indira and her son, Sanjay Gandhi, were 'pushing too hard on the political and constitutional system of India', and reported that he had rebuffed her suggestion to replace the vice president, B.D. Jatti, with her former defence minister, Sardar Swaran Singh.[5]

The cable went on to note that Ahmed was 'uncomfortable with some of Prime Minister Indira Gandhi's actions and certainly with those of her son', and that Indira Gandhi had apologized to Ahmed on behalf of Sanjay for his rude remarks when the President declined to give a statement for the inaugural issue of *Surya*, a magazine run by her daughter-in-law, Sanjay's wife, Maneka Gandhi.

Political Arena

Less than three years into his presidency, Ahmed developed medical issues, having already survived two heart attacks. The reported strained ties with Indira and her son were also taking a toll on his health. On the morning of 11 February 1977, Ahmed was found lying unconscious in his bath. He was declared dead at 8.52 a.m. According to a government announcement, Prime Minister Indira Gandhi was at President Ahmed's bedside when he died.

When the tragedy struck, two of Ahmed's children, Dr Parvez Ahmed and Samina Khan, were in the US. They flew on the same plane as Lillian Carter, President Jimmy Carter's mother and the official US representative to attend the funeral.

Ahmed's death came as a shock to Abida. She became increasingly cranky and often had to be administered heavy doses of tranquillizers. Indira was out of power then. But she made it a point to frequently visit Abida and eventually persuaded her to devote time to active politics. It was with great reluctance that Abida agreed to fight a Lok Sabha by-election from Bareilly, Uttar Pradesh, in 1981 when the local Janata Party MP, Misaryar Khan, died. Abida won, defeating Santosh Kumar Gangwar of the BJP, Mohammad Yunus Saleem of the breakaway Congress (U) and Badam Singh of the Lok Dal. She won again in 1984, making it two in a row from Bareilly, and becoming the first and only First Lady of India to have entered the competitive arena of politics. Indira subsequently appointed her the first president of the newly created All India Mahila Congress.

In May 1984, Abida organized a grand Mahila Congress convention in Bangalore, which was attended by Indira, her son Rajiv Gandhi and 30,000 delegates. After Indira's death in October 1984, Abida faced some difficulties in running the Mahila Congress, which had Margaret Alva as its convener.

Alva was a minister and a favourite of the then prime minister and Congress president, Rajiv Gandhi.

A particularly awkward moment for Abida came when Rajiv, at Congress's centenary celebrations in December 1985 (in Bombay), abruptly sought written plans for what the organization proposed to do in 1986. Abida jotted down a few points which were handed to Rajiv but he was not impressed. He later said that it appeared to him that the Mahila Congress had no concrete plans. Abida sent Rajiv her letter of resignation, which was not accepted.

In 1989, Abida lost from Bareilly, finishing second after the BJP's Santosh Gangwar. While Gangwar would go on to win seven more times from Bareilly and become a Union minister, Abida's political fortune declined. After Rajiv Gandhi's assassination in May 1991, she quietly began focusing more on social work, apart from her involvement with cultural, educational and women's institutions. She served as the chairperson for a host of institutions and committees, such as the Ghalib Institute and Museum, the India–Bhutan Friendship Association, the Indo-Czechoslovakia Cultural Association, Unity International, Hakim Ajmal Khan Girls' School in Darya Ganj, Delhi, the governing body of Kalindi College, New Delhi, and the South Delhi Polytechnic for Women, New Delhi, among others. Abida was the founder chairperson of the Mahila Imdad Committee, Balika Chaman (a Muslim girls' hostel)[6] and the Hum-Sub Drama Group of the Ghalib Institute. She was a member of the National Integration Council, New Delhi, and patron of the

India–Tunisia Friendship Association. She also served as deputy director general of All India Women's Voluntary Service.

Begum Abida Ahmed passed away in New Delhi on 7 December 2003, at the age of 80, barely six months before the Congress returned to power for a ten-year run at the Centre.

9

Noor Bano: Tryst with a Destiny in Politics

Each time Noor Bano stepped out of her house, a retinue of attendants and servants would accompany her. When the erstwhile queen of Rampur toured Ranchi in 2006 as the in-charge of Congress affairs in Jharkhand, party workers were struck by her elegance – her classy white chiffon sari, full-sleeved white blouse and her pearl necklace. The only spot of colour on her being was the red sacred thread tied around her wrist.

The royal background

Begum Noor Bano, originally Mahatab Zamani, is the widow of the former ruler of Rampur. Her husband Nawab Syed Zulfikar Ali Khan Bahadur belonged to the Rohilla dynasty and was popularly addressed as 'Mickey Mian'. Some of the titles that prefixed his name included Major, His Highness

Ali Jah, Farzand-i-Dilpazir-i-Daulat-i-Inglishia, Mukhlis ud-Daula, Nasir ul-Mulk and Amir ul-Umara. Incidentally, the state of Rampur was the first state to accede to the dominion of India after Independence. During the British Raj, Rampur was a 15-gun-salute state – implying that the British government used to offer a 15-gun salute to welcome Rampur's ruler.

Mickey Mian represented Rampur in the Lok Sabha as a Congress nominee from 1967 to 1989, with the exception of 1977, when he lost the elections due to Indira Gandhi's Emergency fallout. The Rampur parliamentary seat, with a sizeable Muslim population, had shot to fame when Maulana Abul Kalam Azad, a prominent freedom fighter, scholar and independent India's first education minister, contested from there in 1951–52.

Some clever manoeuvring and luck shaped Mickey Mian's life in politics. Following the death of his father in 1966, his older brother, Murtaza, became the titular head of Rampur. From 1969 until 1971, Murtaza served as a member in the Uttar Pradesh legislative assembly, but in 1971, he contested the Rampur polls against his own mother, Rafat Zamani Begum, and won. This defiance infuriated Indira Gandhi. Moreover, she was already in favour of ending the privy purse that royals enjoyed. Even though many other royals such as Madhavrao Scindia and Nawab Mansoor Ali Khan Pataudi opposed this, Mickey Mian backed Indira Gandhi's decision to end the system. The privy purse was a payment made to royal families of erstwhile princely states as part of their agreement to integrate with the Indian Union in 1947, and later to merge their states in 1949, whereby they lost all ruling rights. In addition to privileges such as gun salutes and titles, about ₹100 crore of tax-free money was paid to 565 former royals.

His loyalty to Indira was not forgotten and he was rewarded the Congress ticket to the state. He contested from Rampur in 1971, and then again in 1977, 1980, 1984, 1989 and 1991.

Mickey Mian was killed in a freak road accident in 1992 while returning from New Delhi to Rampur. Decades later, his grandson Hamza demanded a CBI enquiry into the road accident, alleging a political conspiracy. Hamza told the media in January 2022:

> Mickey Mian Saheb, who was my grandfather, [and] who died in a road accident in 1992, has greatly benefitted Azam Khan [Samajwadi Party leader and MLA from Rampur] in a political sense. The truck involved in the accident was also stolen. The FIR in the case was registered just a week ago, and when the truck was found, its engine number, chassis number, everything was erased. This is a clear attempt of destroying the evidence, implying that it wasn't a mere accident but a clear attempt to kill him, which they succeeded at. I am trying to get a CBI inquiry initiated in the matter.[1]

The tragedy catapulted Noor Bano into politics. In 1992, while grieving her husband's death, she formally joined the Congress, putting on hold her deep interest in music, and research on Persian and Arabic books. Politics was a familiar territory as Noor Bano's illustrious father, Aminuddin Khan, nawab of Loharu, Rajasthan, was also a member of the INC and served as MLA and state minister from 1967–76, and then became governor of Himachal Pradesh and Punjab.

Foray into Politics

Noor Bano contested the 1996 Lok Sabha polls, and secured 2,71,330 votes, beating the BJP candidate Rajindra Kumar Sharma. The Congress was undergoing much turmoil at this time. The party had lost power at the Centre and the party president and outgoing prime minister, P.V. Narasimha Rao, was thrown out by his own party. While Sitaram Kesri took the mantle of leadership, a powerful group of party leaders led by Jitendra Prasada, Arjun Singh, Pranab Mukherjee and others were calling the shots, with Sonia Gandhi playing a role from behind the scenes. Begum Noor sensed the importance of 10 Janpath and deftly aligned herself with Sonia, ignoring Prasada, who had acted as her mentor in the polls. This clever manoeuvring helped her survive the labyrinth of politics and position her son Kazim as a politician. Kazim, a graduate from Columbia University, served as a minister under both Mulayam Singh Yadav and Mayawati. Noor Bano's grandson and Kazim's son, Haider Ali, too took to the family profession of politics and is currently an MLA from Apna Dal, an ally of the National Democratic Alliance (NDA) led by Prime Minister Narendra Modi.

Throughout her political career, Noor Bano was seen only in a spotless white sari. In Rampur, she was often spotted travelling in an air-conditioned jeep, meeting constituents. In 2004, when the Sonia Gandhi-led United Progressive Alliance (UPA) came to power, Begum Noor Bano suffered a shock defeat to Bollywood star Jaya Prada.

When Noor Bano entered politics, Jaya Prada, some 1,600-odd km away in Hyderabad, was drawing bigger crowds than the Telugu Desam Party (TDP) leader Chandrababu Naidu, dispelling the impression that she was merely a glamorous doll. Jaya Prada was reportedly responsible for influencing Naidu to field about 40 or so women candidates in the 1999 assembly polls, the highest number sponsored by a ruling party till then. In 2002, however, she was denied a second term in the upper house and was replaced by actress Roja as Telugu Desam Party's (TDP's) Mahila president. A miffed Jaya Prada distanced herself from the party and moved to Uttar Pradesh to join the Samajwadi Party. With politician Amar Singh's backing, she was elected to the Lok Sabha from Rampur in 2004 and in 2009.

Jaya Prada joined the Samajwadi Party on 9 March 2004 at the party headquarters in Lucknow – a meet that was attended by 6,000 overawed village-level workers. Speaking at the occasion, Jaya Prada had said she was drawn by the secular credentials of Mulayam Singh Yadav and of General Secretary Amar Singh. The actress added that she would be happy to be an ordinary worker and would not hanker after any post. Explaining her shift from Andhra Pradesh to Uttar Pradesh, she said, 'I think Uttar Pradesh is the soul of India. If the state does not prosper, the country cannot reach anywhere. So I have opted for this state as my field of activity ... Industrialists used to crowd around Chandrababu Naidu but now they are hovering over Netaji [Mulayam Singh].'

Initially, her switch worked. In the 2004 Lok Sabha polls, Jaya Prada stunned Begum Noor Bano by winning over 85,000 votes. From the beginning, Jaya did not behave like a celebrity in her new-found '*karam bhoomi*' of Uttar Pradesh. 'I am Rampur *ki kali*,' she declared as she began her campaign, rejecting the charge of being a political paratrooper in the land of hardboiled politicians. She exhibited a resolve to carve out her own place in voters' hearts by appealing to voters through a developmental agenda. In her election speeches, she said, '*Mujhe maloom hai ki Rampur wale behen aur beti ko khali haath nahi bhejte. Isliye mujhe vote bhi milenge aur dil bhi* [I know the people of Rampur do not send their daughters and sisters away empty-handed. So I will win over both hearts and votes].' Soon, the 'outsider' tag was off, and the predominantly Muslim constituency cheered for her.

Jaya Prada's entry into Rampur made its politics a lot more exciting, and Noor Bano's arch-rival, Samajwadi Party stalwart Azam Khan, became both edgy and aggressive towards the actress. Between 1980 and 2019, Azam Khan was elected as MLA from Rampur nine times. Much of his politics was directed against 'Noor Mahal', the residence of Noor Bano, and the erstwhile rulers of Rampur. While the nawabs and the Begum of Rampur never publicly called Azam Khan their rival, the Samajwadi Party leader, while scaling the ladder of politics, pitted himself as their arch-rival, presenting his typist father's humble background as the antithesis of their wealth and influence. In every election, Azam Khan's campaign would focus on 'mahal [palace] versus people'.

Nafees Siddiqui, who has written several books on the nawabs of Rohilkhand, the region to which Rampur belongs, says:

> Azam's father Mumtaz Khan was a decent man. He used to carry a typing machine on a bicycle. Azam was ambitious and, to carve out his own place in politics, he felt it was necessary to challenge the royal family. So he gave it the form of a battle between *nawab* vs *awam* [king vs people].
>
> During the 1970s and 1980s, the reins of Rampur's politics were firmly in the hands of Noor Mahal. After the Emergency, Azam contested the assembly elections on a Janata Party ticket but lost to Congress' Shannu Miyan. After this, he started to fight for the interests of the beedi-rollers and textile workers. The textile mill, Raza Textile, was started by Nawab Raza Ali Khan. Azam began to stoke a fire there.[2]

Throughout the 1980s and 1990s, Azam, who had initially won assembly polls with the support of Mickey Mian, started to wage a war against the royal family. After the Babri Masjid demolition and the subsequent Meerut riots, Azam transformed his image from a labour leader to that of a firebrand Muslim leader, and went on to become the new 'nawab of Rampur' after he became a minister in the Mulayam cabinet.

Azam, however, remained somewhat restrained while criticizing or attacking Begum Noor Bano. His choicest abuses were reserved for Jaya Prada, who joined the BJP in 2019.

Life After Politics

Both in 2004 and 2009, Rampur witnessed a battle of begums. Noor Bano, as a Congress nominee, and Jaya Prada, as the Samajwadi Party nominee, with an angry Azam Khan saying a lot against his own Party nominee. Also waiting in the wings in 2009 was BJP veteran Mukhtar Abbas Naqvi, who had beaten Noor Bano in 1998.

In the campaign for 2009, Noor Bano, stylishly wearing a white chiffon sari and white sandals, focused on how she was a true Rampuri, and the feud between Jaya Prada and Azam Khan. In a series of street-corner meetings, Noor Bano would say, 'I am from Rampur, I have not come from outside. I am one of you and I will stay here in your midst till my dying day. I know that there are greater forces at work in this election, but I can promise you that if you vote for me, I will never forsake you.'

Noor Bano was also heard accusing Naqvi of doing nothing for the people of Rampur when he had defeated her in the 1998 Lok Sabha polls.

Noor Bano, however, could not help notice that thousands were present at Jaya Prada's public meetings and that many Bollywood veterans like actor Feroz Khan were campaigning for her. Every day, the actress was seen signing hundreds of autographs for her fans. This was well before the era of social media, and autographs were a gauge for a person's popularity.

The outcome in 2004 and 2009 proved Noor Bano's apprehensions. Jaya Prada returned to the Lok Sabha from

Rampur, winning the seat by 30,931 votes, relegating Naqvi to a poor fourth. Noor Bano bagged 1,99,793 votes – not good enough to dent Jaya Prada's margin of victory. In 2004, the margin of Jaya Prada's victory was over 61,000. Since there is no place for those who come second in polls, 2009 marked Noor Bano's last electoral battle.

She remained active for the next five years as an AICC functionary but took a step back after the party suffered an enormous defeat in 2014. She began actively promoting her son Kazim, while resuming her passion for music, books, the Rampur library and her philanthropic work. Kazim finished a poor third in the 2014 Lok Sabha polls, getting just about 16 per cent of votes as a Congress nominee. He was expelled from the Congress in 2016 when he cross-voted during a Rajya Sabha poll.

Rampur had been an active patron of music and the arts when the majestic court of Nawab Wajid Ali Shah of Avadh was abolished. A number of singers, dancers and poets were invited to the Rampur court, and it had become a centre of fine arts, with Nawab Hamid Ali Khan himself being a trained dhrupad singer and poet. Over the past decade, Noor Bano has focused her time and energy in promoting the Naina Devi Foundation and the Rampur gharana for music. Her son and grandson, however, continue taking the family's legacy forward in politics.

10

Rubab Sayda: The Revered Daughter-in-Law of Bahraich

In February 2024, when media outlets reported the death of former Samajwadi Party MP Rubab Sayda, there was an outpouring of grief from the public and from members of the party. The widespread news coverage was not only due to Rubab's identity as an Samajwadi Party leader and former MP – she was also the wife of Dr Waqar Ahmad Shah, the late veteran Samajwadi Party leader, and the mother of young former state minister, Yasar Shah. Back in the 2004 Lok Sabha elections, Rubab Sayda made headlines for being the only Muslim MP from Uttar Pradesh.[1] She had been elected from Bahraich, the political stronghold of her family.

Personal Background

Rubab originally hailed from Meerut and was born on 15 June 1950. Her father, Razaulhaq, was a well-known hakim and he served as a member of the President's panel at that time. Hakims are Muslim practitioners of herbal medicine – especially of Unani and Islamic medicine. Her mother's name was Noorjahan. Rubab demonstrated exceptional sincerity in her education, and completed her MA and BEd from Meerut University. She developed a penchant for teaching and started teaching in a school. She later went on to become the principal of Tara Girls Inter College, located in Brahmnipura, Bahraich. She got married to Dr Waqar Ahmad Shah on 5 January 1975. The couple had one son and one daughter. While their son, Yasar Shah, followed the footsteps of his parents to join politics as a Samajwadi Party leader, their daughter, Alvira, took inspiration from Waqar's earlier stint as a medical practitioner and became a doctor – she now runs a nursing home in Meerut.

Rubab's metamorphosis from an educator to a political leader can be attributed to the illustrious political career of Waqar.

Political Capital

Waqar made an impressive entry into politics, despite coming from a non-political family background. He started his career in education by obtaining a doctoral degree from Kanpur University. He taught in the Ameermah Primary School in Bahraich. Subsequently, he worked as a medical practitioner at the Dargah hospital from 1975 to 1982. In this period, Waqar established himself as a noted doctor and became a member of the Indian Medical Association unit in Bahraich. Later, he became a member of the noted City Azad Inter College, a guardian of the Red Cross Society, Bahraich, a member of the district Eye Relief Committee, and a member of the management committee of the Maharaj Singh Inter College.

He was set for his political debut when he joined the Janata Dal in 1989. His political baptism took place as he consolidated his party in his bastion of Bahraich. Eastern UP's Bahraich is an underdeveloped region for a variety of reasons. Since 1991, after the Babri Masjid was demolished, the region's politics has been marred by communal polarization as the region has a sizeable Muslim population.

Waqar soon switched to the emerging Samajwadi Party in UP under the leadership of Mulayam Singh Yadav. He won his first assembly election from Bahraich Sadar in 1993 and there was no looking back. He continued to win elections from the Bahraich Sadar assembly seat for the next five consecutive terms and served as a Samajwadi Party MLA for more than two decades in the UP Vidhan Sabha. He also served as the deputy speaker for the UP Legislative Assembly, apart from being a member of several legislative committees, including the Public Accounts Committee and the Business Advisory Committee. He also served in the cabinets of Mulayam Singh Yadav and Akhilesh Yadav. As a labour minister, Waqar took several crucial steps to check child labour and emphasized on the education of children from underprivileged backgrounds.

However, he also got embroiled in many controversies during his stint as the labour minister in the Mulayam Singh government due to his continued factional war with another Samajwadi Party leader and the then party general secretary, Beni Prasad Verma. The latter accused Waqar of shielding his loyalists in Bahraich, who were involved in serious offences like murder and sexual assaults – these controversies rocked UP politics in 2007.[2] Waqar effectively navigated this political turbulence to maintain his dominance in the political landscape of Bahraich. He once again became a minister in the Samajwadi Party government under the chief ministership of Akhilesh Yadav in 2012. However, his health deteriorated soon after, and he went into a coma, which led to the end of his ministership and his long stint as the MLA of Bahraich. He passed away in April 2018 after a prolonged illness.

Life in Electoral Politics

Following in Waqar's footsteps, Rubab joined politics in the 1990s and soon became active in Bahraich's public life. In 1995, she became the president of the Zila Panchayat of Bahraich district. Rubab took her first plunge into parliamentary politics in the 1999 Lok Sabha elections on a Samajwadi Party ticket from Bahraich, but was defeated by the BJP candidate, Padamsen Chaudhary, in the constituency. Rubab could only poll in 96,801 votes, with a vote share of 16.28 per cent, and came a distant third in the electoral contest, after Padamsen Chaudhary – who polled a sweeping 2,23,768 votes with a vote share of 37.63 per cent – and Bahujan Samaj Party (BSP) candidate Arif Mohammad Khan, who received 2,18,017 votes with a vote share of 36.67 per cent. However, in the next election, Rubab came prepared and demonstrated her political dominance in the Bahraich Lok Sabha constituency. She successfully polled 1,88,949 votes, with an impressive vote share of 34 per cent, leaving her political adversaries – BSP candidate Ram Bhagat Mishra who could garner 1,62,615 votes and BJP leader, and sitting MP, Padamsen Chaudhary, who got 1,43,780 votes – trailing much further behind. This spectacular electoral performance paved the way for Rubab's entry into the Lok Sabha as the only Muslim woman MP from the state of Uttar Pradesh in 2004.

A Responsible Parliamentarian

As a Lok Sabha MP, Rubab served in crucial parliamentary committees. She became a member of the Committee on Industry in 2004 and, on 5 August 2007, she was appointed as a member of the Parliamentary Committee on Information Technology. As an elected public representative of Bahraich, she raised the pressing issues of infrastructure development in her constituency in Parliament. Her notable contribution to the development of the region has been her relentless push for making the Bahraich–Gonda railway line a broad gauge line. Her strong and continued efforts led to the release of funds for the required survey needed to initiate the project. During her stint as an MP, Rubab also got the opportunity to be part of the delegation in presidential tours.[3]

She also partook in many of the key debates in the Lok Sabha. A few notable ones are her participation in the discussion on the Supplementary Demands for Grants (Railways) for 2005–06, the discussion on the motion for consideration of the Commissions for Protection of Child Rights (Amendment) Bill, 2006, and discussions on the motion of confidence in the council of ministers moved by Prime Minister Manmohan Singh on 21 July 2008.[4] Rubab also made important contributions to the parliamentary consultative committee meeting on the occasion to mark 50 years of ONGC convened in June 2005.[5]

However, Rubab unfortunately couldn't return to Parliament in the next Lok Sabha elections. In the 2009 national election, the Samajwadi Party fielded Rubab not from her family bastion of Bahraich but from the Shravasti Lok Sabha constituency. She came third in that election – the Congress candidate Vinay Kumar won and BSP's Muslim candidate Rizvan Zahir came second in the contest.[6] In the run-up to that contest, *India Today* reported that Samajwadi Party was hand in glove with the BJP to field a Muslim candidate like Rubab in Shravasti in order to cut the Muslim votes of the BSP candidate and help the BJP candidate, Satya Deo Singh. However, it was the Congress candidate who emerged victorious.[7]

Enduring Legacy

Rubab made her final foray into electoral politics by contesting the 2017 Vidhan Sabha elections in UP, a period when the BJP, under Narendra Modi's leadership, was solidifying its position as a potent political force in the state and was all set to dethrone the Akhilesh Yadav–led Samajwadi Party government. Rubab got the ticket from the Bahraich Vidhan Sabha constituency.

However, she was defeated by the BJP candidate, the party's state general secretary, Anupama Jaiswal. Interestingly, Rubab was Anupama's English teacher when she was in Class XI, almost three decades before the contest. Communal polarization in the region and the BJP's massive wave in the 2017 UP elections closed the curtains on Rubab's political life. Thereafter, she mostly stayed in Meerut with her daughter. Her son, Yasar, emerged as one of the leading young leaders in the Samajwadi Party and was an MLA from Bahraich between 2012 and 2022. He also served as the minister of state for power, coal and new and renewable energy, apart from being the minister of state (IC) for transport and minister for commercial taxes in the Uttar Pradesh government under Akhilesh Yadav.

Rubab passed away in February 2024, in Meerut, at the age of 73, after suffering briefly from age-related ailments at a private hospital. Since she had served as an MP, parliamentarians and politicians across party lines paid their respects. The Samajwadi Party condoled her death in their official X (formerly known as Twitter) account[8] and the party chief Akhilesh Yadav visited Yasar in his private residence in Bahraich to pay homage to Rubab and express grief at her death. Rubab was buried at her family graveyard in Bahraich.[9]

11

Mehbooba Mufti: Accidental Politician, Able Leader

It was 2016 and the chief minister of Jammu and Kashmir, Mufti Mohammad Sayeed, had passed away. His party, the Jammu and Kashmir People's Democratic Party, bereft of the veteran's towering presence, was divided down the middle on who would succeed him as leader. There was also the question of alliance – should they press ahead with the late leader's dream or dump their coalition partner, who was, in any case, ideologically incompatible.

It was in this situation that Mehbooba Mufti stepped in. Or, rather, stepped into her father's role with the same sense of duty towards him that, many years ago, had led her to embrace politics as a career. A former Lok Sabha MP, Mehbooba is the only woman so far to have been elected chief minister of Jammu and Kashmir, before she eventually resigned in 2018.

But that's just one part of the story – the bigger part is Mehbooba's evolution from an inheritor of a political legacy to a leader who took over the reins of a turbulent state in an effort to, in her own words, 'bring peace' in a challenging time.

There's also another aspect to Mehbooba's story. She belongs to a category of leaders who would personify Michelle Bachelet's idea of a 'better democracy'. This is what Bachelet, a former president of Chile, said: 'For me, a better democracy is a democracy where women do not only have the right to vote and to elect, but to be elected.'[1]

Bachelet knew what she was talking about. She had lived through it all – the horrors of dictatorship, torture in detention, exile and, finally, her country's transition to democracy. But the words of Latin America's first popularly elected female president – whose political career was established independently of her husband – are also relevant for South Asia, a region where quite a few women leaders have emerged through electoral contests to shape the political discourse within their respective spheres of influence.

Yet, the label of 'dynastic' politics has stuck to most of these women leaders – many of them from established political dynasties, who have, at some point or the other, followed their fathers or husbands into the world of electoral politics. Their tryst with politics too has been marked by what can be called a contradiction. On the one hand, their survival and success not only challenged but also dismantled the rigid patriarchy and gender norms that espouse inequality against women in these regions. On the other hand, their presence in politics has largely been driven by a sense of familial responsibility to support a male relative and carry on their legacy after their death, rather than by any deep-rooted personal desire to pursue a political career.

Mehbooba's entry into the volatile politics of Jammu and Kashmir also mirrors this paradox. To her credit, Mehbooba, who holds degrees in English literature and law, rose to the challenge, taking charge at a time she was already mourning her father's death. Moreover, she had been bequeathed a coalition government in which her Jammu and Kashmir People's Democratic Party (PDP) was in alliance with the BJP, a political force ideologically opposed to the PDP.

To make matters worse, there was much resentment and many differences within the PDP rank and file regarding her leadership and on the continuation of the alliance with the BJP. After three months of political stalemate, the alliance would finally be revived following an intervention from Prime Minister Narendra Modi that set the stage for Mehbooba's coronation as head of the Jammu and Kashmir government in April 2016. That stint would end in June 2018 with the breakdown of the alliance. By then, Mehbooba had cemented her place as the PDP's top leader and party president.

Personal Life

It is often said that Mehbooba's entry into politics was largely accidental. One of the five children of Mufti Sayeed and the eldest of his three daughters, Mehbooba didn't jump straight into politics after she graduated from college. Instead, she worked for some time with the Bombay Mercantile Bank and then with East West Airlines in Delhi, before moving back to Jammu and Kashmir. After completing her LLB, Mehbooba got married in 1984 to Javed Iqbal Shah, a businessman from Bijbehara, who was also a political analyst and animal rights activist. Javed, a first cousin of her father's, is known to have fought against the culling of street dogs in the Valley to control their exploding population. The couple had two daughters, Irtiqa and Iltija. At a relatively young age, in her mid-thirties, Iltija was, in 2023, appointed Mehbooba's media adviser, marking her formal entry into politics.[2]

Mehbooba Mufti and Javed Iqbal Shah's marriage didn't last long. This is what the *Telegraph* newspaper said in a story on Javed:

> [H]is life trajectory might imitate shades of Feroze Gandhi's. Married to the ambitious daughter of a political eminence, then estranged. Uncomfortable with his spouse's foray into politics and unafraid to publicly voice contrarian views. Cynical, even bitter, about political dynasties and their ways, quite content to plough a lone furrow.[3]

In another parallel, Mehbooba – like Indira Gandhi before her – would raise her two children as a single mother, while helping her father manage his political career.

Militancy, Mass Connect and Electoral Politics

The Mufti family has had a long and chequered relationship with Kashmir's politics. Apart from attacks on family members, the Mufti is reported to have survived attacks on his own life by Kashmiri separatists. In 1989, when he was serving as India's first Muslim home minister in the V.P. Singh government, after having broken away from the Congress, his youngest daughter, Rubaiya Sayeed, was kidnapped by Kashmiri separatists in Srinagar. The abductors had demanded the release of five arrested militants of the Jammu Kashmir Liberation Front (JKLF) as a condition for returning Rubaiya to her family. After prolonged negotiations involving both the Centre and the state government, the militants were released and Rubaiya was returned to her family. This incident garnered widespread political and public support for the family.[4]

Mufti Mohammad Sayeed later returned to the Congress fold to lead the party's electoral battle in the 1996 assembly elections in Kashmir, but soon realized that there weren't enough candidates to field. He then got his two brothers-in-law, his wife and his oldest daughter to contest the elections. It was in this context that Mehbooba made her 'largely accidental' entry into politics.

Mehbooba was fielded from the family home turf of Bijbehara and ended up winning. Although the 1996 elections were widely alleged to have been rigged at the behest of the Centre, Mehbooba's victory acted as a catalyst for her ascendancy in the state's politics. Congress had won a total of four seats in the state – Baramulla and Srinagar from the Kashmir Valley; along with Jammu and Ladakh.

Three years later, in 1999, Mehbooba vacated her assembly seat to contest the Lok Sabha polls from Srinagar, but lost to Farooq Abdullah's son, Omar Abdullah. In the same year, her father broke away from the Congress to float his own party, PDP, which was seen as an emerging alternative to the National Conference (NC), the state's most notable regional party, and the Congress.

The Mufti took over as the founding president of the PDP and Mehbooba dutifully slipped into the role of vice president, as the party's second-in-command. While her father remained the party patriarch, it was Mehbooba who hit the ground running to create a strong mass connect for building the party, which she called her father's dream. She went on to strengthen the party's organizational architecture, and emerged as a firebrand and the most well-known woman leader in the Valley.

Mehbooba's sympathetic outreach to families of slain militants and civilians further shaped her image as a valiant mass leader in regions hit by militancy. During the 1990s, when insurgency was at its peak in the state, politicians would generally hesitate to travel to even high-security zones in Srinagar. But Mehbooba would courageously venture into the regions where militancy was rampant. It became a major headline when, in 1999, Mehbooba Mufti visited the home of Hizb-ul Mujahideen's operations chief, Aamir Khan, whose teenage son, Abdul Hameed, had allegedly died in security force custody.[5]

'Healing Touch'

Mehbooba's 'healing touch' outreach to the families of militants, however, attracted severe criticism. The PDP too was accused of practising 'soft separatism' for its call to the Centre to scale down military presence in the state, and for more dialogue and interaction with Pakistan. But the party, led by the Mufti, was able to form its first government in alliance with the Congress from 2002 to 2005. It was during the Mufti's tenure that Prime Minister Atal Bihari Vajpayee initiated the peace process with Pakistan. The PDP's alliance with the Congress during the UPA years, however, collapsed as the state's security situation declined drastically towards the end of the decade. Between 2008 and 2010, over 200 individuals lost their lives in militancy-related incidents.[6] By early January 2009, Omar Abdullah became chief minister and Mehbooba Mufti became the leader of the Opposition in the assembly. The state government, headed by the NC in alliance with the Congress, faced accusations of nepotism and corruption, while the economy struggled, leading to a pervasive sense of despair. In 2014, devastating floods swamped hundreds of villages in the region's most severe deluge in decades. As elections approached in November–December 2014, the PDP posed a formidable challenge to the NC and the Congress.

The results would throw up a fractured mandate. By the time the last vote had been counted, the PDP had emerged as the single largest party with 28 seats in the Kashmir region, but well short of the majority mark of 44 in the 87-member Jammu and Kashmir Legislative Assembly. The BJP, already riding high on Prime Minister Narendra Modi's popularity in the Hindi belt, won 25 seats in the Jammu region. It took the two parties two months to negotiate and form a post-poll alliance – an unlikely tie-up that was derided by the Opposition as 'opportunistic.'[7]

To begin with, the PDP and the BJP had very different ideological positions on the Kashmir question. The PDP, widely seen as a party sympathetic to the cause of militants, supported Kashmiri regionalism as well as peace talks with Pakistan. The BJP, on the other hand, favoured taking a hard line on separatism and approaching Pakistan with an iron fist. The alliance partners also shared divergent views on Articles 370 and 35A, two constitutional provisions that had crafted a special relationship between Jammu and Kashmir and the rest of India. While the BJP had always been ideologically against these special provisions for Kashmir, which it thought had played a role in breeding militancy in the Valley, the PDP's view was that these articles were foundational to the enduring link between Jammu and Kashmir and the rest of the country.

The Mufti, however, saw in the alliance 'a historic opportunity to break a new path in resolving issues of chronic friction between regions and ethnic groups in the state'.[8] So, when the Mufti died on 7 January 2016, it seemed as if the alliance would soon be over. After all, it was his political heft that had acted as the 'Teflon coating' that deflected criticism against such an 'unlikely' coalition. It was in this situation that

Mehbooba's political capital – her years of experience and her image as a carrier of her father's legacy – came to the rescue of the nearly beleaguered alliance.[9]

Tenure as Chief Minister

The Mufti's death was followed by nearly three months of Governor's Rule. Within the PDP, Mehbooba faced the huge challenge of holding her party together but, eventually, was able to not only get complete control over the leadership of her party, but also revive the alliance with the BJP. Then, on 4 April 2016, about a month and a half before her fifty-seventh birthday, Mehbooba took over as the chief minister of Jammu and Kashmir – the first time that a woman would hold the post.

It would hardly be a smooth run. During her tenure, disruptions erupted in the National Institute of Technology, Srinagar, where local students clashed with non-local students following a cricket match between India and Pakistan. She also had to face allegations of nepotism when her cousin's name cropped up as the executive officer of the state's khadi board.[10] But the most difficult time for the Mehbooba government came when Hizb-ul Mujahideen commander Burhan Wani was killed in July 2016 in an encounter with security forces in south Kashmir's Anantnag district. The incident led to violent protests that left over 85 people dead. The protests also created differences within the ruling alliance. While the PDP wanted a more lenient approach to dealing with those who had pelted security forces with stones, the BJP was determined to take a muscular stand to quell the unrest.

Another point of divergence between the two parties cropped up two years later – over the 2018 Ramzan ceasefire with militants. Mehbooba had called for the ceasefire as a gesture of goodwill aimed at winning over the disgruntled sections in the Valley, an idea that was opposed by BJP leader and deputy chief minister Kavinder Gupta.

Although Rajnath Singh, the Union home minister then, announced that the government had issued instructions to security forces and the army not to undertake offensive operations in Jammu and Kashmir during the holy month, the central government later decided not to extend the conditional truce. It said that counterterrorism operations would resume in the Valley in the wake of an increase in militancy-related incidents during the ceasefire period, much to the PDP's disappointment.[11] The differences soon reached a point of no return and, by the end of the third week of June 2018, the BJP had withdrawn its support to the Mehbooba government.

Another possible flashpoint was the murder of senior journalist Shujaat Bukhari, editor of the Srinagar-based newspaper *Rising Kashmir*, who was shot dead outside his office on 14 June 2018. The BJP claimed there was a threat to freedom of speech in the state and justified its decision to end the alliance, citing an overall deterioration in law and order, accusing the Mehbooba government of not being able to control the situation despite Central assistance.[12]

While there were many who had sensed that a collapse was imminent, Mehbooba had tried her best to salvage the situation – possibly to honour her father's last political wish. Former Chief Minister Omar Abdullah had summed up her situation bluntly, saying, 'I have been telling Mehbooba to go. She chose to be dismissed with no dignity.'[13]

Following the BJP's withdrawal of support, Mehbooba submitted her resignation. 'We didn't do this alliance for power; the alliance with the BJP was part of a bigger vision to bring peace in the Valley,' she said, after informing the governor that her party didn't want to explore any other alliances for an alternative government.[14] The state once again came under the Centre's rule.

Disillusionment and Imprisonment

Little did Mehbooba know that the fall of her government wouldn't be the toughest crisis of her political career. More was in store for her. On 5 August 2019, about a year after she resigned as chief minister, the BJP-led government at the Centre revoked Kashmir's special status by the abrogation of Article 370 and Article 35A. Mainstream leaders in the Valley, including Mehbooba, were placed under house arrest amid severe restrictions on movement and Internet communications in the Valley.

Mehbooba had hit back in a tweet: 'How ironic that elected representatives like us who fought for peace are under house arrest. The world watches as people and their voices are being muzzled in J&K.'[15]

She was released in October 2020, after fourteen months of detention in sub-jails and house arrest – six months after the release of two other former chief ministers, Farooq Abdullah and Omar Abdullah. Close allies at the Centre turning into foes is not new to Kashmiri politics. Many years ago, NC founder Sheikh Abdullah was sent to jail by the Jawaharlal Nehru government for eleven years, despite his bonhomie with independent India's first prime minister.

Much has changed in Jammu and Kashmir since that day in August 2019. The erstwhile state has been split into two Union Territories – Jammu and Kashmir, and Ladakh – while the political dynamics in the Valley have been fundamentally altered. In December 2023, the Supreme Court of India upheld the repeal of Kashmir's special status, while directing restoration of statehood 'at the earliest'.

For Mehbooba, the road ahead is tough as she seeks to reignite her political spark and consolidate support for her party – what she calls her father's dream. With the souring of relations with the BJP, the PDP is now part of the national Opposition alliance led by the Congress as she strives to find an idiom and a foothold for her future in the politics of the state.

Battle for Survival?

Mehbooba was in October 2023 elected as the PDP's president for the fourth consecutive term, strengthening her grip over the party.[16] Her tenure has seen the induction of family members, such as her brother Tassaduq Mufti – described as a reluctant politician and known more for his cinematographic achievement in the Bollywood movie *Omkara* – into the party.[17]

In the aftermath of Mehbooba's confinement in August 2019, her daughter Iltija, a journalist by profession, emerged as her mother's spokesperson on Twitter. As already mentioned, Iltija serves as her mother's media adviser.[18]

Maybe Mehbooba's dependence on her family and close relatives indicates a deeper role for the family in the party's future. But for that to happen, she first needs to salvage her party's and Kashmir's political future. Mehbooba's fortunes in electoral politics have faced stumbling blocks in the recent elections in the Valley as her party scored zero seats in the national elections of 2024. Mehbooba Mufti herself lost by 1,81,000 votes from the Anantnag–Rajouri Lok Sabha seat.[19] Making things worse, her party won only three seats with just 8.45 per cent vote share in the October 2024 assembly polls, which was the first election held after the abrogation of Article 370 and splitting of the state into union territories (UTs) in 2019.[20] This was the PDP's worst electoral performance ever since its formation. Mehbooba's daughter, Iltija Mufti, also lost the election in these assembly polls, in which she was contesting for the first time.[21] For Mehbooba, though herculean political challenges stare at her, has earlier shown the spirit and mettle to swing the political tides in her favour. Moving forward, carrying her father's legacy and party's responsibility on her shoulders, she definitely has a lot to do in politics.

12

Tabassum Hasan: Kairana's Daughter-in-Law, Defender of Her Family Legacy

In the scorching month of May 2018, Tabassum Hasan became the most notable headline-maker in the media. The outpouring of attention was linked to her remarkable victory in the Lok Sabha bypolls in the Kairana constituency of Uttar Pradesh.

Tabassum's is not a new name in Uttar Pradesh politics. She was elected to the Lok Sabha in 2009 from Kairana for the first time on a BSP ticket. But the 2018 bypoll victory, which paved the way for her second stint as a parliamentarian, was quite special. The political contest in the Kairana bypoll was seen in the media as a high-stakes prestige battle for the ruling BJP in the state. The election, which was necessitated by the death of the sitting heavyweight BJP MP Hukum Singh became a high-profile battle between the BJP and the

Opposition parties – as political rivals wanted to consolidate their position ahead of the 2019 Lok Sabha elections.

Tabassum, as the Rashtriya Lok Dal (RLD) candidate, was supported by a host of Opposition parties in the state, including the Samajwadi Party, BSP, Congress and Nishad Party. Her victory, a year before the national elections, came as a big boost to the Opposition and it gave these parties a reason to seriously consider putting up a united fight against the BJP in the 2019 Lok Sabha contest.[1] There was another reason there were so many headlines generated by her victory: she also became the only elected Muslim MP from UP since 2014, when the Modi-led BJP swept the state.[2]

Association with Politics

Politics was always a part of Tabassum's life. She was born in Dumjhera village, in UP's Saharanpur district.[3] Her father, Akhtar Hasan, was involved in local politics as block head.[4] She was the second of seven siblings. Later, her younger brother, Wasim Chaudhary, too, joined politics and played an active role in the local panchayat. Tabassum completed her education up to the intermediate level and then got married into the politically influential Hasan family of Kairana. Kairana lies within Shamli district and has a high Muslim population. The town has a rich legacy of artistic tradition. Kairana 'prides itself as being the birthplace of Abdul Karim Khan (1872–1937), a doyen of the Kirana school of music, and for its linkages with artists like Begum Akhtar and Mohammed

Rafi'. The town also 'gave name to the famed Kirana gharana of Hindustani music.'[5]

Tabassum's father-in-law, Akhtar Hasan, was a well-respected Muslim Gujjar leader and served as a Congress party MP from Kairana in 1984. Her husband, Munawwar Hasan, took over the legacy of his father and became the parliamentary representative from their political bastion of Kairana in 1996. He represented the Samajwadi Party. Earlier, Munawwar was elected from the Kairana assembly constituency as an MLA in 1991 and once again in 1993 by defeating their long-time family political rival, Hukum Singh. Munawwar lost the 1998 Lok Sabha elections to Virendra Verma, but was later nominated to the Rajya Sabha by then Samajwadi Party chief, Mulayam Singh Yadav. He was also briefly a Member of the Legislative Council (MLC) of Uttar Pradesh from the Muzaffarnagar–Saharanpur local body authorities constituency in 2003. He emerged victorious in the 2004 national elections and represented Kairana in the Lok Sabha once again.

Munawwar holds the distinction of being a member of both houses of state and both houses of Parliament – the UP Vidhan Sabha and the Vidhan Parishad, and the Lok Sabha and Rajya Sabha. However, his relationship with the Samajwadi Party got strained when he rebelled against the party line in the July 2008 UPA trust vote. Samajwadi Party had filed an expulsion petition against Munawwar with the then Lok Sabha Speaker Somnath Chatterjee. Later, he joined the BSP but died in a tragic road accident in December 2008 – even before the Speaker could act on his expulsion petition.

Tragedy, Turbulence and Politics

Munawwar's tragic and untimely death at the age of 42 left his family deeply shaken. Tabassum, who had already been burdened with the responsibility of taking care of their two children – Nahid and Iqra – alone, was now asked to take the plunge into politics to preserve her family's political legacy. Challenges came aplenty her way. She had barely recovered from the sudden loss of her husband when she had to enter the electoral fray to safeguard her husband's political bastion of Kairana in the 2009 Lok Sabha elections. In her own words about that terrible time, Tabassum said:

> When I recall all that, my heart cries. I have struggled a lot. When MP saheb [Munawwar Hasan] died, everything came to an end all of a sudden. My son, Nahid, was studying abroad and I was in mourning (Iddat), when the time for the nomination for election came. Everyone wanted me to contest. Nahid was young at that time. And, at that time too, many roadblocks were posed [my way]. A lady police officer herself came to our house for filing the nomination. Kairana made me an MP in 2009.[6]

A news report mentions that during the time of Tabassum's electoral debut 'she had not even stepped out of the house because she was observing Iddat [the period of mourning after a husband's death where Muslim women do not meet anyone else than their blood relations].'[7]

A Supportive Family

Her son, Nahid, though just 18 years old at the time, played a very important role in her campaign. Tabassum's youngest brother, Wasim Chaudhary, spoke about Nahid's hard work, 'I can't tell you how hard Nahid worked at that time. He used to not sleep for 48 hours. He had to discontinue his studies.'[8] Wasim is also a four-time district panchayat member and, later on, closely helped Tabassum as her election agent in 2018. For Wasim, Tabassum is a role model. 'When she got married, I was only 12. My life has been influenced by her. She has been a serious and reserved person right from the beginning.' He added that she struggled a lot but he remains proud of her growth as a politician. 'Now, she has matured a lot. The best thing about my sister is that she never tells a lie. She is not crooked as most political leaders are, she is simple and straight.'[9]

Confronting Dynastic Rivalry and More

Tabassum's main challenge has been to retain the political dominance of her family in Kairana, with their long-time political rivals, the family of Hukum Singh, challenging it. The story of the Hukum Singh family and Hasan family is a typical plot of a family friendship vitiated by the exigencies of politics. A news report described it more succinctly as 'the stage for a three-decade feud that could rival a Bollywood script with its elements of "dosti-dushmani-rajneeti."'[10] Hukum Singh, an

Waseem Akhtar

Maimoona Sultan

Begum Akbar Jehan Abdullah

ABP Pvt. Ltd.

ABP Pvt. Ltd.

Mohsina Kidwai

ABP Pvt. Ltd.

Abida Ahmed

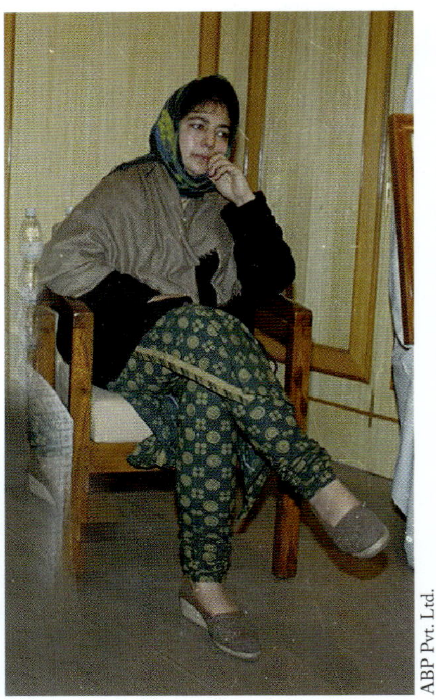
ABP Pvt. Ltd.

Mehbooba Mufti

ABP Pvt. Ltd.

Mausam Benazir Noor

ABP Pvt. Ltd.

Sajda Ahmed

ABP Pvt. Ltd.

Ranee Narah

ABP Pvt. Ltd.

Nusrat Jahan

IABP Pvt. Ltd.

Iqra Hasan

army officer, served as a captain in the Poonch and Rajouri sectors of Kashmir during the 1965 India–Pakistan war before entering politics. He emerged as a seasoned leader in Kairana and served as an MLA from 1980 to 1989, representing the Congress party. He was a friend of Tabassum's father-in-law, Akhtar Hasan. In fact, Munawwar Hasan, in his early years, was mentored by Hukum Singh. However, Munawwar and Hukum parted ways after 1984 – though nobody knows the exact reason behind the souring of their relationship. But there are speculations.

'Some say he [Munawwar] wanted a greater role in the party. Nevertheless, the rivalry began then, and it is now 33 years old,' says Meharban Qureshi, lawyer and adviser to Hukum Singh, in a report published by *DNA*.[11] The rivalry escalated in the early 1990s when Munawwar, a Janata Dal candidate, defeated the Congress candidate Hukum Singh in the Kairana assembly constituency in the 1991 UP state elections. As Kairana has a sizeable Muslim population, Hukum's discord with the Hasans cost him dearly as his Muslim support plummeted. When Kalyan Singh's government made an abrupt exit post the Babri Masjid demolition, necessitating snap polls in UP in 1993, once again Hukum Singh was humbled by Munawwar Hasan. However, in 1996, Munawwar went to the Lok Sabha, and Hukum after joining the BJP, wrested control of the Kairana assembly seat – which he retained until 2012. As the BJP gained political momentum in UP post the Babri Masjid demolition, Hukum's alignment with the party helped his comeback in Kairana politics.

Tabassum's entry into politics after Munawwar's death saw the family rivalry spilling into the Lok Sabha contest as well. In her political debut, Tabassum had to face the tall challenge of contesting against a veteran leader like Hukum Singh. But her relentless efforts in connecting with the people bore fruit and she sailed through that election to victory. She defeated a seasoned politician like Hukum Singh by a margin of more than 20,000 votes in the 2009 Lok Sabha polls.

Tabassum fielded her son, Nahid Hasan, from Kairana in the 2014 Lok Sabha elections but couldn't ensure his victory against Hukum Singh, especially with the strong Modi wave felt across UP. There are reports that Nahid refrained from making personal attacks against Hukum Singh in the election, respecting the fact that he was his late father's mentor once upon a time. Also, trouble brewed for Tabassum, as she faced competition within the family from her brothers-in-law, Anwar and Kanwar Hasan.[12] Her brother-in-law, Kanwar Hasan, an RLD leader, also contested from the Kairana seat in 2014, dividing the votes of the supporters of the family, benefiting Hukum. Nahid is a business graduate from Holmes Institute, Australia. He had to join politics at the age of 18 in order to support his mother in her first election in 2009. He had to discontinue his studies.[13]

Grit Amidst Setbacks

Despite the 2014 political setback, Tabassum didn't give up. She fielded Nahid in the assembly bypolls necessitated by

Hukum Singh relinquishing his MLA seat to go to the Lok Sabha. Nahid won this election against Hukum Singh's distant relative, Anil Chouhan, and became the youngest MLA in the country. Tabassum again decided to hit the electoral fray herself in 2018, scripting the historic victory in the Lok Sabha bypolls after Hukum Singh's death. Tabassum effectively weathered public sympathy after Hukum Singh's death and defeated her opponent, Mriganka Singh, Hukum Singh's daughter, by a sizeable margin of almost 50,000 votes.[14] This time, Tabassum could also deftly handle the political competition from within her family and rallied the support of her brothers-in-law for her candidature, as Kanwar withdrew his nomination and threw his weight behind Tabassum.

Tabassum has faced not only high-pressure political competition but also social conflict that emanated from the Hindu–Muslim rifts in the area. BJP MP Hukum Singh levelled a serious allegation that 250 Hindu families had to flee from Kairana because of threats and intimidation from the 'gangsters of a particular community' (implying the Muslim community, which constitutes the majority in that region).[15] Such allegations made way for communal polarization and vitiated the political atmosphere in Kairana. Later an National Human Rights Commission (NHRC) report confirmed the exodus of people from the region.[16] This issue became a major political flashpoint as the ruling BJP accused the Opposition, the Samajwadi Party, of indulging in minority appeasement politics. Tabassum, during her 2018 election campaign, tried to douse the communal heat by reaching out to the Jat community in the area. A news report said, 'Fifty-year-old Tabassum had been struggling to save the Hindu–Muslim unity.' Tabassum was reported to have said to the people there, 'I have come to tell you when my husband died in an accident, his head was resting on the knees of a Jat, who was crying profusely. The two Jat friends of my husband, Munawwar Hasan, were with him till his last breath. Please do not withdraw your support.'[17]

However, despite winning the 2018 bypolls, there were more struggles coming Tabassum's way. In 2022, her son, and sitting MLA, Nahid, was arrested under the Gangster Act by the UP Police. Family properties were seized, and there were serious financial constraints that Tabassum and her family faced. And Tabassum, despite her historic win in the 2018 bypolls, lost the 2019 Lok Sabha polls to the BJP in the midst of the Modi wave.[18] But Tabassum has been fortunate enough to have her children on her side whenever she has been engulfed in a crisis. It was during the Covid-19 pandemic in 2021 when her younger child, Iqra, returned to India after completing her MSc in London, just as her family was besieged by crisis. Iqra Hasan, along with Tabassum, took up the campaign on behalf of her brother in the 2022 Vidhan Sabha elections and ensured his remarkable victory, despite him being in jail. The mother-daughter duo also fought for more than a year to get Nahid released by appealing at all three levels of the judiciary.

With her baptism by fire in managing her brother's career, Iqra came of age in politics. She contested the Kairana Lok Sabha polls in 2024 and registered a spectacular political victory on the Samajwadi Party ticket against the BJP's veteran leader

Pradeep Kumar. As she made history as one of the youngest MPs in the present Lok Sabha, we have a separate chapter on Iqra in this book. Iqra considers her mother as a role model and recognizes her contributions in guiding her through the various technicalities of public outreach – instrumental in public life, especially with regard to giving speeches and holding public meetings. She shares that her 'mother told ... that responsibilities teach you everything you need to know. Politics was never in my plans, though I come from a political family. As a shy student, I avoided public speaking.'[19]

Looking Ahead

Tabassum has come a long way in politics. From being a first-time MP in 2009, propelled into parliamentary politics by a personal tragedy and a call for family duty, she has seen and endured many turbulences of political life. She and her two children have been each other's rock-solid support in difficult hours of crises. She has gained enormous experience in public life and administration in the course of her journey. During her stint as MP, she was a member of the Committee on Health and Family Welfare, and the Standing Committee on Social Empowerment and Justice. She has also been a member of the UP Central Sunni Waqf Board.[20]

Now, with both her children firmly placed in active politics as sitting MLA and MP, Tabassum has the tall task of mentoring them. Since politics is a game of possibilities, she might also throw herself in the electoral fray some day if the situation demands it.

13

Mausam Benazir Noor: Illustrious Political Legacy, Promising Political Future

Just before the Lok Sabha elections of 2024, there was reportedly a storm in the political circles of Malda, a district in the northern part of West Bengal. And in the eye of the storm was the Rajya Sabha MP from the ruling Trinamool Congress (TMC) in the state, Mausam Benazir Noor. Noor, the only active TMC leader from the first political family in Malda – Ghani Khan Choudhury's family, who switched to the TMC a few years ago – couldn't be traced in Malda. She had also not been campaigning ahead of the Lok Sabha elections, as the TMC hadn't fielded her in either of the two parliamentary seats in Noor's family bastion of Malda. There was serious discomfort and apprehension in the TMC about an unhappy Noor switching over to another party as she hadn't received a ticket. More tongues wagged when she went incommunicado and was spotted in Delhi. However, ending all speculations, Noor returned to Malda without switching over to any other party and she cited viral fever as the reason for her disappearance from Malda.[1] This incident established just how important she is in the political landscape of Malda.

Noor completed her education in Kolkata from the city's premier school, La Martinière, and graduated in law from Calcutta University. She met her husband, Mirza Kayesh Begg, during her stint at Calcutta University and they got married in 2009. Noor has had a distinguished parliamentary career, representing the Malda Uttar constituency in the Lok Sabha for two consecutive terms as a Congress MP, spanning a decade. After she switched to the TMC, she was made the Rajya Sabha MP from the state. She has said in interviews that while she was quite interested in public service and planned to join politics later in life, she chose to pursue a career as a lawyer in Delhi as part of the Supreme Court panel and in a private firm, Fox and Mandal. Only after the death of Noor's mother, Rubi Noor, did she take the plunge and enter politics.[2]

Mother's Legacy

Rubi Noor, Ghani Khan's sister, had an impressive political career as the long-time MLA from the Sujapur Vidhan Sabha constituency of Malda – from 1991 to 2008. She holds the distinctive record of not losing any election from Sujapur. In 1991, Rubi Noor, at the age of 46, embarked on a career as a Congress leader under the guidance of the charismatic political patriarch of Malda, Ghani Khan Choudhury. Rubi, in the initial days after her marriage to her college friend, Syed Mohammad Noor, went to Canada with her husband as he had a job there. Apart with Noor, Rubi and Syed had two more daughters – Syeda Saleha Noor and Sonya Sarah Noor. The couple returned to India in 1972. This was when Rubi plunged into the political waters of Malda. Apart from being an MLA, Ghani Khan also made Rubi the district president of the Malda Congress unit in 2001 – a post she held till her death. After Rubi's death in 2008, an obituary in the *Telegraph* read: 'Over the years, her brother ingrained in her an insight into Bengal politics, which in turn helped her feel the pulse of electoral politics. Under her able leadership, the Congress came to power in the Malda zila parishad this year without having to clutch on to other anti-Left parties.'[3]

Noor's family legacy is deeply intertwined with the politics of Malda and understanding her family lineage is crucial for us to understand her public life.

A Coveted Political Lineage

The politics of Malda in north Bengal has, for a long time, been dominated by the political dynasty of Ghani Khan Choudhury, popularly called 'Barkat-da'. Ghani Khan Choudhury started his political career in mid 1950s as a Congress MLA from the region, and his influence thrived from the 1970s onwards until the early 2000s – he served eight terms as the MP from Malda, and became minister in the Indira and Rajiv Gandhi governments from 1982 to 1984 at the Centre.[4] Ghani Khan is credited with the development of Malda as he ensured jobs for the local youth, and played a key role in establishing educational institutions and setting up the Malda town railway station.[5] Ghani Khan also got embankments built in a region affected by river erosion, 'schools and colleges set up, madrasas recognized, rural banks and public health care dispensaries set up. Malda also has the Ghani Khan Choudhury Institute of Engineering and Technology.'[6] His influence and goodwill is so deeply entrenched in the memory of the people of Malda that Ghani Khan's family members – his siblings, niece and nephew – continue to win assembly and parliamentary elections in his name even 18 years after his demise. His three siblings – Abu Nasar Khan, Abu Hasem Khan and Rubi Noor – all joined politics as members of the Congress party.

After his death in 2006, and following the division of the Malda seat into the North and South Malda political constituencies, his younger brother, Abu Hasem Khan Choudhury, and his niece, Mausam Noor, continued to win both the Malda Lok Sabha seats on Congress tickets, largely riding his legacy. However, there has been a split in the family as Ghani Khan's younger brother, Abu Nasar, and his nieces, Shehnaz Quadery and Mausam Noor, have all shifted to the TMC over the years.[7] In 2019, the family's hold over the two seats appeared loose for the first time as Noor defected to the TMC and fought against her cousin (Abu Hasem's son), Isha Khan Choudhury, in Maldaha North, resulting in the defeat of both Noor and Isha to the BJP candidate, Khagen Murmu, due to split of votes. Abu Hasem retained the Malda South seat with a very slender margin of 8,000 votes. In the 2024 election, the BJP's Murmu retained his seat in Maldaha North and Isha Khan won the Maldaha South seat on the Congress ticket by an impressive margin, after his father gave up the seat due to his frail health.[8]

Political Journey So Far: A Mixed Record

Immediately after her mother's death in 2008, Noor had to contest from Rubi's long-held assembly constituency, Sujapur, in Malda. She won – impressively defeating the CPI(M) candidate. That very year, she won the Lok Sabha election from the Maldaha North parliamentary constituency at the age of 30. She earned the distinction of being the youngest Muslim woman to be elected to Parliament and one of the five youngest members in the Lok Sabha. Noor, known to be close to Congress leader Rahul Gandhi, became the president of the West Bengal Youth Congress with his support in 2011. In 2013, she also took over as the president of the Malda district Congress from her uncle and veteran Congress leader, Abu Hasem Khan Choudhury.

However, Mausam's differences with the party's state leadership grew over the question of having an alliance with the TMC, with Noor being in favour of the alliance for the 2019 Lok Sabha elections as the BJP was emerging as a potent force in Malda as well as in many other regions of Bengal. Even before the 2018 panchayat elections in the state, Noor had batted for a TMC–Congress–CPM alliance by reaching out to both the TMC and the Left leadership in order to prevent the BJP from making political inroads in her pocket borough of Malda. However, the alliance proposal with the TMC was not accepted by the CPI(M). Noor then switched to the TMC and contested the Maldaha North Lok Sabha seat under the Trinamool ticket in 2019. However, she lost the election as the voters of her support base got divided between Noor and her cousin Isha Khan, who was on the Congress ticket. As the support base of the Ghani Khan Choudhury family got divided between the two cousins, the BJP's Khagen Murmu won the election amidst the BJP's overall spectacular election performance in West Bengal in 2019. Noor was later elected to the Rajya Sabha from the TMC in 2020. She has been made the general secretary of the party and the president of the Malda district unit of the TMC. She also serves as the TMC's party in-charge in Uttar Dinajpur, Dakshin Dinajpur and Malda districts.

Mausam has described her decision to leave the Congress party as 'a difficult choice, a difficult decision'.[9] In their native, iconic, family home in Malda, a wall has been erected after her switch to the TMC. A news report by NDTV during the 2019 Lok Sabha elections said:

> After Ms Noor joined TMC, the wall was built, dividing the compound where Ghani Khan used to meet his supporters and assured them his support. Ms Noor maintains her decision to join TMC has not harmed her personal relations with her cousin or her uncle. She may be right. Isha Khan's wife was

looking after Ms Noor's children as they rode bikes inside the campus when reporters visited the ancestral home.[10]

The ground report also noted that 'despite the political divide, supporters said, the family members have managed to live in the same compound. They also share their kitchen.'[11]

Though there were party workers who were disappointed with Noor's decision to jump ship – leading to a political split in the first family of Malda – others have been more considerate towards her decision. One of her associates who worked closely with Noor when she was in the Congress said that she couldn't be blamed – she simply wanted to serve her constituency better by aligning with the ruling party in the state.

This reasoning bears credence given the rising clout of the BJP in the state. Moreover, a sizeable section of traditional Congress voters in Malda, largely minorities, were shifting to the TMC as revealed in the zila parishad and panchayat samiti elections in the region in 2018. Also, during her stint as a Congress MP, she alleged a lack of cooperation from the TMC-led state government in the implementation of development projects in Malda. Hence, her association with the TMC by deviating from her family's long-held glorious association with the Congress could be seen as an act of political expediency in light of the rapidly changing political dynamics in Malda, as well as in the larger context of West Bengal.

A Committed Parliamentarian

Noor has had a distinctive career as a parliamentarian. She served as a member in the Parliamentary Standing Committees of Labour and Women Empowerment, the Committee on Papers Laid on the Table, as well as the Standing Committee on Rural Development. She has also been part of the Consultative Committee of the Ministry of Youth Affairs and Sports, and later served as a member of the Consultative Committee of the Ministry of Minority Affairs.

During her first stint as a Lok Sabha MP, 1,500 km of roadways was built in her constituency under the Pradhan Mantri Gram Sadak Yojana. Under the Rajiv Gandhi Grameen Vidyutikaran Yojana, she got funds allotted for her seat, Maldaha North. She also got impressive developmental funds sanctioned for National Highway 81 (running from Gazole to Harishchandrapur), for building the Ratua–Nakatti Bridge. She secured the allotment of the Backward Regions Grant Funds to address the erosion caused by the Mahananda river and for the construction of the Samsi railway overbridge.

The issue of river erosion that has severely impacted the lives of the people in Malda has been taken up very seriously by Noor in Parliament. In July 2024, Noor raised the issue of riverbank erosion in Malda in the Rajya Sabha, highlighting how the confluence of the Ganga and Fulhar rivers was claiming lives, destroying livestock and damaging crops each year. She earned praised from the sitting Rajya Sabha chairman Jagdeep Dhankhar, and other members for raising this pertinent issue on the floor of the house. Noor also took on the central government for not allocating funds for tacking the perennial devastation caused by floods in the riverbanks of Malda. She informed the upper house with visible anguish that 'a huge area will be engulfed by the rivers causing loss of land, farms and mango orchards rendering lakhs of people homeless'.[12]

Apart from raising this issue during question hour repeatedly on the floor of Parliament, both as a Lok Sabha and Rajya Sabha MP, Noor has also been quite vocal about it in the media and has called for the Centre's intervention for the creation of embankments in the region, which she feels can mitigate this problem. Not only in Delhi, Noor has been very much on the ground to help people impacted by the river erosion. During a flood in Malda in 2020, she visited the area and raised her voice against this problem, which could be resolved through proper governmental intervention and administrative alertness. Noor said in her statement during her visit: 'It is the barrage authorities who are responsible for this situation. We will raise the issue at necessary quarters and also take up political activities in protest.'[13]

Noor, as a young representative with a legal background, has also been vocal about the detrimental repercussions of Artificial Intelligence (AI) on labour rights and individual privacy. In 2023, she had tabled two bills in the Rajya Sabha in this regard: the Workforce Rights (Artificial Intelligence) Bill, 2023 and the Deep Fake Prevention and Criminalization Bill,

2023. A news report in the *Deccan Herald*, elaborately covering the important merits of Noor's proposed legislations, said:

> Noor's Bill on rights of workforce insists that employers must obtain 'explicit and informed consent' from employees before implementing AI technologies that directly affect their work or rights. Implementation of AI should also ensure that biases in AI algorithms that could have an impact on employees are erased.[14]

The news report also commended the vision of the second bill tabled by Noor:

> Noor's Bill on deep fakes proposes setting up a National Deep Fake Mitigation and Digital Authenticity Task Force to evaluate the prevalence of deep fakes affecting the citizens, businesses in India and the functioning of the union and state government and the influence of digital content forgery and deep fake on civic participation, including the electorate.[15]

This reflects Noor's involvement, sincerity and vision, which is not only confined to the challenges of her own region but also addresses the broader concerns of society emanating from AI-induced misinformation.

With political capital, young age, family legacy and impressive developmental vision on her side, Mausam Noor is posited to consolidate herself as a potent political figure not only in Malda but in the larger landscape, despite her political setbacks and challenges in recent years.

14

Kaisar Jahan: A Political Life Shaped by Circumstances

'*Yeh ek ittefaq hai ... iske agey sab alag hai* [This is merely a coincidence ... beyond this, everything else is different],' says Mohammad Jasmir Ansari, a tea vendor-turned-politician and the husband of parliamentarian Kaisar Jahan. Ansari does not like his life's trajectory being compared to the success story of Narendra Modi, who started his career, by his own admission, as a chaiwala in Vadnagar, Gujarat. As Jasmir himself admits, his likeness to Modi's story is both insipid and coincidental.

Jasmir's induction into politics and BSP supremo Mayawati saw destiny playing a role. The tea vendor hailed from a poor Momin (weaver) family and never received the benefits of a formal education. After joining politics and becoming an elected representative, he had to struggle for four months to master his signature.

Setting the Context

While working at a tea stall, Jasmir met Zafar Farooqui, local zamindar and *muttawalli* (custodian) of local waqf properties, who rose to become chairman of the Uttar Pradesh Waqf Board. Farooqui took a shine to Jasmir, asking him to contest the municipal elections from Laharpur, which has a substantial population of the Momin community. Jasmir grabbed the opportunity and served Farooqui his finest tea laced with a liberal dose of malai.

There was no going back for Jasmir as he went on to head the Nagar Palika after being elected as chairman of the municipal board. His sense of industry, perseverance and plain living was such that the Laharpur Nagar Palika bagged the award as the 'aadarsh' (model) municipal corporation. This recognition not only earned Jasmir a lot of goodwill but also resulted in the Laharpur Nagar Palika doubling its budgetary allocation. More funds meant more municipal work, ranging from the upkeep of graveyards to better water and sanitation services.

This was the time BSP supremo Mayawati was trying to get her electoral mathematics right for the 2007 Uttar Pradesh assembly polls. When word about the 'Laharpur model' reached her, she dumped her nominee, Jalis Ahmed Ansari, in favour of Jasmir. The grapevine has it that Jasmir upstaged Jalis in terms of marshalling better resources, which gladdened the heart of Mayawati.

In 2006, the Laharpur municipal seat was reserved for women, bringing Kaisar Jahan into public life as she won the seat with ease.

A year later, Jasmir contested the assembly polls as a BSP nominee and Laharpur saw Kaisar Jahan during the electioneering, moving from door to door, house to house, locality to locality without a veil or the hesitation of a simple housewife from the Momin community. Here was a woman who, by her appearance, may not stand out in the crowd, but could intermingle with one and all easily through her empathy, care and attention. Soon, the couple became the toast of Laharpur town and a household name. The election result on 7 April 2007 saw Jasmir getting 41.6 per cent of votes (57,179 votes). His nearest rival, Anil Kumar Verma, of the Samajwadi Party was way behind with 32 per cent of votes (44,314 votes). The BJP finished a poor fourth in that election.

Ascent to the National Stage

Mayawati became the chief minister of Uttar Pradesh, the country's largest and most populous state, and went on to create a history of sorts by completing a full term in office. She scored over Govind Ballabh Pant, Kamalapati Tripathi, Sampurnanand, Sucheta Kripalani, Narayan Datt Tiwari, Mulayam Singh Yadav, Kalyan Singh and the other chief ministers of the state who had, until now, never completed a full term in office.

Then came the Lok Sabha elections of 2009. Mayawati – riding high on popularity and the social engineering of bringing together Dalits, Muslims and Brahmins – was looking for a suitable nominee for Sitapur, a prestigious battle for her because local Congress stalwart Ram Lal Rahi was a Dalit and a four-time MP.

Mayawati summoned Jasmir and Kaisar Jahan to Lucknow. Jasmir and Kaisar stopped at 'Sharmaji ki Chai' in Hazratganj before heading to the chief minister's residence. Jasmir was anticipating a ministerial position, but instead, Mayawati came straight to the point by asking him to contest the polls. The lingering taste of chai vanished quickly as Jasmir struggled, looking tentatively at his wife for an answer. Mayawati, a politician among politicians, sensed his unease. She directly asked Kaisar: '*Tu ladegi?* [Would you contest?]' The answer came immediately and spontaneously from both Jasmir and Kaisar – yes.

In a fiercely fought four-corner contest among the former union minister Ram Lal Rahi of the Congress, Mahendra Singh Verma of the Samajwadi Party and Gyan Tiwari of the BJP, Kaisar Jahan emerged victorious – even though she had barely thirty-five days to prepare and campaign. And like that, Kaisar's career in national politics began.

In September 2009, during the month-long Ramadan fasting period, Jasmir and Kaisar hosted iftar for over 1,000 persons, with a spread of many vegetarian and non-vegetarian cuisine. In fact, even now, many Laharpur residents, including Dr Mohammad Haneef, remember the lavish iftar parties hosted every year without fail, particularly catering to the poor and daily wage earners. 'I have known the couple and their parents. They are modest, well-meaning persons who have stayed away from the trappings of power. I have been their family doctor as well and I can vouch for Kaisar Jahan's integrity and sense of purpose in life,' Dr Haneef said in a telephonic interview.

He added that several beautification projects in Laharpur were carried out by the couple. 'We have seen the widening of roads, sanitation work and street lights,' he said, adding, 'I wish there was greater thrust on employment and industry coming to our town.'

In Laharpur and Sitapur, Jasmir is still remembered as a neta (politician) who does not forget a face. In fact, his phone book's contact list has photos against every name and entry. This way, he remembers everyone he has ever met.

Kaisar Jahan is known as a leader of few words. After serving the BSP in UP for around two decades, the couple was suddenly expelled from the party. Kaisar remains taciturn about this turn of events and joined the Congress. She simply said about the Congress, '*Woh log achche lage, hum unke saath aagaye* [We liked them and so we joined them].'[1]

Political Record

Kaisar served as MP from Sitapur from 2009 to 2014, when she was still relatively young in her thirties. Though she dropped out of school after Class VIII, she rose to political prominence in a complex region like Sitapur – known for its diverse electorate and socio-economic challenges. Her tryst with politics has much to do with the seats reservation policy for women in the local self-government, leading to her political debut in electoral politics. Her contributions in the former laid the groundwork for her ascent to national politics.

Kaisar Jahan's tenure in the 15th Lok Sabha (2009–14) saw her serving on the Committee on Science and Technology, Environment and Forests as well as the Committee on Housing and Urban Affairs. Her parliamentary performance, however, reflected a mixed record, with her attendance at 62 per cent, which is below the national average of 76 per cent.

She also asked questions to the government on more than thirty issues during her stint as MP. As a representative from Sitapur, she raised significant issues in Parliament, including flood prevention in Sitapur, railway development and welfare schemes for weavers in her constituency.

According to records in Parliament, Kaisar Jahan also raised several questions on issues such as the implementation of the Justice Ranganath Misra Commission on Religious and Linguistic Minorities, funds allocated by the government for the Indian Community Welfare Fund in the past years, and special arrangements for imparting training for improved and commercial goat rearing. She also raised queries relating to the appointment of Urdu teachers, the purchase of offices and residential accommodation for officers and employees of Indian embassies functioning abroad, investment in textiles, allocation of funds to minority institutions, the Jawaharlal

Nehru National Solar Mission, the functioning of Central Madrasa Board, flood control and complaints against recruitment agencies.

Ups and Downs

Her political journey saw fluctuations in her electoral success. After winning the Sitapur seat in 2009, she contested again in 2014, increasing her vote share to 35.69 per cent but losing to BJP's Rajesh Verma. By 2019, as an INC candidate, her vote share declined to 9.02 per cent, placing her in third position, with the Modi wave in UP dampening her political prospects in both the 2014 and the 2019 Lok Sabha elections.

Her transition from the BSP to the INC in 2018 was marked by controversy, as she was expelled from the former allegedly for anti-party activities. This political shift demonstrated her adaptability and political resilience but also reflected the challenges of maintaining a stable foothold in a competitive political landscape. As she didn't contest the 2024 Lok Sabha elections, Kaisar has a tall task of reorienting her political career. However, under the right circumstances and opportunity, she can definitely turn the tide for herself and her family in the politics of Sitapur.

In 2020, the couple, having served both the BSP and the Congress, switched to the Samajwadi Party, professing loyalty to Akhilesh Yadav.[2] In 2022, Jasmir and Kaisar Jahan could not get assembly tickets as the Samajwadi Party fought a difficult election against Yogi Adityanath from the ruling BJP.

Akhilesh, however, kept his word by bringing Jasmir into the legislative council as the MLC to serve a six-year term. In 2027, the Uttar Pradesh assembly polls are due. In Laharpur, there is considerable speculation whether Jasmir, with less than a year to go as MLC, will fight or will it be Kaisar, who enjoys an excellent rapport with the voters cutting across caste and religion. With age and political capital on their side, this couple still has a long way to go in the world of politics.

15

Mamtaz Sanghamita: The Good Doctor

Mamtaz Sanghamita, now in her late seventies, has built an impressive legacy in Indian medicine and politics. She is celebrated for her exceptional contributions to healthcare, education and social welfare in times of great social and political upheaval in the country. She was born in 1946 into a family steeped in intellectualism and public service. Her upbringing in Burdwan, West Bengal, laid the foundation for a remarkable career marked by dedication, compassion and unwavering commitment to community welfare.

Bengali Muslims from Burdwan defy many of the monolithic stereotypes we are programmed to look for in the community. This defiance also holds true for Muslims in districts like Malda and Murshidabad. You could be completely off the mark if you conclude that Bashar is the name of a Muslim boy, or, for that matter, Milon the name of a Hindu boy. In these districts, as well as in large parts of Bengal, a Bashar can be a

Hindu and Milon, a Muslim. There are several reasons for this. First, many Muslims in these districts are descendants of the elite, landed gentry. Next, since everyone is Bengali-speaking, one cannot use linguistic markers to identify a community on the basis of religion. And lastly, Muslim or not, they are deeply entrenched in Bengal's rich and inclusive cultural tapestry. Being an integral part of a linguistic and cultural majority, it is no longer surprising to see a Hindu Bashar and Muslim Milon. It is this context which allows a Mamtaz and a Sanghamita to happily coexist as a single marker of identity.

Family's Calling Towards Public Service

From an early age, Mamtaz was nurtured in an environment where education, civic responsibility and political awareness were not just encouraged but deeply ingrained. Her family ensured that she was exposed to the principles of justice, equality and activism – values that would later define her career. Born into a household where political discourse was a part of everyday life, she had the privilege of witnessing first-hand the mechanisms of governance, policymaking and grassroots activism.

Her father, Sayyad Mansur Habibullah, was a towering figure in West Bengal politics and law. A veteran leader associated with the CPI(M), Mansur was not only a committed advocate for farmers' rights but also a key player in the state's political landscape. As a legislator in the West Bengal assembly, he championed policies aimed at empowering marginalized communities. His tenure as the state law minister from 1982 to 1987 under the Left Front government solidified his reputation as a leader dedicated to progressive reforms, particularly in the domains of agrarian rights and legal empowerment. His commitment to the cause of the working classes and rural populations left a lasting impression on Mamtaz, instilling in her a sense of duty towards working for social equity.

Equally instrumental in shaping her worldview was her mother, Maqsooda Khatoon. An educator and a tireless advocate for women's rights, Maqsooda worked to break down barriers that restricted women's access to education and economic independence. At a time when societal norms imposed severe restrictions on women's roles outside the household, she emphasized the importance of intellectual empowerment and self-reliance. Her work in promoting gender equality and her insistence on education as the ultimate tool for social mobility had a profound influence on Mamtaz, who grew up internalizing the belief that knowledge was the most powerful catalyst for change.

Growing up in a culturally rich, politically engaged and socially conscious household, Mamtaz imbibed the principles of activism and advocacy almost by osmosis. She was raised to question authority, challenge injustice and stand up for those whose voices were often ignored. The fusion of her father's political acumen and her mother's passion for social reform created an environment where Mamtaz naturally gravitated towards public service. This unique upbringing not only shaped her career but also positioned her as a formidable advocate for justice, equity and democratic rights in contemporary West Bengal.[1]

Education and Medical Career

Mamtaz's academic journey commenced at the Burdwan Municipal Girls School, where she laid the groundwork for her future achievements. Her mother's workplace in Kolkata allowed her admission to the renowned Brahmo Balika Vidyalaya, from where she graduated, setting the foundation for her pursuit of higher education in medicine. The values of a secular and spiritualist education were evident in her growing passion for community welfare.

Having finished her schooling, Mamtaz enrolled in the Bethune College for her pre-medical studies and earned her MBBS degree from the Calcutta Medical College in 1968. Several milestones mark her exemplary journey as a woman gynaecologist. Her quest for knowledge and specialization led her to obtain a Diploma in Gynaecology and Obstetrics (DGO) from Calcutta University in 1970, followed by an MD in Obstetrics and Gynaecology from Delhi University. She augmented her expertise with international training in ultrasound at King's College, UK. She specialized in gynaecological laparoscopy and colposcopy (a procedure to detect precancerous conditions and cervical cancer) in Delhi, solidifying her reputation as a leader in women's health.

Mamtaz joined the West Bengal Health Services Department, where she served in various capacities, each marked by her exemplary dedication and expertise in women's health. Her tenure included key roles at the Calcutta National Medical College and the North Bengal Medical College. Later, she became a professor and subsequently, the head of department at the Calcutta Medical College until her retirement in 2006. Her contributions, however, extended beyond clinical practice – she served as a consultant to the Government of India's Health and Family Planning Department and held advisory roles at a prestigious Delhi-based medical college.

Throughout her career, Mamtaz Sanghamita remained unwavering in her dedication to advancing women's healthcare, particularly in the fields of maternal and reproductive health. At a time when women's health issues were often sidelined or considered secondary to broader public health concerns, she emerged as a strong advocate for policies and initiatives that placed these issues at the forefront of medical and governmental discourse.

One of her primary areas of focus was maternal and child health, where she worked tirelessly to reduce the maternal mortality rate and improve healthcare access for expecting mothers, particularly in rural and underserved communities. Recognizing that systemic changes were required to bring about significant improvements, she pushed for policy reforms that emphasized better prenatal care, institutional deliveries and postnatal support. She also played a pivotal role in advocating for reproductive rights, ensuring that women had greater autonomy over their reproductive choices, along with access to safe abortion services and awareness about family planning measures. Importantly, beyond just championing solutions, she was instrumental in bringing these concerns into the national conversation, ensuring that issues such as maternal deaths, lack of access to contraception and gender disparities in healthcare were addressed at both the policy and grassroots levels.

Her expertise and leadership were widely acknowledged, earning her prestigious positions in national and international medical organizations. She served as the president of the Bengal Obstetrics and Gynaecological Society, where she led efforts to modernize gynaecological practices, and create awareness about emerging healthcare challenges faced by women. Her contributions to the field extended to perinatology and reproductive biology, leading to her appointment as the vice president of the Indian Society of Perinatology and Reproductive Biology, where she helped formulate research-driven policies and interventions to improve neonatal and maternal health outcomes.

Beyond these roles, Mamtaz was also deeply involved in medical education and policy formulation. As a key figure in professional bodies such as the Indian Medical Association (IMA) and the Calcutta Medical Club, she worked to bridge the gap between medical research and real-world healthcare implementation. She actively promoted the training of healthcare professionals, emphasizing the need for continuous medical education and interdisciplinary collaboration to keep pace with the evolving needs of women's health.

Foray into Parliamentary Politics

Mamtaz recognized the need for galvanizing public action for large-scale development. As she had seen in her family, such development was impossible to implement without working from within the legislative system. Parallel to her medical achievements, she carved out a niche for herself in the political arena. Her election as an MP from the Burdwan–Durgapur constituency in West Bengal in the 16th Lok Sabha (2014–19) reflected her deep-rooted connection with her constituents and her ability to translate healthcare expertise into effective policies. To know her popularity, we only have to look at her landslide victory with over 1,00,000 votes in the election.[2]

As a member of the TMC, she brought a specialized perspective to national debates on healthcare, education and women's empowerment. Some of her memorable speeches in the Lok Sabha include questioning the provenance and efficiency of the dispersal of central funds during discussions on national health accounts, debating the impact of the Indian Medical Council (Amendment) Bill, 2018, and stressing the urgency of commencing construction work on National Highway 2 (NH2).

According to records in Parliament, Mamtaz Sanghamita also asked many questions in the 16th Lok Sabha. She expressed concern over the sanctioned railway projects under the Howrah and Asansol division, and questioned a proposal to issue licences to people looking to open naturopathic wellness centres, she asked about the tariff exemptions to IT start-ups and the cancellation of flights by airlines. She also tabled questions on the sale of medicines at a higher price, the sufficient supply of some life-saving drugs, and measures being taken by the Centre for regular production and supply of these drugs. She also questioned the shortage of veterinary surgeons for the protection and preservation of wildlife and wondered about the planting of fruit-bearing trees alongside national highways.[3]

Life Dedicated to Social Service

Mamtaz's contributions extend far beyond healthcare and politics; her deep commitment to education, culture and social reform has left a lasting impact on Bengal's socio-cultural fabric. Recognizing that education is the foundation for empowerment, especially for marginalized communities, she has played a pivotal role in establishing institutions that cater to the educational needs of young girls and underprivileged students.

Her efforts in founding the Mansur Habibullah Memorial School in Ashok Nagar and Asleha Girls, College in Nalhati were driven by a vision to provide access to quality education in regions where opportunities were scarce. These institutions were designed not only to impart academic knowledge but also to instil values of self-reliance, confidence and leadership in young students. Additionally, her involvement in the establishment of Sophia Girls College reflects her unwavering belief in the transformative power of education. Through these institutions, she has enabled countless young girls to break barriers and pursue careers in fields that were once considered out of reach.

Beyond traditional education, Mamtaz has been a strong advocate for digital literacy. Understanding that the future lies in technological advancements, she introduced initiatives to promote computer literacy among students, ensuring that they are equipped with the skills necessary to navigate an increasingly digital world. This forward-thinking approach has helped bridge the educational divide, particularly in rural Bengal where access to technology remains a challenge.

Her cultural contributions are equally noteworthy. She has been deeply invested in preserving and promoting Bengal's rich cultural heritage. She has played a crucial role in the development and restoration of temples and mosques across Murshidabad, Birbhum and Burdwan, fostering communal harmony and reinforcing the importance of religious coexistence. Her belief that culture serves as a unifying force is evident in her various initiatives aimed at celebrating Bengal's artistic traditions.

One such initiative is Surangana, a cultural group dedicated to teaching singing, dancing and the arts. Through Surangana, she has provided a platform for young artists to explore and express their creativity, while ensuring that Bengal's artistic legacy is passed down to future generations. Her unwavering commitment to cultural preservation has reinforced the significance of music, literature and performing arts in shaping societal values.

Mamtaz's humanitarian efforts are just as impactful. She actively lends her support to various NGOs focused on women's welfare and child development, advocating for policies that promote social equity. Her activism against gender-based violence, female foeticide and discrimination remains a cornerstone of her social work. She has been a vocal proponent of legislative measures aimed at protecting women's rights, ensuring their equal participation in all spheres of life –from education and employment to politics and governance.

Personal Life Shaped by Sense of Duty

Mamtaz's personal life has been deeply intertwined with her professional and social commitments, creating a legacy that spans generations. In 1975, she married Nure Alam Chowdhury, a distinguished barrister, who later rose to the position of acting Chief Justice of the Calcutta High Court. His illustrious career in law and governance saw him serve as a cabinet minister in the West Bengal government between 2011 and 2016, during the TMC-led administration. His legal acumen and political contributions significantly shaped Bengal's legal and judicial landscape, and his influence further cemented Mamtaz's own dedication to public service.

Their partnership was built on the shared values of justice, education and social reform. Despite their demanding careers, both Mamtaz and Nure Alam Chowdhury remained committed to the causes they championed. Their combined presence in the fields of law, governance, healthcare and social activism made them a formidable force in Bengal's intellectual and political circles.

Their daughter, Shabana Roze Chowdhury, inherited her parents' deep-rooted sense of duty and commitment to social welfare. Following in her mother's footsteps, she pursued a career in medicine, a field where she could make a tangible impact on people's lives. From an early age, Shabana was exposed to the realities of rural healthcare, often accompanying her mother on medical visits to remote villages in Bengal. These trips were more than just professional engagements for Mamtaz – they were an extension of her commitment to providing free and accessible medical care to underprivileged women.

For young Shabana, these visits were eye-opening experiences. She witnessed first-hand the struggles of women in rural Bengal – stories of maternal health complications, lack of medical infrastructure and deeply ingrained societal challenges preventing these women's access to medical care. She also listened to harrowing accounts of domestic violence and harassment, often shared in hushed tones by women who had no other outlet for their pain. These encounters left an indelible mark on her, shaping her resolve to work towards advancing maternal and child healthcare in the state.

Shabana's commitment to this cause has led her to advocate for improved healthcare policies and services, ensuring that vulnerable women and children receive the care they need. Like her mother, she believes that healthcare is not just a profession but a form of service, and she continues to build on the foundation laid by Mamtaz.

Devoted Life in Service

Mamtaz Sanghamita is an unsung hero of Bengal, whose life and career exemplify the transformative power of dedication, compassion and leadership. From her early years shaped by a family legacy of service to her multifaceted contributions in medicine, politics, education and social activism, she remains an inspiration and a role model for future generations – especially for women and the rural communities for whom she has worked so passionately. Her legacy continues to resonate through the lives she has touched, the institutions she has nurtured and the causes she has championed, leaving a prominent mark on Bengal and beyond.

16

Sajda Ahmed: Navigating Personal Tragedy and Political Trepidation

In Sajda Ahmed's office in Kolkata, there is a big photograph of her late husband, Sultan Ahmed, with Sajda's party chief and West Bengal Chief Minister Mamata Banerjee. This imagery is a powerful embodiment of Sajda's political trajectory.

Sajda was elected to the Lok Sabha from the constituency of Uluberia in West Bengal in 2018 after the sudden death of her husband, senior TMC leader Sultan Ahmed. Mamata decided to field the late veteran leader's wife, Sajda, from his Lok Sabha seat and she won by a record margin, carrying forward her husband's illustrious legacy. Sajda's political ascent has been remarkable since her electoral debut in 2018 when she won by 4,74,000 votes. Sajda managed to increase the vote share by a massive 13 per cent in 2018 from the previous Lok Sabha elections in 2014, when Sultan Ahmed won from the Uluberia seat by a margin of 2,00,000 votes.

After that, there was no looking back for Sajda as she successfully got re-elected from her seat in the subsequent national elections in both 2019 and 2024, winning by impressive margins once again. She could effectively navigate the turbulent political waters even as the BJP posed serious challenges to her in recent years. She has effectively taken forward her family's political legacy in their bastion of Uluberia.

Sultan Ahmed's Legacy

It is important we begin with Sultan's political journey as it provides the foundation for Sajda's career in the later years. Sultan Ahmed boasted of a distinguished political career at the very top of Bengal politics in the last few decades. A career politician, Ahmed carved his path through student politics to begin with. During his days as a graduate student in Maulana Azad College in 1969, he joined the student wing (Chhatra Parishad) of the then dominant party in the state, Congress. Sultan steadily rose through the ranks as he joined the Youth Congress and eventually became its district secretary in the 1970s.

He successfully established himself as a popular and credible Muslim face in the state's politics. Sultan, a close confidante of Mamata Banerjee, shifted from Congress to the TMC as one of its founding members, when the party was formed under Mamata's leadership in 1998. Eventually, Sultan made his foray into legislative politics by serving as an MLA from his Vidhan Sabha seat, Entally, in Kolkata from 1987 to 1991, and again from 1996 to 2001. Ahmed entered parliamentary politics in 2014 by getting elected as a Lok Sabha MP from Uluberia – a stint he couldn't complete due to his untimely demise.

Sultan's political clout stemmed from his social capital for he was deeply engaged in welfare activities for the Muslim community. He was associated with a number of notable and influential minority organizations in Kolkata. He served as the secretary and president of the Mohammedan Sporting Club, Kolkata. Formed in February 1891, it is one of the oldest active football clubs in the country and after Independence, it became the first Indian club to win a football tournament on foreign soil – achieving the remarkable feat of winning the Aga Khan Gold Cup in 1960. The club is a powerful embodiment of the progressive Muslim identity amongst the elite that emerged in the communally sensitive post-Partition era. The club remains a point of pride for the elite Muslims of Bengal.

Sultan was also a member of the All-India Muslim Personal Law Board. He was the secretary, and later president, of the Muslim Institute – a thriving socio-cultural platform engaged in political, social, cultural and sporting activities in Kolkata, which was founded in 1902. At the time of his death, he was the vice chairman of the All India Hajj Committee and also headed the state's Minority Development and Finance Corporation.

His association with a prestigious charitable institution, the Calcutta Muslim Orphanage (CMO), led to much acclaim and Sultan is credited for bringing in a slew of progressive reforms in the organization. The CMO is widely regarded as the leading Muslim elite welfare organization in Kolkata, and political parties have often battled hard to gain control of the organization. In a *Telegraph* report from 2012, Salman Akhtar, who had served as the honorary secretary of the organization, said, 'It is probably the oldest orphanage in Asia and one of the very few Muslim institutions in the city and that makes it coveted.'[1] The report further delves into the reach and importance of the institution, as it 'boasts [of] property worth over ₹100 crore, including four schools, and a healthy cash cushion'. One of its members at that time said of the funding for the organization, 'Besides rent from its various properties, aids and grants, one of the major sources of the orphanage's income is the zakat [an Islamic levy paid by Muslims to charitable organizations] that Muslims give out.'[2]

The organization's influence and clout can also be seen from the fact that two panels of a sizeable number of members compete to control the body. Sultan's status amidst the Muslim elite had already increased as he gained control over the Islamia Hospital and Mohammedan Sporting Club, even during the dominant rule of the Left in Bengal. True to his political mobilizational skills, Sultan, along with another TMC leader, Iqbal Ahmed, could take control of the CMO from CPI(M) stalwart and former MP Mohammed Salim once his party came to power in the state. One member highlighted in the report that 'being part of such institutions helps politicians have a direct channel of communication with the members of the community. It also gives them a chance to showcase their work in the community.'[3] Sultan could successfully capitalize on his control over such premier social institutions to further consolidate his political stature as a major Muslim leader both in the TMC and West Bengal.

Foray into Public Life

Sajda's foray into public life began with Sultan's plethora of social welfare activities. Sajda Ahmed received impressive education as she completed her BA (Honours) degree in English from the University of Calcutta after passing out from Loreto School in Kolkata. She eventually began coordinating her husband's welfare activities and businesses, serving as his support in his public life. In one of her Facebook pages, which has a sizeable number of followers, a post from around the time Sajda entered politics succinctly describes her transition.

> An educator and social worker, Sajda Ahmed is the wife of the late Sri Sultan Ahmed, a prominent parliamentarian who represented the constituency of Uluberia in the 15th and 16th Lok Sabha. For several decades, Sajda Ahmed had an unwavering presence and provided constant support to her husband through his illustrious socio-political career. Their shared vision for Bengal was one of holistic socio-economic development, communal harmony and equity among all sections of society, and that Ahmed aims to further pursue as the Trinamool Congress' candidate for the Uluberia Lok Sabha by-poll election.[4]

Sajda, who has created a distinguished identity for herself as an educator and active social worker, served as the principal of the Oxford Primary School for eight long years. In 2018, she also served as the convenor of the Islamia Nursing College and secretary of the Madrasah-Tus-Sabaya in Kolkata. Additionally, she was a governing body member of Islamia General Hospital, where she focused on the development and expansion of a new multi-speciality block in Park Circus, Kolkata. The social media post also said that Sajda 'possessing a deep empathy for marginalized persons [and] has been an active contributor through her involvement within such local communities, especially the Calcutta Muslim Orphanage, providing access to secular educational opportunities'.[5]

Sajda and Sultan have two sons: Dr Taha Ahmed is an established doctor in the city and his wife, Zeba Khan, is a lecturer. Their younger son, Sharique Ahmed, is more active in public life and is serving as the finance secretary of the Mohammedan Sporting Club. After Sultan's death, before the party officially declared Sajda as their candidate for the Uluberia Lok Sabha seat, speculations were rife that Sharique would get the ticket. However, it was Sajda who took the responsibility of carrying forward Sultan's political glory.[6] Regarding Sharique's entry into politics, Sajda had said in 2018: 'Well, to be honest, he is too young to enter this field. However, if he wants to and the party approves of him then, of course, he can contest sometime later. We will do what our party supremo, Mamata didi, wants. If she has shown confidence in me then I shall deliver.'[7]

Sultan's sudden death due to a cardiac arrest became a contentious issue between his party, the TMC, and the BJP, with the party leadership accusing Central agencies like the CBI of humiliating him and causing so much stress that it led to his death. Sultan was being interrogated by the agencies as part of the Narada bribery sting row.[8]

Life as an MP

Sajda has demonstrated adequate energy, interest and sincerity in her role as an MP and is seen as a vocal three-time parliamentarian of her party. As a Lok Sabha MP, she has so far served as a member of the Standing Committee on Science and Technology, Environment, Forests and Climate Change; a member of the Standing Committee on Energy; and a member of the Standing Committee on Rural Development. She has also served as a member of the Consultative Committee for the Ministry of External Affairs.

Sajda has been quite active in her role as MP and has asked relevant questions and demanded accountability from the Centre on diverse and extremely important policy issues. She has prioritized issues affecting her state by addressing concerns about the development of the tourism industry in West Bengal, the problem of erosion and the railways' allocation for the state. She has also shown concern for issues concerning the education sector, such as the New Education Policy 2020 (NEP 2020), the issue of student suicides in coaching centres and academic integrity in research education. She has also raised her voice regarding Covid-19–related healthcare challenges such as potential side effects of the vaccine, and the illegal marketing and sale of AYUSH medicines in the open market for Covid-19 treatment across the country.

Sensitive issues like the development of unused Waqf properties for revenue generation, the deaths of Indian Hajj pilgrims and the lynching incidents in the country have been brought up by her. She also raised questions on the fencing work along the India–Bangladesh border, and the need for verifying the accuracy and integrity of the voting process through electronic voting machines (EVMs). Making a strong pitch for social inclusion, she also raised the need for a policy on menstrual leave for women, and the development of Anganwadi Centres (AWCs) and the rights of workers there.

She has also shown interest in diverse modern and evolving developmental concerns at the national level including the question of freight transportation through inland waterways, reforms made to improve the regulatory environment for electronic manufacturing in the country, foreign investment in the electronic manufacturing sector and employment generation in civil aviation, to name a few.

Call of Duty

Sajda's entry into mainstream politics was driven by a personal tragedy. But she quickly demonstrated remarkable political skills to do justice to the formidable task entrusted to her as a leader, parliamentarian and social worker. Despite her accolades, Sajda dedicates her political life to the wish of her late husband. She once said in an interview, 'Long back, my husband had wanted me to join politics. But I had declined. There were already two politicians in the family and I had my kids to groom. So many years down the line, today, when I will be contesting this election, in a way will be fulfilling his wish.'[9] She also tries to strengthen her long association with public life, despite her late entry into politics, and her rock-solid support to Sultan's political life as a dutiful wife: 'I might not have campaigned, but I have been like a shadow for my husband, during his 30 years of political career.'[10] As Sajda has comfortably placed herself as the rightful successor of Sultan's legacy in politics, it would be interesting to see how her stint in Bengal's parliamentary politics unfolds in the days ahead.

17

Ranee Narah: Bat, Ball and Politics

Three days before Ranee Narah turned 47, on 28 October 2012, her then party colleague Himanta Biswa Sarma had tweeted, 'Congratulation to Shrimati Rani Narah for her induction into the Union Council of Ministers.'[1]

At 11.56 a.m. that day, Ranee had taken oath as a junior minister in the Ministry of Tribal Affairs in the Manmohan Singh-led UPA government. Sarma's congratulatory tweet was sent exactly 36 minutes after the ceremony.

To date, Ranee has not responded to the tweet.

Many would have viewed Sarma's courtesy tweet as an attempt to bury an old hatchet. The series of events that followed over the next twelve years reveals that the hatchet remained exactly where it was, though the stature of these two protagonists in this saga has changed. A former Congress leader, Sarma has since joined the BJP and is now the chief minister of Assam. While his career graph in the current political scenario has been rising, Ranee has all but taken a back seat in the public memory since her exit from the Rajya Sabha in 2022.

Ranee, it seemed for a long time, was destined for bigger things. Born Jahanara Choudhury, she took the name 'Ranee Narah' following her marriage. Her husband, Bharat Narah, is a six-time member of the Assam Legislative Assembly and a former Congress minister in the Assam government.

Rise of a Sportswoman

If her husband was drawn to politics as a young man, cricket was Ranee's calling before she threw her hat into the political ring as well. Old newspaper reports describe her as a 'stingy left-arm orthodox bowler' and a 'hard-hitting left-handed batter'.[2] Women's cricket in India has only recently drawn the kind of attention that it has always deserved. When Ranee started out in the 1970s, there was hardly any incentive for a girl to pick up the willow or the red cherry. Ranee picked up both. She was an all-rounder – a middle-order batter and a left-arm spinner – and showed plenty of aggression on the field, said a Guwahati-based journalist, who did not wish to be named. He is among the very few who still remember Ranee as a player. Most sports journalists today cannot even recall her playing days, though Ranee captained the Assam state cricket team, according to her Wikipedia profile.[3] There are no records available of Ranee's exploits on the cricket pitch. When we searched ESPNcricinfo, considered one of the most comprehensive websites for all things cricket, we found an article from 13 November 2006 that said that the Board of Control for Cricket in India (BCCI), the game's national governing body, had decided to disband the Women's Cricket Association of India (WCAI). The name 'Jahanara Choudhury' draws a complete blank.

Ranee, president of the WCAI for three terms, was asked to resign along with the secretary, Shubhangi Kulkarni, a former captain of the women's cricket team, and join the BCCI's women's committee. The WCAI would later be absorbed by the BCCI, following the merger of the International Women's Cricket Council with the International Cricket Council to form one unified global body to manage the game. Earlier, in 2005, when Ranee was still heading the WCAI, the Indian women's cricket team had reached the final of the Women's Cricket World Cup, where they lost to Australia by 98 runs.

Ranee, who also represented Assam in volleyball, weightlifting, shot put and discus, says it was politics in sports and cricket administration that drew her to state and national politics as a career option. During a personal interaction with the author, she said: 'I was happy to be a sportswoman and [was] about to don Indian colours having played in the junior team, but the Assam cricket body kept me out without taking into account my on-field talent. In short, it was a gross injustice and discrimination of the worst kind.'

She appeared calm while reminiscing about those days decades later at the lounge of New Delhi's India International Centre. But back then, anger and frustration had pushed her into the comforting arms of politics.

From Cricket to Politics

On the political turf, there were at least three veteran Congress leaders who played a pivotal role in her ascent – Hiteswar Saikia, Santosh Mohan Dev and Tarun Gogoi. Ranee's formal entry into politics happened in the mid-1990s and she would be, in quick succession, appointed as the general secretary, then vice president and finally president of the Assam Pradesh Youth Congress.

About a decade before Ranee's entry into politics, a young leader from the All-Assam Students' Union was creating waves in the state. When the Asom Gana Parishad (AGP) formed the government under Prafulla Mahanta, a 27-year-old Bharat Narah from the ethnic Mising group of people was made a minister.

Apparently, it was Hiteswar Saikia who had introduced Ranee – then known by her birth name, Jahanara – to Bharat. The young couple fell in love and their relationship blossomed with the blessings of Saikia. Former student leaders who had taken oath as chief minister and ministers in the new AGP government were among those who attended their wedding. Ranee said that she and Bharat had a nikah ceremony, a court registered marriage and a celebration in keeping with the Dugla Lanam (elopement marriage) system – a popular form of marriage among the Misings.

Months later, the Mahanta government would run into a storm of dissent over myriad issues. Among them was Bharat's decision to invite Saikia to his wedding. His then party colleagues were also upset with him for marrying a Muslim woman.

Saikia, who was chief minister of Assam for two terms, died in 1996. By then, the Narah couple were firmly in the Congress fold and have remained steadfast in their loyalty towards the grand old party.

Another Saikia Protégé

Like the Narahs, Himanta Biswa Sarma also considers himself a protégé of Saikia. Younger than both Bharat and Ranee, Sarma had cut his teeth in student politics while he was still in school and would rise to be number two in the Tarun Gogoi government before leaving the Congress to join the BJP in August 2015.

As an up-and-coming Congress politician in the mid-1990s, Sarma's proximity to Saikia and his growing clout within the organization had created a rivalry among several young leaders who had similar ambitions. Then, in 2001, Sarma entered the assembly for the first time as an elected member, taking his first step towards what has been an unbroken run till date. By then, Ranee had already become a two-time MP, winning her first election in 1998 from the Lakhimpur Lok Sabha seat in Upper Assam.

Ranee's critics say she had 'managed' the ticket from the Congress high command despite several complaints against her. 'I remember the late Santosh Mohan Dev had introduced her to us at the Circuit House,' recalls a now retired journalist, who didn't wish to be named.

Ranee is candid about her loyalty to the Congress high command, especially Sonia Gandhi. 'I owe everything to Sonia Gandhi. She liked me and trusted my political acumen. Even Chief Minister Tarun Gogoi would often gently chide me and say he had to accommodate me because of Sonia Gandhi,' Ranee said to the author during a personal interaction.

In 1999, Ranee won from Lakhimpur again – this time defeating the AGP nominee, Sarbananda Sonowal, who would, a decade and a half later, go on to become Assam's first BJP chief minister in May 2016.

'But, as in cricket, politics sometimes does not work to a game plan,' Ranee says. 'The best bowling goes unrewarded and you lose despite scoring a century. But all's well that ends well.'[4]

After Gogoi became the chief minister for the first time in 2001, he made two appointments, one of which would have far-reaching consequences for him, the Congress and for Ranee. While Ranee's husband, Bharat, was appointed a cabinet minister, a post he would hold for ten years, Sarma was made the junior minister for planning and development in 2002. Ranee was by then largely preoccupied with cricket administration. But unknown to her, resentment was brewing against her within the party, which ultimately cost her the Lakhimpur Lok Sabha seat.

In 2004, the year the Congress had upset the BJP's 'India Shining' campaign, and Manmohan Singh, a Rajya Sabha MP from Assam, was sworn in as the prime minister, Ranee lost the Lakhimpur seat following a full-blown rebellion from local MLAs against the party's official nominee. Four MLAs refused to campaign for Ranee. She was also accused of not submitting formal accounts of a session of the Assam Sahitya Sabha held at Lakhimpur in 2003. Ranee was the reception committee president. The amount was reported to be around Rs 50 lakh. The local MLAs were also unhappy with her failure to do anything 'substantial' for the constituency.

Her 'proximity' to the late Hiteswar Saikia also came back to haunt Ranee, as several of her colleagues in the Assam Congress accused her of 'spying' for Saikia when he was the chief minister.

Two years later, in 2006, the feud between her and Sarma was out in the open. 'Things have gone a bit too far and since the department and the chief minister have ignored my complaints of kickbacks being demanded for funds meant for development, I have decided to move Madam Sonia Gandhi in the greater interest of the party,' Ranee had declared. 'What I am doing is for the party. I am not working against any poll candidate or criticising the government or the party leadership. I am only highlighting corruption in one specific department, and that too, after a former executive of the Mising Autonomous Council (MAC) wrote to the MAC chief about the wheeling-dealing in the department to get funds released.'[5]

Ranee's announcement that she would seek an audience with the then party chief in New Delhi came a day after Sarma had called for an impartial enquiry into the corruption allegations levelled against him by the former MP. Ranee's husband, Bharat, however, described Sarma as an asset for the party and what went on within the four walls of the Narah residence never saw the light of day.

But there is a day deeply entrenched in Ranee's memory. It was a day she cried herself to sleep, resting her head in her mother Nurjahan Choudhury's lap. She woke up the next morning numb and broken to see both Bharat and Gogoi supporting Himanta, who dismissed her as 'mentally disturbed'.

Brief Spell of Glory

Her little act of rebellion aside, Ranee bagged the ticket for the Lakhimpur Lok Sabha seat in 2009 and, despite the initial reluctance of the local MLAs, she managed to bring them around. This marked a brief spell of all-round resurgence for the former all-rounder. Ranee was made the deputy chief whip and three years later, in 2012, replaced the National Congress Party's (NCP's) Agatha Sangma as the Northeast's only woman representative in the Union cabinet. Her luck, it seemed, turned again, especially after her narrow escape from what could have been a fatal crash. On 22 July 2011, Ranee, accompanied by the then Assam Congress president and Rajya Sabha MP, Bhubaneswar Kalita (who has since moved to the BJP), were on board a Delhi–Guwahati flight which reportedly avoided a mid-air collision over Patna. 'It was God's hand that saved us,' Ranee said after that close brush with death.[6]

Although she lost in the 2014 parliamentary elections, Ranee went on to serve another stint as a parliamentarian in

2016, this time as a Rajya Sabha member. Six years later, her exit from the Rajya Sabha in 2022 would be etched in the record books, as her replacement helped the BJP cross the 100-member mark in the upper house.

But even before her six-year term ended, vexing developments had cast a shadow over her. In September 2020, Ranee was named as the first accused in a case of alleged misappropriation of around Rs 1 crore from funds she was entitled to spend as an MP under the Members of Parliament Local Area Development Scheme. The move followed a complaint filed against Ranee in 2017 after a report submitted by the Comptroller and Auditor General (CAG) of India to the Assam Legislative Assembly's Public Accounts Committee. The alleged misappropriation, according to the complaint, took place in 2013–14 when Ranee was Lakhimpur MP.

Around a decade after his congratulatory tweet, Sarma, by then the chief minister of Assam, sent another note to Ranee. This one she could not ignore. In September 2023, Ranee appeared before the chief minister's special vigilance cell.

That was not the only allegation against Ranee. In 2023, once again, Manab Deka, a BJP MLA from the Lakhimpur assembly segment, a part of the Lok Sabha constituency, accused Ranee and Bharat of encroaching upon government land and setting up a tea estate in her name in Lakhimpur. Bharat is the sitting MLA from the Naoboicha assembly segment, which is also part of the Lakhimpur parliamentary constituency.

'Bharat Narah and his wife, Ranee Narah, have set up a tea estate [Ranee Narah Tea Estate] at Balijan, Lakhimpur, after encroaching upon government land and forcefully evicting some landless farmers [who] were staying there after losing their homes to floods. They did this when Bharat Narah was a minister in the past Congress government,' Deka alleged and claimed that the Narah couple had also applied for possession of 128 bighas of land there through a person claiming to be Bharat's nephew.[7] Ranee and Bharat have both rubbished the allegations, as has the Congress.

Even in matters related to cricket, things haven't played out the way Ranee would have wanted them to. On 12 November 2016, Sarma, then finance minister in the Sarbananda Sonowal government, was selected as the president of the Assam Cricket Association, while Ranee was replaced as a vice president in a revamp of the state cricket body's panel of office-bearers. Her proposal to create a quota or reserve the post of vice president for women's cricket was vehemently opposed by those present.

After the meeting, a smirking Sarma was seen walking out of the Barsapara Cricket Stadium in Guwahati, followed by a crestfallen Ranee. One wonders if a 'thank you' response to the 2012 tweet would have made a difference to her life and Assam's politics.

18

Nusrat Jahan Ruhi: Being Her Own Woman

Elizabeth Monroe Richards Tilton, the nineteenth-century American suffragist who went through a damaging social scandal over an alleged relationship with a preacher, is believed to have said that women should be allowed to do whatever men were allowed to do.[1] They were bold words for that era, when women in America didn't even have the right to vote or petition for divorce on the same terms as men.

Nearly a century after her death, a girl born into a Muslim family in Kolkata would go on to live exactly the way the late suffragist, poetry editor and women's rights activist believed women should live.

Nusrat Jahan Ruhi, the first Muslim superstar in Bengali cinema on this side of the border and a directly elected MP, didn't stop at simply living that life. She would flaunt it too. 'Women should get a hold of themselves. Start living their lives their way and stop listening to what other people have to say about them. We have seen the world pulling us down because of our gender, but if we start accepting it and doing the same to ourselves, that's wrong,' she would say in an interview in June 2020, a year after her election from the Basirhat Lok Sabha constituency in West Bengal.[2]

June has always been an important month for Nusrat. On 3 June 2011 – two weeks after Mamata Banerjee became Bengal's first woman chief minister – Bengali cinema got its first female superstar from a Muslim family. *Shotru* did well enough to be later dubbed into Hindi. Eight years later, and still in her twenties, Nusrat would make her debut speech in the Lok Sabha on 26 June as an elected member of the lower house of Parliament. Two years later, in 2021, on another June day, she would share a photograph showing a hint of a baby bump, announcing to the world that she was pregnant, along with a clarification that her then 'husband', Nikhil Jain, was not the father of the unborn child.

Nikhil, a Kolkata-based entrepreneur, and Nusrat had got 'married' in Turkey after she became an MP. A court in Kolkata later declared the purported wedding legally invalid. That was when Nusrat publicly claimed that the two were in a live-in relationship.

Nusrat's June 2021 public announcement had set off feverish speculation on who the father of her child was. Neither Nusrat, nor her current beau, Yash Dasgupta, rumoured to be the father, has since confirmed or denied the baby's paternity.

Unwelcome Attention

Such interest in her personal life has been constant since the time Nusrat was beginning to get a taste of stardom following her debut in *Shotru*. Barely seven months later, she would be accused of helping Kader Khan, one of the accused in the Park Street gang-rape case of February 2012, escape arrest. Nusrat did not deny that she and Kadir had been 'seeing each other for three–four years', but said they had 'split' a few months before the incident and had remained friends.[3]

It is said that Nusrat came in contact with the ruling Trinamool Congress at that time, which led to her entry into politics. Although she was brought in for questioning, Nusrat was eventually let off. While it must have been a testing time, the incident had a favourable outcome for the young woman who had just turned twenty-two. Suddenly, people were asking Nusrat Jahan was.

In the recent past, Nusrat has been in the news over matters that had little to do with her life in films or politics. It was her personal life that seemed to generate interest – questions about her marital status, her child's paternity and whether she had been married twice or thrice. It was the same intrusive obsession that was at play when, just after she was announced as a Trinamool Congress nominee for the 2019 elections, a businessman from Jamshedpur was declared as her childhood friend whom she had married in secret. Nusrat had promptly issued a denial. She was then dating Nikhil.

The actor-MP is not bothered by such unwelcome interest in her personal life. As for criticism, she simply shrugs it off. Such is her self-confidence that she can make her maiden appearance in the Lok Sabha in a pair of pants and a peplum zip top, thumb her nose at Muslim clerics and display Hindu marriage symbols, or play the dhak, an instrument synonymous with Durga Puja in Bengal.

Whether in her deliberate silences, her bold sartorial choices or unabashed acknowledgement of her relationships with men, Nusrat's message has been clear. Women have the right to lead their own lives as they wish to. In fact, a brief preview of that spunk had come ten years earlier when she firmly turned down suggestions of adopting a Hindu name for her cinematic debut.

Muslim Superstar

Till Nusrat appeared on-screen in 2011, Bengali cinema had largely been dominated by upper-caste Hindus. Take, for example, the two biggest superstars of Bengali cinema – Uttam Kumar and Soumitra Chatterjee. Both were Brahmins. Among actresses, Sabitri Chatterjee, a living legend, is also a Brahmin. So was the late Supriya Devi, while Suchitra Sen, Bengali cinema's topmost female star, came from an upper-caste Baidya family.

'Sociologists have not yet explained why there have been no Muslim superstars in Bengal. There have been [Muslim] writers, poets, sportspersons, musicians and painters but no one in the film industry,' says journalist and screenplay writer Arnab Ganguly in a conversation with the author. 'There was an educationist and social reformer, Begum Rokeya, who championed gender equality in the early twentieth century, but acting remained tauba tauba [a taboo]. I don't know why.' Ganguly has closely followed Nusrat's career in both politics and cinema.

Nusrat's acting career has, however, slowed down since 2019.[4] Between 2020 and 2024, she had just six releases, possibly due to her presence in parliamentary politics as an MP from Bengal. Yet, Nusrat has grown professionally, turning into a producer with Yash Dasgupta. Even if she did not have a single film in a year, she would still be very much in the reckoning, which is precisely what had happened in 2019 when she won from Basirhat by a mammoth margin of over 3,50,000 votes. (Incidentally, the first MP from the Basirhat Lok Sabha seat was also a woman. Renu Chakravartty, a niece of Bengal's then Congress chief minister Bidhan Chandra Roy, won the seat in 1952 as a member of the CPI.)

Comments and Controversies

While Nusrat has lived by her own rules in her personal life, she has carried that approach into politics too, sometimes courting controversy in the process. In 2021, the year assembly elections were held in Bengal, Nusrat, one of the star campaigners of her party, had refused to participate in a roadshow. 'I have been doing this for an hour. I don't do this even for the chief minister,' she was caught saying on camera while stepping off a vehicle in Guma, in North 24 Parganas district.[5]

Two years later, in May 2023, ahead of rural elections in the state, she had provoked party supporters to attack the Opposition. 'Why will the people of Bengal vote for you? What have you done for them?' she was quoted as saying, adding that the Opposition would be thrashed with 'bamboo sticks'.[6]

Months later, she was embroiled in a corruption scandal, like many of her party colleagues accused of alleged financial irregularities. A complaint filed before the Enforcement Directorate had alleged that a company in which Nusrat was one of the directors had duped 415 individuals of Rs 23 crore by reneging on a promise to deliver residential flats. Nusrat was questioned by the central agency for nearly six hours on 13 September 2023.

As a Politician

As a first-time MP, Nusrat's track record on the floor of the house was ostensibly not looking very encouraging – barely 22 per cent attendance and participation in only eleven debates in the 17th Lok Sabha. The ruling BJP even accused her of staying away from her constituency.

But a closer look at her parliamentary record would reveal otherwise. According to PRS Legislative Research, the parliamentary research wing, the Basirhat MP asked 144 questions on a range of subjects, including the state of tertiary care cancer centres in Bengal, infrastructure facilities of minority institutions, inspections by track recording cars leading to railway accidents and the need to invest more in the country's defence expenditure.[7] She also asked how farmers were benefiting from mega textile parks set up in the country.

Nusrat's brief speech on the government's bid to privatize public sector undertakings (PSUs) showed her understanding of economic issues that had a bearing on the common man. In February 2022, she had said the following in the Lok Sabha:

> [W]e all know, the public sector was structured to spearhead a chain of revolutions leading to the path of economic growth … In the initial years of planning, the public sector was used as a strong tool by the government to maintain its control over key industries. The public sector was, in fact, seen as an instrument to move towards the ideal of a so-called socialist society. The wages given in the public sector industry are supposed to be the model for private sector enterprises. But, now, the government, at this juncture, is considering the possibilities of raising revenue by very aggressively disinvesting shareholdings in major Maharatna and Navratna public sector units, like Coal India, IOC, HPCL, SAIL, GAIL, BHEL, [and] Air India, etc.[8]

A commerce graduate from Bhawanipur College, Calcutta, the MP then went on to ask the government why it had chosen to sell off profit-making industries.

> Rather, if the government wants to disinvest, then disinvest the loss-making industries. Due to such aggressive disinvestment policy, all the employees are in a state of total uncertainty. The whole country is very proud of our major government-owned industries. Thus, I would humbly request the government to, at least, sell the loss-making PSUs in PPP [public–private partnership] model and not opt for the total sellout of the PSUs. My party and I strongly oppose the disinvestment of profit-making PSUs by the government.

MPs cutting across party lines had thumped their desks to show their support after her speech.

Former Krishnanagar MP Mahua Moitra, who had also made her debut in Parliament in 2019, is also a rebel but in a way different from Nusrat's. Nonetheless, both women challenged the deep-rooted patriarchy and the male mindset. For Nusrat, however, her identity made the uphill climb even steeper when compared to Moitra, who comes from an upper-caste Hindu family.

Earlier, in 2019, Nusrat had sought the Narendra Modi government's help to prevail upon the government of Bangladesh to start dredging the Ichhamati, which flows from the neighbouring country into India, while drawing attention to the plight of around 20 lakh people badly affected by the silting of the river. Following Nusrat's intervention in the Lok Sabha, a Joint Technical Committee made up of members from both India and Bangladesh conducted a hydrographic survey to assess the Ichhamati's navigability and inclusion in the Protocol on Inland Water Transit and Trade as the new Indo-Bangladesh Protocol route from Basirhat to Hemnagar covering a distance of 82.5 km.

On 3 February 2022, Nusrat, along with three other parliamentarians, sought details of 'hate crimes' against minorities, a state- and year-wise break-up of religion-based atrocities since 2019 and the number of deaths due to such atrocities. She asked whether the government was aware that cases of communal riots had risen by 96 per cent and caste riots by nearly 50 per cent in 2020 as compared to 2019 and, if so, the reasons behind such a drastic increase. She also pointed out that crimes against the Scheduled Castes (SCs) had increased by 9.4 per cent and those committed against the Scheduled Tribes (STs) by 9.3 per cent in 2020.

The reply from Union Minister Mukhtar Abbas Naqvi was evasive. Naqvi, who was the minister for minority affairs, replied that public order and police were state subjects, according to the Seventh Schedule of the Constitution.

The responsibility of maintaining law and order, registration and prosecution of crimes against all citizens, including minorities, rests with the respective state governments. As such, specific data regarding attacks against an individual community is not maintained centrally. The Government of India monitors internal security and the law and order situation in the country and issues appropriate advisories from time to time to maintain peace, public tranquillity and communal harmony. The Central Armed Police Forces (CAPF) are deployed to aid and assist state governments, on their request, to maintain law and order and public tranquillity.[9]

Doing Things on a Larger Scale

Like many before her, especially women who excelled in other fields, Nusrat too did not plan her entry into politics. 'I had no plans for politics, and I did not want to be a part of it either in the beginning, but when I realised that I have an opportunity of doing things at a larger scale, [it] did not sound like a bad idea. People, including me, had forgotten the real meaning of politics, which is to bring about a change,' Nusrat said in an interview a year after her election.[10]

During the Covid-19 pandemic, Nusrat, like many of her colleagues in Parliament, used her MP's Local Area Development Fund to set up test facilities. She has also been vocal against domestic violence in her constituency, which has 86.5 per cent rural voters and around 46.3 per cent Muslim voters, according to the 2011 census.

Visibility on the ground becomes a factor in politics when public representatives are seen more on social media apps like Instagram, where she has 3.2 million followers. Nusrat has claimed that she was video conferencing with authorities in Basirhat in North 24 Parganas, some 72 km from the state capital Kolkata and, around the same time, she was also posting life updates on Instagram. The thrust of her argument is that films, glamour and her social media presence have not affected her commitment to being a social worker and the people's representative.

still, you will always see me supporting my colleagues who are in politics.'[16]

Reflecting upon her future, Nusrat asserted that one need not have a political position to make a difference. 'I do believe that if you need to do something for somebody, you don't really need to have a post or be in the middle of the political game. Good work can be done without being a post-holder. I am doing exactly what I need to do right now,' Nusrat Jahan said.[17]

In politics, Nusrat's contribution was significant. While she identified with the Muslim community, she was equally admired by all other communities. She was often seen celebrating Durga Puja and taking part in rath yatras with the same enthusiasm and fervour with which would celebrate Eid. 'I genuinely believe in secularity. I believe all festivals need to be celebrated and all religions should be respected. My principles and ideologies tell me to respect all religions, and I will continue doing that. In Bengal, we celebrate all festivals together,' Nusrat told the interviewer.[18]

When asked about the issue of online trolling, she said, 'Trolling happens to every second person. You can combat them only by ignoring them. Everybody can say what they want, and you can't stop them. But you can stop yourself; you can control your mindset. It is not required to give them so much importance.'[19]

'I won't be remembered as a woman who can keep her mouth shut and I'm ok with that,' she wrote on her Instagram account on 9 June 2021. She is far, far away from being silenced. One might even say, Nusrat has just started.

19

Iqra Hasan: A Silver Lining for Progressive Politics

In the days immediately after 4 June 2024, the day of the Lok Sabha election results, the media was understandably abuzz with reports and analyses. Amongst many other aspects of the Samajwadi Party's impressive show in UP, the reportage on newly elected Samajwadi Party MP, Iqra Hasan Choudhury, stood out for a reason. From earning the distinction of being one of the youngest MPs after defeating a veteran leader from the BJP to becoming the centre of social media discussion as a young, London-educated Muslim woman leader, Iqra appeared to have carved out a space for herself in the public imagination.

Iqra's entry into electoral politics has been celebrated in all quarters – from social media channels to traditional media houses to her premier institution's students' blogs. When Iqra was asked about the social media attention she received, her response was that she wanted to be known by her work and not due to social media traction. After her win, a student at her alma mater, School of Oriental and African Studies (SOAS), wrote a blog on the university website, highlighting her victory. The blog post said: 'In the 2024 Indian General Election, SOAS alum Iqra Hasan Choudhury, 29, made history as the youngest Muslim woman to be elected.'[1]

Balancing Contradictions

Iqra's electoral debut has the unique distinction of balancing many common perceptions often seen as contradictory. First, though Iqra belongs to a political dynasty, with the privilege of a long family legacy in Kairana town in UP, her entry into politics has been marked by herculean challenges and crises. Second, although Iqra has a distinctive education background of pursuing a master's degree in International Politics and Law at SOAS, on entering electoral politics, Iqra started covering her head with a dupatta, conforming to a cultural practice followed by both Hindu and Muslim women in her constituency.

Iqra explained this in an interview with *Frontline* in July 2024. She insisted that her headwear was not a traditional hijab: 'I cover my head because it is a cultural practice in our area; Gujjar or Jat women do the same. My friends jokingly call my way of covering the head an extremely secular gesture,' she said. Also, mindful of the defamation that women in politics are subjected to, she explained: 'Covering my head helps me concentrate on my duties and ensures that I am judged by my actions, not by my appearance ... I don't want conversations about my clothes to hamper real talks about progress and what really needs to be done.'[2]

Trial by Fire

Iqra belongs to a prominent political family in western UP. Her grandfather, Chaudhary Akhtar Hasan, was elected MP from the Congress Party in Kairana in 1984, defeating Mayawati, who was contesting her first Lok Sabha election. Aktar was the patriarch of the Hasan political dynasty of Kairana. He passed away in 2017.[3] Iqra's father, Munawwar Khan, continued the family legacy and became MP on a Samajwadi Party ticket in 1996. Munawwar, who later joined the BSP, died in a road accident in 2008 when Iqra was only thirteen years old. Iqra's mother, Tabassum Hasan, joined politics and contested the Lok Sabha election from Kairana to become an MP on a BSP ticket. Her brother, Nahid Hasan, contested the 2014 Lok Sabha election and was defeated by the Hasan family's arch-rival, the BJP leader Hukum Singh. After Hukum Singh's death, Tabassum won the 2018 by-election and re-entered the Lok Sabha, but lost to BJP leader Pradeep Kumar Chaudhary in the 2019 elections. Nahid Hasan is now a three-time MLA representing the Samajwadi Party.

Despite their electoral wins, the Hasan family came under a cloud. In 2022, the UP Police arrested Nahid under the Gangster Act. Iqra's mother lost her seat to the BJP. Family properties were seized and there were serious financial constraints placed on them. This was the scenario into which Iqra returned in 2021, after completing her studies abroad. During an interview, she said the following about this time: 'This was the time when my mother and brother were falsely implicated in gangster cases. I came back ten days before everything fell apart. It was fortuitous that I was here to take charge of our home and handle my family's political legacy.'[4]

Iqra took up the campaign on behalf of her brother during the 2022 Vidhan Sabha elections and ensured his remarkable victory, despite him being in jail. Although Iqra planned to pursue a PhD, she stayed back not only to save the political legacy of her family but also to manage the crisis that they were grappling with. With her brother imprisoned and the family's bank accounts frozen, Iqra had to come of political age and confront this multi-pronged adversity. She fought various court battles for more than a year to get her brother released by appealing to all the three levels of the judiciary. She also had to manage the work of her brother's assembly constituency.

She said, 'For about a year, I also had to oversee my brother's MLA term as he was still in jail. He couldn't be available to the people, so I was. That gave me a lot of experience and the confidence to do this.' It is during this time of crisis that her determination to fight the BJP strengthened. 'That's when I thought, since we are fighting the BJP anyway, why not fight against them openly in an election?'[5]

Taking the Plunge

Like many other women in politics, Iqra also regards her family's support as a major impetus which made it possible for her to plunge into electoral politics. Iqra looks up to her brother and mother for guidance. She praises her brother for his courage to stand up against the intimidation unleashed by the government. 'There were several fabricated charges against my brother, including those involving Section 324 of the Indian Penal Code [voluntarily causing hurt by dangerous weapon or means], all filed during the tenure of Chief Minister Yogi Adityanath. Despite these challenges, my brother has continued his political journey to keep our father's legacy alive.'[6]

'My brother does not mind stepping back to give me more space,' she said.[7] She also recognizes the contribution of her mother in guiding her through the various technicalities of public outreach, especially when it comes to public speeches and holding public meetings. 'My mother told me that responsibilities teach you everything you need to know. Politics was never in my scheme of things although I come from a political family. As a shy student, I avoided public speaking.'[8] Iqra considers her mother a role model for women in leadership positions along with other leaders like Anuradha Chaudhary and Gayatri Devi, who have represented Kairana in the past. Iqra, quite early in her career in politics, has been mindful of the privilege that comes with being a part of an established political family. She doesn't get defensive or refute the dynastic charge. Rather, she has a measured response to it as she feels she can use this privilege in a positive manner. She adds, 'Through my hard work, I hope to erase the fact that I am a dynast.'[9]

Harbinger of 'Good Politics'?

Iqra's journey through top-tier colleges and institutions raises expectations that she will only indulge in 'good politics'. She did her schooling from Queen Mary's School, New Delhi, and moved to Lady Shri Ram College (LSR) to study history and law, before getting her master's degree from SOAS. On hitting the streets for her election campaign, she has touched upon two important aspects about the constituency she represents. One is communal harmony and the other is education. Before Iqra's entry into politics, she took part in an anti-Citizenship Amendment Act protest rally in London and spoke strongly against religious discrimination. With her 'educated woman' image, Iqra wants to overcome the challenge posed by divisive politics with 'positive' politics, addressing the issues of empowerment and governance cutting across divides.

'This is my first Lok Sabha election. I am grateful for the respect and love I received from 36 biradaris [castes]. Iqra means taalim [education]. Education is very important to keep harmony in our society,' she told the *Indian Express*.[10] Through her secular appeal and message of social harmony, Iqra could garner support from not only Muslims but also from Hindus in her constituency. After the results, it became clear that she defied all odds to garner support from several social segments to win the election. Muslims and Hindus of different communities, including Rajputs, Sainis, Jats and Gujjars, had voted for her.

When the Rashtriya Lok Dal (RLD) moved out of the Indian National Developmental Inclusive Alliance (INDIA) just before the elections, Iqra was apprehensive about Jat voters moving away from her. But the challenge made her work even harder, which finally resulted in her victory against the incumbent MP and senior BJP leader Deepak Chaudhury by an impressive margin of 70,000 votes. 'The biggest challenge was to fight a party with huge resources, administrative support and money. We tried to be consistent with our efforts on the ground,' she reminisced on her experience.[11]

Building Bridges, Healing Divisions

Iqra's secular image has been extremely crucial in a communally sensitive region like Kairana. The region was hit by a communal riot in 2013 that is believed to have benefited BJP leader Hukum Singh's electoral prospects during the 2014 Lok Sabha elections. The BJP had alleged that there was a constant exodus of Hindus from the region. To stop such alleged 'intimidation' of Hindus, the UP government planned to establish a Provincial Armed Constabulary (PAC) camp and a firing range in the region. In 2018, just before the by-election in Kairana after the death of Hukum Singh, Chief Minister Adityanath announced the establishment of the PAC camp and firing range, and tweeted, 'Today no one dares [to] scare away anyone from Kairana and Kandhla.'[12]

However, with Iqra in the political fray in 2024, the campaign narrative that dominated was that it would not be the Hindu–Muslim issue.[13] Iqra herself viewed the communal polarization pervasive in Kairana with utmost concern. While campaigning, she said, 'There has been a huge religious divide, of the kind I never saw growing up. My attempt here and effort is to bring everyone together which is why I have campaigned extensively in non-Muslim villages so that they can connect to me and I to them. This is what the area needs most.'[14]

Iqra effectively tapped into the wave of discontent with the sitting MP Pradeep Choudhary even within the BJP supporters in the region. She later spoke about getting support from all sections: '[The] anti-incumbency sentiment worked against the sitting MP. He was not accessible to the people and did not deliver on his promises. People were tired of him. Perhaps that's why they overlooked the fact that they were voting for a Muslim woman.'[15]

'Like her father, there is something charismatic about this girl [Iqra],' says Mukesh Rana, a local Samajwadi Party worker.[16] In the course of the campaign, Iqra could emotionally connect with the people by calling herself their 'beti'. Well aware of debates in the feminist discourse on the individual identity of women versus identity within the family, Iqra clarified her position in an interview to The Wire. 'I know it may not sound feminist to some people to hear beti or bahen, but these are important identities and a lot of progressive change can come about even while invoking these identities.'[17]

Iqra, as a woman, could seamlessly connect with the women of the region. According to her, she could reach out to the women staying indoors to listen to them and understand their problems. As an MP, she is committed to improving the educational and healthcare facilities for women in the area. She has said that 'a major personal focus will be on women's education. Many girls are forced to drop out because their parents are uncomfortable with co-educational settings in schools. I plan to establish dedicated higher education facilities for women since I believe that when a woman is educated, an entire family benefits.'[18] Not only women's issues, Iqra has also quite adeptly addressed the major local issues of economic challenges that have affected her constituency. She attributed the support that she received to the farmers, agitation that swept the western parts of UP, especially the issues of delayed payments to sugarcane farmers in sugar mills and low minimum support price.

A Ray of Hope

Despite being a new entrant in Indian politics, Iqra has made all the right noises. Mindful of her dynastic privilege, she knows that she has to work at the grassroots level and stay on the ground to carry forward her family's legacy of service. Unlike the common discourse, she refuses outright to project herself as a victim. 'It is unfortunate that women are often depicted as helpless [bechari] to gain acceptance in politics in our region.'[19]

The blog post from her university in London, written after her victory, carried a quote from SOAS faculty Subir Sinha, which read: 'It should be a matter of pride for SOAS that one of its alumnae is now among the youngest members of the Indian Parliament and that the progressive campaign she ran was on issues facing the people of her constituency, across caste, class, gender and religious divides.'[20]

The question remains: Can Iqra maintain the momentum of 'progressive' politics in the by-lanes of Kairana, still reeling under patriarchy and communal discord?

Epilogue

This work is a testament of women's empowerment, inspiring leadership and human resilience. The effort comes as a reminder that despite the fact that there have been only 18 Muslim women MPs elected to the Lok Sabha till now, it does not make their stories any less inspiring. The book is a modest attempt to start a much-needed conversation on the political journeys, achievements and challenges that mark the careers of the women politicians discussed in this book.

We would like to stress the fact that this work is not aimed at apportioning blame to any individual or political party, ideology, and so on. As authors, we have attempted to tell the stories of individuals whose inspiring and formidable legacy has hitherto remained unsung. Barring a few, the lives of most of the women discussed in this book have remained under-explored in the public imagination until now, despite their careers in the Lok Sabha.

We must remember that Indira Gandhi became the Prime Minister of India in 1966, much ahead of elected women leaders in many Western democracies. Even so, her presence only highlighted the limited space for women in power in their own country. The late Khushwant Singh used to say that most women in political-public spaces came from anglicized, upper-class gentry while the working classes did not have the same ease and access. While the BJP under Modi is trying to change this, a cursory look at all women MLAs and MPs shows a disproportionate representation of the dynasty and fewer working-class woman leaders. Out of the 18 Muslim women who made it to the Lok Sabha, 13 of them belong to political families in the sense that their close relatives were in politics prior to their entry and success in the electoral fray.

Yet women politicians, not just Indira Gandhi, have been successful in transforming politics in a big way. Take Sheila Dikshit, for example. As Delhi's chief minister, Sheila Dikshit was a politician from Uttar Pradesh. In 1998, Sonia Gandhi brought her to Delhi politics, projecting her as Congress' chief ministerial candidate. Gandhi had then turned to Dixit when she had just taken over as the Congress president amid mild rebellion over the manner in which her successor Sitaram Kesri was dumped and how the General Elections in 1998 had given the Congress fewer seats than post-Emergency 1977 Lok Sabha polls.

Unpacking the Title

The title of the book uses the phrase 'missing from the house' for two crucial reasons. First, it is to reinforce the fact that 18 Muslim women in the lower house of the Indian Parliament is a low number and it is an imperative to ensure higher representation of Muslim women in parliamentary politics. Second, even those who did get elected to the Lok Sabha so far, have mostly remained outside the dominant public discourse. This book makes a serious attempt to address this lacuna by shedding light on the political journey of these 'missing' women as most of them have hitherto remained at the margins of public attention and outside the critical realm of analytical and research.

Profiling of political personalities can be done in diverse ways. Many of the politicians included in this book have had more illustrious careers in politics than the others, and deserve a more elabourate account of their long and eventful political journeys. However, this work chooses to largely maintain a somewhat equal length of all profiles – not because we felt that all profiles are similar in nature, but because this book offers a collective account of the life stories of all the Muslim women MPs without prioritizing one over the other. Definitely, interested researchers can and should take up more in-depth studies of any of these women, which would be a great contribution to India's political history.

Identifying the Impediments

Now, coming to the two key glaring revelations about women's participation in Indian politics that unfolded as we worked on this book. First, political parties have a long way to go in order to provide adequate representation to women, in not only parliamentary politics but also in party positions. There have been few women chief ministers and notable female leaders as party presidents, and the overall participation of women in politics has remained inadequate.[1] The low representation of Muslim women in politics is a part of a larger issue – an inconducive environment for women, in general, to participate more actively in politics.[2] There are many structural and procedural factors that impede women's political participation, and need focussed policy interventions and societal reforms.[3]

Second, the representation of women across regions has been skewed, and many of the states with better socio-economic indicators have remained in the backseat in sending a greater number of Muslim women to Parliament.[4] This raises many key questions about women's empowerment, in general, and the political participation of women, in particular. Can better socio-economic indicators ensure a greater scope for women to enter and participate in electoral politics? Even with socio-economic empowerment, what are the factors that deter women to thrive in electoral politics? How do diverse regions and political parties deal with the contexts and dynamics as well as unique challenges in encouraging more women to participate in competitive electoral politics? Finding answers to these questions is the need of the hour.

Coming back to our experience with this book project, it is important to concede that researching human lives, which are replete with subjectivities, contradictory perceptions and contested episodes, is a daunting task. Keeping into consideration the fact that the personalities in the focus of our research were political leaders, our task was all the more challenging, given the turbulence, contentions and sensitivities a political life is engulfed in. However, our commitment to make a novel attempt to tell the stories of these brave and ambitious political personalities helped us overcome the hurdles in our journey. We must also confess with all humility that due to the paucity of space in a single book, we had to keep our chapters brief. Spatial constraints compelled us to make conscious cuts in our stories, which has left many other facets of the women's lives untouched or under-emphasized. However, we feel it takes immense strength to acknowledge the limits of individual capacity in a single endeavour. We would encourage interested researchers to take up a deeper analysis of the political legacies of these personalities, which deserve more attentive and in-depth research. This book is just a starting point of this challenging journey.

Missing Bits at a Glance

We must confess that this work has its own set of limitations, which are entirely ours. We have not included Subhashini Ali and Afrin Ali née Aparupa Poddar in this book. Though we researched and wrote their chapters, we couldn't include their important political profiles in this book due to their lack of 'Muslimness' – something that they shared with us. Just the way Mahesh Bhatt and Sanjay Dutt faced many challenges and opposition in the Bollywood industry on account of their mothers being 'Muslim', Subhashini Ali and Aparupa Poddar were neither born Muslim nor did they ever convert to Islam.

Hence, we felt it best to leave them out of the purview of this book.

Authors Parama Roy and Rosie Thomas, in her book *Bombay before Bollywood*, have argued that public interest in Bhatt's mother, Shirin, and years earlier, in Dutt's mother, Nargis, was focussed not only on their scandal-tinged lives, but on their 'Muslimness'.[5] Roy even posed the question: 'How are we to read the process by which Sanjay Dutt becomes Nargis, and becomes Muslim?'[6] Thomas argued that many found the revelation of Sanjay having a Muslim mother 'shocking', particularly in the context of his involvement with guns during the 1993 Mumbai riots and in the subsequent blasts. Sanjay, when confronted by his father Sunil Dutt, had, according to *The Times of India*, said he had done so 'because [he has] Muslim blood in [his] veins. [He] could not bear what was happening in the city.'[7] Throughout April 1993, after Sanjay was arrested and booked under the stringent Terrorist and Disruptive Activities (Prevention) Act (TADA), he faced hatred from all quarters and was branded a 'traitor' and an 'anti-national'. Even as he languished in jail, his alleged girlfriend of the time, Madhuri Dixit, who was among the era's much-in-demand stars and belonged to a Maharashtrian middle-class family, publicly called off their relationship and denounced him. The film industry unofficially boycotted the Dutts, and in cities like Pune, films featuring either Sanjay or his father, Sunil, were not screened. As far as Bhatt is concerned, there is also a subtext identifying him with his mother, Shirin, and her 'Muslimness', though in his case, it might well be one that he himself has partially crafted.

Coming back to this work, though we were unable to include separate chapters on Subhashini Ali and Afrin Ali, we felt it would be grave injustice to these extremely important political personalities as well as to our readers if we do not include few important and interesting snippets about their political journeys.

Subhashini Ali

Subhashini Ali has, for long, been a well-known political leader of the Communist Party of India (Marxist) or CPI(M). However, in recent years, she made headlines for something extremely important. In 2022, the Gujarat government released 11 convicts in the horrific Bilkis Bano case – nearly 22 years after the then pregnant Bilkis was gang-raped and 14 members of her family were killed in the aftermath of the Godhra train burnings that led to the Gujarat riots of 2002. Subhashini Ali was the first of three petitioners to approach the Supreme Court to overturn this decision. Finally, in 2024, the top court struck down the remission, stating that the government of Gujarat could not free the convicts, and that only the state government of Maharashtra – where the trial was held – could do so.[8]

Just days after the verdict, instead of celebrating, Subhashini, a former Lok Sabha MP from Kanpur, Uttar Pradesh and one of the strongest Marxist voices in the country, was on her way to Madhepura, Bihar, to lend her support to a thousand-odd tribals agitating in front of the district collectorate. The protesters had gathered to demand the arrest of those responsible for the murder of one of their leaders, Rajesh Hansda, months earlier in October, allegedly by the local land mafia.

There is no cause that is too small for Subhashini. Well into her seventies now, she has spent most of her life trying to give a voice to the oppressed. One end of her sari folded over her shoulder, a fabric bag slung on the other, Subhashini has moved from battle to battle in the five decades she has spent in public life.

Others may have given up at her age, but Subhashini was born to two freedom fighters – soldiers, at that. Her parents were at the battlefront in Burma (now known as Myanmar) in the Second World War, against the full might of the British army. Colonel Prem Sahgal and Captain Lakshmi Sahgal, soldiers of the Indian National Army led by Netaji Subhas Chandra Bose, are legends in their own right. Bose handpicked Captain Lakshmi to raise the women's regiment of the INA. Lakshmi, a doctor, promptly locked her clinic and cut her hair short to join the INA and lead the Rani Jhansi regiment.

After Independence, the Sahgals settled down in Kanpur, where Subhashini was born. Her father, Prem Sahgal, went on to become a mill manager. Captain Lakshmi, who would eventually join the CPI(M), continued with her chosen profession as a doctor. A majority of her patients were from the poorer sections of society and received free treatment from her. Subhashini grew up watching her mother attend to the poorest and provide them with care.

Subhashini's marriage to filmmaker Muzaffar Ali, a descendant of the royal family of Kotwara in Awadh, made her a member of the minority community, although, in all likelihood, the atheist-Marxist Subhashini merely took on the surname of her husband. Religion hardly played any role in her life. Possibly, the only instance when Subhashini wore a burqa was in 1971, when she needed to avoid the police while organizing a strike at Kanpur's Power House, where the party had sent the young, twenty-something to form a new union of electricity sector workers.

Apart from being a social activist and a Marxist, Subhashini has donned many hats. In 1981, she designed the period costumes for her husband's celebrated movie, *Umrao Jaan*. She won much praise for her attention to detail and, with her connections, could have easily made a career in costume designing. But she didn't.

She also tried her hand at acting and played the role of Shah Rukh Khan's mother in Santosh Sivan's 2001 film, *Asoka*. 'It's a bit role,' Subhashini, who had initially turned down the offer, had said then. 'But it was wonderful playing mother to the world's best-known practising pacifist.'[9]

Subhashini went on to appear in two more films, including one (*Amu*) with fellow CPI(M) politburo member Brinda Karat, but working for the people would always be her first calling. This was probably the reason she and Muzaffar chose to go their separate ways. 'We never divorced and are just separated. She was too much into her politics and I was too much into my own madness, and our lives were just not fitting in,' Muzaffar Ali had said in 2015.[10] The couple's son, Shaad Ali, is a well-known filmmaker.

Subhashini has always had more than one life to lead, but her story cannot only be a summation of the things she has said or done, or the elections she won or lost. Hers is a generational story that goes back a little over a hundred years, to the time of the 1921 Malabar Rebellion – or the Moplah Rebellion, as it is also called – when members of the Moplah (Muslim) community requested her maternal great-grandmother, A.V. Lakshmikutty Amma, to stay back and not leave for Madras, as she had planned to do.

The rebellion had started as a form of resistance against the British in parts of the old Malabar District of modern-day Kerala. The popular uprising also saw clashes between the peasantry and the feudal, elite Hindus.

Lakshmikutty Amma, the Nair matriarch, had deferred to the request of the Moplah community. When she slept indoors, two members of the community stood on guard outside.[11] Subhashini carries that legacy of strong-willed solidarity.

Her story is also the story of her maternal grandmother, Ammu Swaminathan, who served as a member of the Constituent Assembly of India and later as a Member of Parliament (MP). She was also the first woman in the erstwhile Madras Presidency to have a driver's licence. That, in itself, was no less a revolution at that time. Subhashini's story is also that of her mother, Lakshmi Sahgal (neé Swaminathan) – in short, she is the product of these strong-willed women on her maternal side. Hers is all of their stories and more.

However, this shared quality of fearless individuality did not mean that all these women had the same political leanings, too. While Ammu Swaminathan was a member of the Congress, her daughter, Lakshmi, was always more attracted to the militant nationalism that Subhas Chandra Bose stood for. Subhashini opted for the CPI(M), in turn. Political differences aside, what bound them together was their independent minds and spirits, and their compassion for the downtrodden.

Speaking about her mother once, Subhashini recalled that Lakshmi Sahgal was in the habit of giving away food and clothes at home to patients at the government hospital where she was an intern. 'When Ammu was old and very ill, lapsing into a coma off and on, Lakshmi Sahgal was in Madras looking after her. One night, the nurse removed [Ammu's] gold chain and ring which she thought were chafing [against] her skin and gave them to Lakshmi for safekeeping. Ammu recovered during the night and started searching for the chain and the ring. The nurse told her reassuringly, "I have given them to your daughter." This made Ammu wake up with a start and she said, "Take them back quickly, otherwise she will give them to the communists!"'[12]

For over three decades, the Sahgal couple – Prem and Lakshmi – would bear animosity towards the communists for their assessment of the Netaji as an agent of Nazi Germany. Before reaching Singapore in July 1943, where Lakshmi Swaminathan had first met him, Bose had escaped to Berlin from Calcutta via Afghanistan with the aim of raising an army to fight the British for India's independence.

Subhashini, however, had a more nuanced appraisal of her parents' opinions. 'My parents, though critical of the communists because of their violent distaste for Subhas Chandra Bose's relationship with the Axis powers [led by Hitler's Germany], had a great regard for all freedom fighters and, of course, EMS [former Kerala chief minister E.M.S. Namboodiripad, the first elected communist leader in India to head a popularly elected government]. My Malayali mother was very supporting of the role EMS had played in transforming the hide-bound, caste-ridden Kerala society. EMS was happy to stay with Indian National Army veterans,' she wrote later.[13]

It was EMS who convinced the young Subhashini to become a member of the CPI(M) in 1970–71. The CPI(M) was then only a few years old, after having split from the Communist Party of India (CPI) in 1964. Subhashini had filled in the form while EMS was still a guest of the Sahgals, much to the couple's dismay. A year later, Lakshmi Sahgal herself would become a member of the CPI(M) and go on to be an MP. This might be the only instance of a mother following in her daughter's footsteps.

Earlier, when she was very young, Lakshmi had come in close contact with Suhasini Chattopadhyay, Sarojini Naidu's sister and the first woman to join the undivided CPI. Chattopadhyay had spent a few days in hiding at Ammu's house in Madras (now Chennai), but ties between the Sahgal couple and the communists would remain frosty for decades till Subhashini broke the ice.

The gathering at Madhepura in 2024 would have brought back memories of her early days in politics, when the twenty-three-year-old Subhashini, fresh out of college, was determined to join either of the three mainstream communist parties in India (CPI[M], CPI and CPI[ML]), much to the annoyance of her parents.

Subhashini had returned to Kanpur from a trip to Calcutta, in the early 1970s, when political violence was at its peak and the CPI(M) was gaining ground. One afternoon, she boarded a rickshaw from Kanpur's privileged and protected Mall Road, and went to Kursawan, a lower-middle-class neighbourhood that was home to mill workers. That would be the first port of call for young Subhashini as she stepped into the world of trade unionism – organizing the mill workers in Kanpur.

One of the first movements that Subhashini took part in was the re-opening of the New Victoria Mills, where her father, Prem Sahgal, worked as a manager after his INA days. The mill had been closed since the early 1960s. Old-timers still recall the slogan that a section of political workers had raised then: '*Sahgal mill bandh karvaye, uski beti chalu karvaye* [Sahgal has closed the mill whereas his daughter has helped in reopening the mill].' These words are a measure of how fraught the situation was.

This was also the first time Subhashini witnessed poverty from up close, the appalling living conditions of the workers, their tumultuous lives, as well as their everyday humour to deal with the precarious uncertainty of their situation. At that point in time, Subhashini, with her pedigreed background – born to parents known across the country – was an outsider there. It became a watershed moment for her. Her entire life from then on was spent becoming an insider, moving as far away as she could from the privilege that she was born into.

Many years later, in 2014, that outsider tag resurfaced, when Subhashini unsuccessfully contested the Lok Sabha elections from Barrackpore, in West Bengal's North 24-Parganas district, a decaying industrial settlement much like Kanpur, with a sizeable Hindi-speaking population. The Trinamool Congress had wrested the seat from the CPI(M) in 2009 and the incumbent was another Hindi-speaking MP, Dinesh Trivedi.[14]

It was the CPI(M)'s North 24-Parganas secretary and a former minister in the Left Front government, Gautam Deb, who had suggested Subhashini's name with the support of former chief minister, Buddhadeb Bhattacharjee. But murmurs of an 'outsider' being pushed on Marxist cadres in Barrackpore were heard in the CPI(M) offices, while the Trinamool Congress went to town on it.

The area, though, was not an entirely unknown territory for Subhashini. In 2010, she had addressed meetings during a sixty-three-day jute mill strike from Barrackpore to Kanchrapara, also in North 24-Parganas.

'I knew her through Capt. Lakshmi Sahgal. A formidable, strong woman. When Gautam Deb suggested her name, I was not certain that she would agree. Surprisingly, she not only agreed but put up a good fight too. She fights for different causes and is the most prominent face from our party in the

Hindi belt,' Biman Bose, former secretary of the CPI(M)'s Bengal unit, said.[15] (Incidentally, the 1938-born Biman Bose was the first all-India secretary of the party's students' wing, the Students' Federation of India, when Subhashini was taking her first step in trade unionism.)

Although Subhashini had been an MP and a former president of the All-India Democratic Women's Association, the glass ceiling within the Marxist fold did hold her back for many years. It was only in 2015 that the CPI(M) inducted her into the party politburo, making her the second woman after Brinda Karat to enter the Marxists' male-dominated club.

That the Marxists had revised their views on Subhas Chandra Bose, too, was evident when Subhashini's mother, Lakshmi Sahgal, not only went on to represent the party in Parliament, she was also their nominee for India's president against A.P.J. Abdul Kalam.

Subhashini today is fighting a whole other battle – for the story of women to be told to future generations.

In an interview with the Malayalam channel Kairali News, Ali highlighted that generally, history didn't do justice to women. She said that she read *Who Cooked the Last Supper? The Women's History of the World* by Rosalind Miles, and explained that while everyone knew the people who supposedly *participated* in the 'Last Supper' (alluding to a freedom struggle), nobody knew who 'cooked' this 'Supper'. That, according to Ali, was quite telling of the fact that there were thousands of women – apart from those who fought, received some kind of recognition and became big leaders – who supported freedom struggles and did all the necessary chores to sustain important movements, however, their contributions were sidelined and not documented anywhere. In a conversation with the authors, she also said that 'this is the story of women from the poorest sections. They were raped, brutally beaten, shot at, but they stood strong. Thus, this story needs to be told. What they dreamt of is not the India of today. We certainly are not living in the India of their dreams. We have to once again fight and be prepared to sacrifice to realise the India of those dreams.'

That is why Subhashini had to travel to Madhepura soon after the Bilkis verdict. That India of her dreams is still far away.

Afrin Ali née Aparoopa Poddar

Another personality whose story we missed including separately in this book is of Afrin Ali née Aparoopa Poddar. Afrin Ali began her life's journey as Aparupa Poddar in 1986. She pursued her education in Hooghly Mohsin College and obtained a Master of Arts degree from the University of Burdwan. She also completed her Bachelor of Laws (LLB) and Master of Laws (LLM) from Dr B.R. Ambedkar Open University, Hyderabad. Aparupa ventured into politics after completing her postgraduate studies. In politics, she experienced remarkable success at an early stage, securing consecutive victories in the Lok Sabha elections of 2014 and 2019 as a candidate of the All India Trinamool Congress (TMC). She represented the Arambagh constituency, a politically significant region located in the Hooghly district of West Bengal. The constituency is centred on the town of Arambagh and comprises seven assembly segments, six of which fall within the Hooghly district, while one extends into the Paschim Medinipur district. Historically, Arambagh was an open seat, but, in 2009, it was designated as a reserved constituency for SCs, altering the electoral dynamics of the region. Aparupa's successive victories highlighted not only her personal popularity but also her ability to mobilize grassroots support in a constituency known for its complex political undercurrents. Her electoral success reflected the broader appeal of the TMC in West Bengal during this period, particularly in rural and semi-urban areas where the party's influence was growing. Her campaigns focused on local developmental issues, accessibility to governance and the broader welfare schemes initiated by the Mamata Banerjee-led state government.

However, as her political career gained momentum, her personal life increasingly came under public and political scrutiny. Her marriage and religious identity became subjects of intense debate, with various factions using her personal choices to further their own narratives. In a political landscape where personal lives often intertwine with public perception, Aparupa found herself at the centre of controversies that sometimes overshadowed her legislative work. These debates were fuelled by both social and political forces, highlighting the intersection of gender, religion and personal autonomy in Indian politics.

Despite the challenges posed by these controversies, her early successes in the Lok Sabha elections remains a testament to her initial political acumen and the trust reposed in her by the electorate of Arambagh. The trajectory of her career underscores not only the volatile nature of Indian electoral politics but also the unique challenges faced by women leaders in navigating public life while contending with deeply entrenched societal expectations.

Born a Hindu woman from a scheduled caste (SC), in 2007, Aparupa married a Muslim man – Mohammed Shakir Ali, a TMC leader and councillor of the Rishra Municipality – and subsequently adopted the name Afrin Ali. This became a point of friction during the 2014 Lok Sabha elections, when the BJP complained to the Election Commission (EC) that her marriage and name change invalidated her SC status, which was a bureaucratic caveat Afrin Ali was accused of exploiting. BJP's contention was that after her marriage and conversion to Islam, Aparupa – now Afrin – could no longer claim to be from a SC. This made her ineligible for contesting and representing Arambagh, a constituency reserved for SC candidates. She offered a feeble defence – that after her marriage, she merely changed her name and not her religious beliefs.

In raising objections to Aparupa Poddar's candidature, the BJP adhered to the letter of the law. But did it truly uphold its spirit? The fundamental question here was whether caste-based discrimination – a deeply entrenched social reality in India – could simply vanish overnight through marriage or religious conversion. Could an individual born into a historically marginalized community suddenly become free of generational inequities merely by changing their name or faith? The answer, as sociological and historical evidence suggests, is far from straightforward.

Extending this argument further, India has long witnessed individuals and communities seeking refuge in inter-caste marriages or religious conversions as a means to escape the rigid confines of caste-based discrimination. Dalits and other backward caste (OBC) groups, in particular, have often embraced new identities in an attempt to break free from the deeply entrenched social hierarchies that limit their opportunities. However, societal structures do not change as quickly as individual identities. The stigma and systemic inequalities faced by marginalized groups remain pervasive, regardless of the technicalities of personal transformation.

Aparupa, or Afrin, as she changed her name to, did not explicitly engage with this larger, more philosophical debate. Her defence remained focused on countering the immediate legal challenge rather than questioning the deeper social contradictions at play. While the BJP attempted to discredit her legitimacy under the reserved category by citing her personal choices, it overlooked the broader reality: caste-based disadvantages do not simply dissolve through a change in documentation. The big-picture debate of whether the reservation system should acknowledge the persistence of historical discrimination beyond formal labels was left unaddressed.

As an MP, Afrin took part in several national debates. Some of her significant inputs were on the need for taking juridical action against human trafficking convicts in 2015, on the need to address malnutrition in the country in the same year, and, in 2016, on the maintenance of the culturally important Tarakeshwar Temple in West Bengal. Her more recent involvement as an MP was during a demand for grants for road transport and highways in the Lok Sabha in 2022. She put forward a claim for facilitating the development of the Varanasi–Kolkata Expressway, which would pass through the Hooghly district (which was a part of her constituency).

She also asked a wide range of questions about the measures taken by the government to boost wholesale and retail trade, about companies engaged in meat processing and its export, about posts lying vacant in the National School of Drama (NSD), and the increase in unemployment across the country. She expressed concern about conducting a single entrance test in the form of the National Eligibility cum Entrance Test (NEET) for admission to medical colleges across the country. She also brought up the issue of complaints regarding missing body parts from the mortal remains of Indians who had died abroad and asked what the government was doing about it.

But controversies, both within her party and outside, soon engulfed her. In the run-up to the 2024 Lok Sabha elections, when the TMC denied her a ticket from Arambagh or anywhere else, Afrin told a section of the media that the party did not nominate her because she did not have sufficient financial resources. She was implying that the party only nominated those with money and this did not go down well with TMC's top leadership. Afrin's detractors within the party quickly leveraged this to isolate her. During a public meeting before the 2024 Lok Sabha elections, a section of TMC workers physically prevented her from getting on to the podium to campaign, even though she was the sitting MP and the meeting was taking place in her constituency. True to her style, Afrin accused her party colleagues of discriminating against SCs and minority communities. The TMC decided to read the riot act to Afrin since SCs and minorities brought in the bulk of their votes. The incident also brought to the fore the steady erosion of public support for Afrin.

The erosion of TMC's voter base in Arambagh was not lost on the party's election strategists, who were supported by the meticulous data analysts of the Indian Political Action Committee (I-PAC). They closely tracked the constituency's shifting political tides, well aware that the once-formidable TMC stronghold was slipping. Arambagh had been a bastion of the CPI(M) since 1980, but Afrin Ali – then known as Aparupa Poddar – shattered that legacy in 2014, when she secured a decisive victory with a commanding margin of 3.46 lakh votes.

However, the landscape changed dramatically over the next five years. By the 2019 Lok Sabha elections, Afrin's once-comfortable lead had dwindled to a razor-thin margin of just 1,042 votes. The stark decline sent alarm bells ringing within the TMC. In a high-stakes contest, even a minor shift in voter preferences – amounting to a swing in just two polling booths – could have resulted in a loss for the party. This dramatic drop in support was seen as a direct reflection of the rising BJP wave in Bengal, which capitalized on the growing religious and political polarization in the state.

Afrin's justification for her position – asserting that she remained a SC Hindu, despite adopting a Muslim name – failed to resonate with either her party or the electorate. In a climate where identity politics played an increasingly dominant role, her continued candidacy risked providing the BJP with a potent weapon to attack the TMC. The BJP's campaign in Bengal is allegedly fuelled by aggressive polarization and Afrin's contested identity could have become a rallying point for their narrative.

Recognizing this risk, the TMC leadership made the calculated decision to replace Afrin with Mitali Bag as its candidate for Arambagh in 2024. The move paid off – Bag secured victory for the party, albeit with a relatively narrow margin of 6,399 votes. While not an overwhelming win, it was a clear indication that the TMC had managed, at least temporarily, to stem the tide of BJP's advance in the constituency.

Afrin's ouster symbolized a broader shift within the TMC's electoral strategy – one that prioritized pragmatism over loyalty. In an era where margins were shrinking and political battlegrounds were becoming increasingly volatile, even a single candidate's controversy could tip the scales against the entire party.

There is no straightforward explanation for Afrin's dwindling political fortunes even as her party increased its Lok Sabha tally from 22 (in 2014) to 29 (in 2024). In fact, even as her party consolidated its position, Afrin was no part of it. So, what pushed her into a corner as a politician? Apart from her personal issues, we must keep in mind that politicians like Afrin are second-generation leaders who made a lateral entry into the party hierarchy. Many of these leaders joined politics from various other professions. While we do not doubt their sincerity and integrity, they lack activism and street-fighting experience. Most core leaders from the TMC have emerged through a violent political retribution unleashed by the CPI(M) or the Congress. Compared to such leaders, the generation that Afrin represents is more transactional in approaching their political career, which also makes them less resilient to withstand the blows – literally.

Aparupa Poddar's transformation into Afrin Ali has been anything but smooth. Her political journey, once marked by steady electoral success, has, in recent years, been overshadowed by controversies, speculation and a failure – wilful or otherwise – to fully grasp the shifting political undercurrents of West Bengal. Once a rising star in the TMC, her trajectory has taken a tumultuous turn, with personal and political upheavals casting a shadow over her future prospects. However, despite the challenges she has faced, she appears far from retreating into political obscurity.

In her public statements, the former MP continues to exude optimism, hinting at an unwavering belief in her ability to stage a comeback. With the crucial West Bengal state elections slated for 2026 and the next Lok Sabha elections soon after, in

2029, she may see an opportunity to re-establish herself within the TMC ranks. Her social media presence strongly reflects this intent: her posts are filled with images and updates of her attending TMC's internal strategy meetings, party events and public gatherings, all in a clear attempt to signal her continued relevance and allegiance to Mamata Banerjee's leadership.

Yet, the political landscape in West Bengal has completely changed from what it was when she first entered electoral politics. The TMC, while still a formidable force, faces increasing pressure from the BJP and a resurgent Left-Congress alliance. The party's internal dynamics, too, are evolving, with new leaders emerging and old loyalties being tested. Whether Afrin can successfully navigate this changing landscape remains to be seen. Will her past successes, coupled with her continued engagement with the party, be enough to secure her a place in its future plans? Or will the controversies that have dogged her in recent years act as a roadblock to her political resurgence? Regardless of the outcome, her journey remains a compelling one – an embodiment of the unpredictability and personal stakes that define Indian politics. Whether she reclaims a prominent position within the TMC or fades into the backdrop of Bengal's evolving political narrative, her story will undoubtedly leave a mark on the political terrain. Supporters and detractors alike will watch closely as she attempts to script the next chapter of her political career in a landscape that is as dynamic as it is unforgiving.

Signing Off

We took the liberty to take some space in the epilogue to share some interesting insights from our research on these two political profiles.

The epilogue of a book is usually a reflection on the closure that the book would like to offer. But the theme of this book is the beginning of a long journey which is far from over. In our understanding, the future that this book envisages is marked by endless possibilities for this work and beyond. A possibility of greater empowerment of women, stronger political representation, better governance and much more. It holds immense hope for Indian democracy and its ability to produce an able leadership even in extremely difficult and challenging circumstances. This book is a tribute to the fighting spirit of the many women leaders, and not just Muslim, who braved difficult situations to assert their claims to leadership several decades ago, at a time when male-dominance in the world of politics was much more entrenched. The book also offers an account of positive changes that women can bring in governance, and builds a compelling case of why more women should be given the space and opportunity to enter and thrive in the domain of electoral politics.

At a time when women as voters have become more politically aware and active, and the Women Reservation Bill has been enacted, this work is another vocal push for a greater participation of women of all faiths and communities in India's parliamentary politics. Even in the domain of research, this work can be a potent foundational pillar to looks at several other aspects of women's political representation in India. For instance, the journeys of Muslim women representatives in the Rajya Sabha, state legislative assemblies, and in the municipal corporation and panchayats, are extremely important stories which are waiting to see the light of the day. Similar work on women from other minority communities as well as backward groups and regions can be valuable subjects of scholarly attention.

As already mentioned, there might be shortcomings in this work which are entirely and only ours, and we are determined to learn from them. However, documenting the political lives of personalities by moving beyond biographical genres is a crucial analytical exercise which we feel should be taken up more seriously by scholars and commentators of Indian politics. Ours is a humble effort in this regard.

Notes

Authors' Note

1. Tayyen, Sana. 'From Orientalist Sexual Object to Burkini Terrorist Threat: Muslim Women through Evolving Lens.' *Islamophobia Studies Journal*, vol. 4, no. 1, 2017, pp. 101–114, tinyurl.com/bdjecdhs, https://doi.org/10.13169/islastudj.4.1.0101.
2. Ohlan, Ramphul. 'Muslim Women in India: Status of Demographic, Socioeconomic and Health Inequalities.' *Journal of Muslim Minority Affairs*, vol. 40, no. 3, 9 September 2020, pp. 1–12, tinyurl.com/2tbda6ee, https://doi.org/10.1080/13602004.2020.1813991.
3. al-Turabi, Hasan. 'The Islamic State.' *Voices of Resurgent Islam*, edited by John Esposito, Oxford University Press, 1983, pp. 244.
4. Jones, Justin. 'Muslim Feminism as Islamic Modernism: Women's Activism in India between the Quran and the Constitution.' *Modern Asian Studies*, vol. 58, no. 2, March 2024, pp. 421–447, tinyurl.com/2hcn3b44, https://doi.org/10.1017/s0026749x23000495.
5. 'Ashoka Fellow Noorjehan Safia Niaz', Ashoka, 2025, www.ashoka.org/en-us/fellow/noorjehan-safia-niaz#accordion.
6. "All India Muslim Women Personal Law Board." *shaistaambar.com*, 2024, www.shaistaambar.com/.
7. Singh, Vijaita. 'Women's Reservation Bill Will Be Implemented Only After 2029: Amit Shah.' *The Hindu*, 20 September 2023, tinyurl.com/3pr6f2ak.

Introduction

1. Rinehart, Sue Tolleson. *Gender Consciousness and Politics*. 1st ed., Routledge, 1992, doi.org/10.4324/9781315866482.
2. Bergeron, Ryan. '"The Seventies": Feminism Makes Waves', CNN, 22

July 2015, edition.cnn.com/2015/07/22/living/the-seventies-feminism-womens-lib; *Second Wave Feminism Primary Sources & History*. Gale, 2022, www.gale.com/primary-sources/womens-studies/collections/second-wave-feminism.

3. UN Women. 'Political Participation of Women.' UN Women Asia and the Pacific, https://asiapacific.unwomen.org/en/focus-areas/governance/political-participation-of-women.
4. Freeman, Jo. *A Room at a Time: How Women Entered Party Politics*. Rowman and Littlefield, 2000.
5. Inter-Parliamentary Union (IPU). 'Women in Politics: New Data Shows Growth but Also Setbacks.' Inter-Parliamentary Union Press Release, March 2021, https://www.ipu.org/news/women-in-politics-2021.
6. Erickson, Lynda. 'Making Her Way In: Women, Parties, and Candidates in Canada.' *Gender and Party Politics*, edited by Joni Lovenduski and Pippa Norris, Sage Publications, 1993.
7. Conway, M. Margaret. 'Women and Political Participation.' *Political Science and Politics*, vol. 34, no. 2, June 2001, pp. 231–233.
8. Zenger, Jack, and Joseph Folkman. 'Research: Women Score Higher Than Men in Most Leadership Skills.' *Harvard Business Review*, 25 June 2019, https://hbr.org/2019/06/research-women-score-higher-than-men-in-most-leadership-skills.
9. Chamorro-Premuzic, Tomas. 'If Women Are Better Leaders, Then Why Are They Not In Charge?' *Forbes*, 7 March 2021, https://www.forbes.com/sites/tomaspremuzic/2021/03/07/if-women-are-better-leaders-then-why-are-they-not-in-charge/.
10. McDougall, Gay. 'Meeting the Challenges of Discrimination Against Women from Minority Groups.' United Nations Human Rights, 7 March 2006, Statements and Speeches, https://www.ohchr.org/en/statements-and-speeches/2009/10/meeting-challenges-discrimination-against-women-minority-groups.
11. Coffe, Hilde, and Selin Dilli. 'The Gender Gap in Political Participation in Muslim-Majority Countries.' *International Political Science Review*, vol. 36, no. 5, 2014, https://doi.org/10.1177/0192512114528228.
12. Rolland, Abby M. "Muslim Women Political Leaders and Electoral Participation in Muslim-Majority Countries." *What All Americans Should Know About Women in the Muslim World*, 2015, cupola.gettysburg.edu/islamandwomen/5.

13. Bayes, Jane H., and Nayereh Tohidi. *Globalization, Gender and Religion: The Politics of Women's Rights in Catholic and Muslim Contexts*. Palgrave Macmillan, 2001.
14. Joly, Daniele, and Khursheed Wadia. *Muslim Women and Power: Political and Civic Engagement in West European Societies*. Palgrave Macmillan, 2017.
15. Bourque, S., and J. Grossholtz. "Politics an Unnatural Practice: Political Science Looks at Female Participation." *Politics and Society*, vol. 4, no. 2, pp. 225–266; Lovenduski, Joni, and Pippa Norris, editors. *Women in Politics*. Oxford University Press, 1996; Lovenduski, Joni, and Jill Hills, editors. *The Politics of the Second Electorate: Women and Public Participation*. Routledge & Kegan Paul, 1981; Pateman, Carole. *The Disorder of Women: Democracy, Feminism and Political Theory*. Polity Press, 1988; Randall, Vicky. *Women and Politics: An International Perspective*. 2nd ed., Palgrave Macmillan, 1987.
16. Tadros, Mariz. *Women in Politics: Gender, Power and Development*. London: Zed Books, 2014.
17. Sawer, Marian, Manon Tremblay, and Linda Trimble. *Representing Women in Parliament: A Comparative Study*. Routledge, 2006.
18. Urbinati, Nadia. *Representative Democracy: Principles and Genealogy*. University of Chicago Press, 2008.
19. Kohli, Atul, editor. *The Success of India's Democracy*. Princeton University Press, 2001; Vora, Rajendra, and Suhas Palshikar. *Indian Democracy: Meanings and Practices*. Sage, 2003; Guha, Ramachandra. *India After Gandhi*. Penguin India, 2007.
20. 'Hindu Muslim Population in India.' *The Census 2011*, Census Organization of India, 2011, www.census2011.co.in/religion.php.
21. Khalidi, Omar. *Indian Muslims Since Independence*. Vikas Publishing House, 1998.
22. Sen, Ronojoy. *House of the People: Parliament and the Making of Indian Democracy*. Cambridge University Press, 2022.
23. Chatterjee, Sanchari. 'Muslim Representation Increases to 27 from Its Lowest Margin in Previous Lok Sabha.' *India Today*, 26 May 2019, https://tinyurl.com/msarvhkh.
24. Dalwal, Hamid. *Muslim Politics in India*. Nachiketa Publication, 1968; Farooqui, Adnan. 'Political Representation of a Minority: Muslim Representation in Contemporary India.' *India Review*, vol. 19, no. 2, 2020, pp. 153–75. https://doi.org/10.1080/14736489.2020.1744996; Shairgojri,

Aadil Ahmad, and Rashid Manzoor Bhat. 'Muslim Women and Politics of India.' *Multidisciplinary Output Research for Actual and International Issue*, vol. 2, no. 4, 2023, E-ISSN 2808-6635.

25. Francis, Nikita, and Vignesh Radhakrishnan. 'Data | Eighteenth Lok Sabha Has Lowest Share of Muslim MPs in Six Decades.' *The Hindu*, 18 June 2024, https://tinyurl.com/h9tt6pmy.
26. Bhandare, Namita. 'Muslim Women Are 6.9% of Population. In Lok Sabha, 0.7%.' IndiaSpend, 26 April 2019, https://www.indiaspend.com/muslim-women-are-6-9-of-population-in-loksabha-0-7/.
27. Tewari, Ruhi, and Abhishek Mishra. 'Every Second ST, Every Third Dalit & Muslim in India Poor, Not Just Financially: UN Report.' *The Print*, 12 July 2019, https://theprint.in/india/every-secondst-every-third-dalit-muslim-in-india-poor-not-just-financiallyun-report/262270/; Gupta, Monobina. 'Interview: "Post Sachar Report, Condition of Indian Muslims Unchanged."' *The Wire*, 20 February 2019, https://thewire.in/rights/interview-post-sachar-report-conditionof-indian-muslims-unchanged.
28. Calman, Leslie J. *Toward Empowerment: Women and Movement Politics in India*. Routledge, 2018.
29. Rajput, Pam, and Usha Thakkar. *Women in State Politics in India: Missing in the Corridors of Power*. Routledge, 2023.
30. Hassan, Zoya, and Ritu Menon. *Unequal Citizens: A Study of Muslim Women in India*. Oxford University Press, 2004.
31. Kidwai, Rasheed. 'Women's Reservation Bill May Open Pandora's Box.' *India Today*, 20 September 2023, https://www.indiatoday.in/opinion/story/womens-reservation-bill-may-open-pandorasbox-2437970-2023-09-20.
32. Dimitrov, B. E. George, and Noblelyne Nongkynrih. 'A Study on Muslim Women Political Participation in India.' *International Journal of Research*, vol. 4, no. 9, Aug. 2017, ISSN: 2348-6848.
33. Yunus, Saba, and Manorama Gupta. 'Role of Indian Muslim Women in Politics.' Proceedings of the International Conference on Law, Education, Business and Corporate Social Responsibilities (LEBCSR-17), 4–5 September 2017, Budapest, Hungary, https://www.eares.org/siteadmin/upload/6486ED0917024.pdf.
34. Jaffrelot, Christophe, Virginie Dutoya, Radhika Kanchana, and Gayatri Rathore. 'Understanding Muslim Voter Behaviour.' *Seminar*, no. 602, October 2009, https://www.india-seminar.com/2009/602/602_christophe_et_al.htm.

35. Shukla, Shashi, and Sashi Shukla. 'Political Participation of Muslim Women.' *The Indian Journal of Political Science*, vol. 57, no. 1/4, 1996, pp. 1–13, https://www.jstor.org/stable/41855734.

1. Setting the Context

1. Lahiri, Deepanjali, and Ruha Shadab. 'Muslim Women in India's Workforce: Where Are They?' *India Development Review*, 30 July 2021, https://idronline.org/article/diversity-inclusion/muslim-women-in-indias-workforce-where-are-they/.
2. Chattopadhyay, Raghabendra, and Esther Duflo. 'Women as Policy Makers: Evidence from a Randomized Policy Experiment in India.' *Econometrica*, vol. 72, no. 5, Sept. 2004, pp. 1409–1443.
3. Beaman, Lori, et al. 'Political Reservation and Substantive Representation: Evidence from Indian Village Councils.' *India Policy Forum*, 2010–11, https://www.ncaer.org/wp-content/uploads/2022/09/4_Lori-Beaman_Esther-Duflo_Rohini-Pande_Petia-Topalova.pdf.
4. Katz, Ariel. 'Margaret Thatcher, Golda Meir, and Indira Gandhi's Actions and Rhetoric Regarding Feminism and Gender During Their Ascent to Power.' Senior thesis, Claremont McKenna College, Fall 2012, submitted to Professor Hilary Appel and Dean Gregory Hess, https://scholarship.claremont.edu/cgi/viewcontent.cgi?article=1515&context=cmc_theses.
5. Ibid.
6. Ibid.

2. Mofida Ahmed: The Forgotten Begum of Assam

1. 'Mofida Ahmed.' Wikipedia, 22 January 2025, https://en.wikipedia.org/wiki/Mofida_Ahmed.
2. 'Assam's First Woman MP Mofida Ahmed.' *India Today,* 8 April 2024, https://www.indiatodayne.in/visualstories/webstories/assams-first-woman-mp-mofida-ahmed-124383-08-04-2024.
3. *Mofida Ahmed vs The State of Assam and 4 Ors.* Gauhati High Court, 17 December 2019, https://indiankanoon.org/doc/76682332/.
4. 'Mofida Ahmed – First Woman MP of Assam.' MPositive.in, 4 December 2018, https://www.mpositive.in/tag/mofida-ahmed-first-woman-mp-of-assam/.

5. Kumari, Khusboo. 'Paying Tribute to Pathbreaking and Forgotten, Muslim Women from the 20th Century.' *The Wire*, 30 May 2018, https://thewire.in/women/paying-tribute-to-pathbreaking-and-forgotten-muslim-women-from-the-20th-century.

3. Zohraben Akbarbhai: Service Before Self

1. A Mahamandleshwar is a respected title within Hinduism, specifically for leaders within the 13 recognized monastic orders (Akhadas). Mahamandleshwars hold a position of authority and responsibility, managing spiritual, cultural, and administrative affairs of their respective Akhadas.
2. 'National Herald', Part 1 (Questions and Answers), Parliament Digital Library (PDL), 30 April 1964, https://eparlib.nic.in/handle/123456789/1011153?view_type=browse.

4. Maimoona Sultan: The Life and Times of a Congress Insider

1. Gustasp, and Jeroo Irani. 'The Begums of Bhopal: A Tale of Royal Women and Their City.' *Outlook Traveller*, 2 November 2024, www.outlooktraveller.com/experiences/heritage/the-begums-of-bhopal-a-tale-of-royal-women-and-their-city.
2. 'Rocking at 72: Doordarshan News Anchor Salma Sultan Graces Ramp.' Mpositive.in, 18 September 2019, www.mpositive.in/tag/salma-sultan/.
3. This refers to the diplomatic stance regarding the Vietnam War (1955–1975).
4. Singh, Shashi Kumar. 'Immortal Saga of Courage and Struggle: Indira Gandhi.' *Indian National Congress*, 7 November 2024, inc.in/congress-sandesh/tribute/immortal-saga-of-courage-and-struggle-indira-gandhi.

5. Begum Akbar Jehan Abdullah: Kashmir's 'Madr-e-Meharban'

1. Khan, Nyla Ali. 'Remembering Begum Akbar Jehan Abdullah.' *Daily Times*, 3 September 2018, https://dailytimes.com.pk/291905/remembering-begum-akbar-jehan-abdullah/.

2. 'Vajpayee, Advani to Attend Funeral of Begum Akbar Jehan.' *Rediff.com*, 11 July 2000, https://m.rediff.com/news/2000/jul/11begum.htm.
3. Omar became the chief minister for the second time at the end of the 2024 elections, which were held almost a decade after the abrogation of Article 370 which changed Kashmir's status from a state to union territory (UT).
4. Khan, Nyla Ali. *The Life of a Kashmiri Woman: Dialectic of Resistance and Accommodation*. Palgrave Publication, 2014.
5. Ibid.
6. Ibid; p. 25.
7. Abdullah, Sheikh Mohammad. *The Blazing Chinar*. Gulshan Books, 2023, p. 138.
8. Khan, Nyla Ali. *The Life of a Kashmiri Woman: Dialectic of Resistance and Accommodation*. Palgrave Publication, 2014.
9. Khan, Nyla Ali. *Sheikh Mohammad Abdullah's Reflections on Kashmir*. Palgrave Macmillan, 2018, http://ndl.ethernet.edu.et/bitstream/123456789/61742/1/303.pdf.pdf.
10. Khan, Nyla Ali. *The Life of a Kashmiri Woman: Dialectic of Resistance and Accommodation*. Palgrave Publication, 2014, p. 39.
11. Ibid.
12. Ibid.
13. Ibid.
14. Khan, Nyla Ali. *The Life of a Kashmiri Woman: Dialectic of Resistance and Accommodation*. Palgrave Publication, 2014, p. 5.
15. Khan, Nyla Ali. 'Until Lions Have Their Historians, Tales of the Hunt Shall Always Glorify the Hunters: Sheikh Mohammad Abdullah, History Retold.' *CounterPunch*, 22 January 2015, https://tinyurl.com/m5aes76f.
16. Ibid; p. 29.
17. Khan, Nyla Ali. *The Life of a Kashmiri Woman: Dialectic of Resistance and Accommodation*. Palgrave Publication, 2014, p. 108.
18. Khan, Nyla Ali. *The Life of a Kashmiri Woman: Dialectic of Resistance and Accommodation*. Palgrave Publication, 2014, p. 109.
19. Khan, Nyla Ali. *The Life of a Kashmiri Woman: Dialectic of Resistance and Accommodation*. Palgrave Publication, 2014, p. 114.
20. Khan, Nyla Ali. *The Life of a Kashmiri Woman: Dialectic of Resistance and Accommodation*. Palgrave Publication, 2014, p. xvi.
21. 'NC Pays Tributes to Begum Akbar Jahan.' Two Circles.net, 12 July 2007, https://www.twocircles.net/2007jul12/nc_pays_tributes_begum_akbar_jahan.html.

22. Khan, Nyla Ali. *The Life of a Kashmiri Woman: Dialectic of Resistance and Accommodation*. Palgrave Publication, 2014, p. 5.

6. Rashida Haque Choudhury: From Political Prominence to Oblivion

1. As reported by Rashida Haque Choudhury's close acquaintance.
2. 'Profile of Political Leaders: Moinul Haque Choudhury (1923–1976).' Wayback Machine, https://web.archive.org/web/20141224090937/http:/www.unishemay.org/english-pages/geography-content/Profile%20of%20Political%20Leaders.pdf.
3. 'About Moinul Hoque Choudhury.' Moinul Hoque Choudhury Memorial Science College (Official College Website), https://mhcmsc.in/about-moinul-hoque-choudhury.
4. 'Death Anniversary of Moinul Haque Choudhury.' *Assam Tribune*, 15 September 2010, https://assamtribune.com/death-anniversary-of-moinul-haque-choudhury.
5. 'Choudhury, Smt Rashida Haque.' Datais.info, https://tinyurl.com/3f5b3x48.
6. Bhardwaj, Ashutosh. 'Why Alliance with Ajmal's AUDF May Not Help Assam Congress Resolve Its "Muslim Dilemma"'. *The Wire*, 4 April 2021, https://tinyurl.com/nvpkffv7.
7. Wright, Jr., Theodore P. 'Muslims and the 1977 Indian Elections: A Watershed?' *Asian Survey*, vol. 17, no. 12, December 1977, pp. 1207–1220.
8. 'Worldwide Guide to Women in Leadership: Republic of India/Bharat.' https://www.guide2womenleaders.com/India.htm.
9. 'Chairpersons of National Bal Bhawan'. National Bal Bhawan, https://nationalbalbhavan.nic.in/aboutus/nbb-chairperson.html.
10. 'Rashida Haque Choudhury – Hindustan Times Report.' https://tinyurl.com/muebbkuc.
11. 'HT This Day: Jan 10, 1980 - Cong-I Gets Two-Thirds Majority.' *Hindustan Times*, 9 January 2022, https://tinyurl.com/yuxrtv4p.
12. In conversation with Rashida Haque Choudhury's close acquaintance.

7. Mohsina Kidwai: A Life Lived with Dignity

1. Kidwai, Mohsina, and Rasheed Kidwai. *My Life in Indian Politics*. HarperCollins, 18 October 2022.

2. Ibid.
3. Ibid.
4. Ibid.
5. Ibid.
6. 'Meerut Burns in Communal Fire Ignited by Squabble for 200 Sq Ft Property.' *India Today*, 31 October 1982, https://www.indiatoday.in/magazine/special-report/story/19821031-meerut-burns-in-communal-fire-ignited-by-squabble-for-200-sq-ft-property-772302-2013-08-26.
7. Kidwai, Mohsina, and Rasheed Kidwai. *My Life in Indian Politics*. HarperCollins, 18 October 2022.
8. Ibid.
9. Ibid; Source: Daryabadi, Maulana Abdul Majid. *Tafsir ul Qur'an: Translation and Commentary of the Holy Qur'an*. 4 vols., Darul Ishaat, 1991.
10. Ibid.

8. Abida Ahmed: First Lady as Politician and Parliamentarian

1. Uma Vasudev. 'First Lady Begum Abida Ahmed Organizes International Art Exhibition of Women Artists.' *India Today*, 25 June 2014, https://tinyurl.com/mv647y49.
2. Ibid.
3. Prakash, Gyan. *Emergency Chronicles: Indira Gandhi and Democracy's Turning Point*. Penguin Viking, 2018; Mohan, Manasa. 'President Who Took a Tranquiliser after Signing Away India's Democratic Rights to Indira.' *The Print*, 11 February 2019, https://theprint.in/theprint-profile/president-who-took-a-tranquiliser-after-signing-away-indias-democratic-rights-to-indira/190303/.
4. Majumdar, Neera. 'Indira Gandhi's Emergency Era through Cartoons.' *The Print*, 25 June 2018, https://theprint.in/last-laughs/indira-gandhis-emergency-era-through-cartoons/74536/.
5. 'President Fakhruddin Resented Indira, Sanjay's Family Planning Policy: WikiLeaks.' *The Times of India*, 10 April 2013, https://tinyurl.com/4kydnnbu.
6. 'British Governor Used to Rest Here before Boarding Train.' *Hindustan Times*, https://tinyurl.com/bdcphjvw.

9. Noor Bano: Tryst with a Destiny in Politics

1. 'UP Polls: Now Haider Khan Claims Threat to Life, Demands CBI Probe in Grandfather's Death.' ETV Bharat, 31 January 2022, https://tinyurl.com/2p9rc6tr.
2. Arnimesh, Shanker. 'New Election, Old Rivalry: Jailed Azam Khan, Son Make It People vs Nawabs in Rampur, Suar.' *The Print*, 7 February 2022, https://tinyurl.com/yn5ek6zk.

10. Rubab Sayda: The Revered Daughter-in-Law of Bahraich

1. Mirza, Azim. 'Former SP MP Rubab Saida Passes Away, Last Rites Will Be Performed in Bahraich Late Tonight.' *Navbharat Times*, 6 February 2024, https://tinyurl.com/3zt7ys2j.
2. Hasan, Masoodul. 'Women Panel Refutes SP Leader Charges.' *Hindustan Times*, 5 February 2007, https://tinyurl.com/24rju4hu.
3. Mirza, Azim. 'Former SP MP Rubab Saida Passes Away, Last Rites Will Be Performed in Bahraich Late Tonight.' *Navbharat Times*, 6 February 2024, https://tinyurl.com/3zt7ys2j.
4. 'Further Discussion on the Motion of Confidence in the Council of Minister Moved by Dr. Manmohan Singh on the 21st July, 2008 (Concluded).' Lok Sabha Digital Library, Parliament of India, https://eparlib.nic.in/bitstream/123456789/732817/1/10243.pdf.
5. 'Parliamentary Consultative Committee Discuss 50 Years of ONGC.' Press Information Bureau (PIB), 24 June 2005, https://www.pib.gov.in/newsite/erelcontent.aspx?relid=9840.
6. 'Assembly Election Race in Shrawasti.' Election Fate, 2009, https://www.electionfate.in/constituencies/Shrawasti.
7. Srivastava, Piyush. 'SP Paving Way for Rajnath's Victory.' *India Today*, 16 April 2009, https://www.indiatoday.in/election-news/story/sp-paving-way-for-rajnath-s-victory-44533-2009-04-15.
8. Samajwadi Party [@samajwadiparty]. 'Heartfelt Condolences on the Demise of Former MP Rubab Sayda.' X (formerly Twitter), 6 February 2024, https://x.com/samajwadiparty/status/1754754749906252213.
9. Harun Khan [@iamharunkhan]. 'Akhilesh Yadav Visits Yasar Shah's Residence to Offer Condolences After Rubab Sayda's Demise.' X (formerly Twitter), 23 February 2024, https://x.com/iamharunkhan/status/1761329386924781667.

11. Mehbooba Mufti: Accidental Politician, Able Leader

1. 'Evaluating Challenges Women Face.' *The New York Times*, 6 March 2012, https://www.nytimes.com/2012/03/07/us/07iht-letter07.html.
2. 'Mehbooba's Daughter Iltija Mufti Appointed Her Media Advisor.' *The Indian Express*, 30 August 2023, https://tinyurl.com/4spmmrdu.
3. 'Insider Tears into Muftis and Family Party.' *The Telegraph*, 2 March 2016, https://tinyurl.com/bp77h48h.
4. Narayan, Priyanjali. 'How 5 Terrorists Freed for Home Minister's Daughter Set a Benchmark.' *India Today*, 13 September 2024, https://tinyurl.com/yyhu2ytu.
5. Majid, Zulfikar. 'Mehbooba Mufti Unanimously Re-Elected PDP Chief.' *Deccan Herald*, 26 October 2023, https://www.deccanherald.com/india/jammu-and-kashmir/mehbooba-mufti-unanimously-re-elected-pdp-chief-2742668.
6. Rashid, Toufiq. 'Why the Kashmir Protests in 2010 and 2016 Are Different.' *Hindustan Times*, 18 August 2016, https://www.hindustantimes.com/india-news/kashmir-s-summers-of-discontent-why-the-protests-in-2010-and-2016-are-different/story-xy9w5KiPO7VGSehQcwJ2bM.html.
7. 'Opportunistic BJP-PDP Alliance Cost India Strategically: Rahul.' *Business Standard*, 19 July 2018, https://www.business-standard.com/article/news-ians/opportunistic-bjp-pdp-alliance-cost-india-strategically-rahul-118061900962_1.html.
8. Hebbar, Nistula. 'Analysis: BJP Didn't Want to Face 2019 Polls as PDP's Ally.' *The Hindu*, 30 Sept. 2023, https://www.thehindu.com/news/national/other-states/analysis-why-the-pdp-bjp-alliance-ended/article61824478.ece.
9. Ibid.
10. Ahmed, Mudasir. 'Nepotism Row Erupts as Mehbooba Mufti's Cousin Named Executive Officer of Khadi Board.' *The Wire*, 24 February 2018, https://thewire.in/politics/nepotism-row-erupts-as-mehbooba-muftis-cousin-named-executive-officer-of-khadi-board.
11. 'BJP-PDP Split In J&K: Here's a Look Back at Their 3-Yr Alliance.' *The Quint*, 20 June 2018, https://www.thequint.com/news/politics/bjp-pdp-alliance-split-timeline#read-more.
12. Bose, Shohini. 'BJP Lists 5 Reasons for Dumping the PDP in Jammu & Kashmir.' *The Quint*, 20 June 2018, https://www.thequint.com/videos/

news-videos/bjp-lists-5-reasons-for-dumping-the-pdp-in-jandk#read-more.

13. Aiyar, Mani Shankar. 'Mehbooba Was Burdened by Her Father with an Impossible Legacy.' *NDTV*, 22 June 2018, https://www.ndtv.com/opinion/mehbooba-was-burdened-by-her-father-with-an-impossible-legacy-by-mani-shankar-aiyar-1871474.
14. 'BJP Ends Alliance with PDP; Can't Treat J&K as Enemy Territory, Says Mehbooba after Resigning.' *The Economic Times*, 19 June 2018, https://economictimes.indiatimes.com/news/politics-and-nation/bjp-ends-alliance-with-pdp-in-jammu-and-kashmir-presidents-rule-likely-in-the-state/articleshow/64646710.cms.
15. 'J&K on Edge: Omar Abdullah, Mehbooba Mufti Under House Arrest.' *The Quint*, 5 August 2019, https://www.thequint.com/news/india/jammu-and-kashmir-crisis-mehbooba-mufti-omar-abdullah-under-house-arrest.
16. 'Mehbooba Mufti Elected PDP President for Fourth Consecutive Term.' *The Hindu*, 26 October 2023, https://www.thehindu.com/news/national/mehbooba-mufti-elected-party-president-for-fourth-consecutive-term/article67461064.ece.
17. Masood, Bashaarat. 'Mufti's Son Rise in Kashmir Politics: Dynasty Is Destiny?' *The Indian Express*, 20 January 2016, https://indianexpress.com/article/explained/muftis-son-rise-in-kashmir-politics-dynasty-is-destiny/.
18. Hussain, Ashiq. 'PDP Appoints Mehbooba's Daughter Iltija Mufti as Her Media Adviser.' *Hindustan Times*, 31 August 2023, https://www.hindustantimes.com/cities/chandigarh-news/pdp-appoints-mehbooba-s-daughter-iltija-mufti-as-her-media-adviser-101693421952220.html.
19. 'PDP Suffers Worst Electoral Result Since Its Formation 25 Years Back.' *Hindustan Times*, 8 October 2024, https://www.hindustantimes.com/india-news/pdp-suffers-worst-electoral-result-since-its-formation-25-years-back-101728374957059.html.
20. Ibid.
21. Ashiq, Peerzada. 'PDP Faces a Rout in J&K, Retains Only Three Seats.' *The Hindu*, 8 October 2024, https://www.thehindu.com/elections/jammu-and-kashmir-assembly/pdp-faces-a-rout-in-jk-retains-only-three-seats/article68733849.ece.

12. Tabassum Hasan: Kairana's Daughter-in-Law, Defender of Her Family Legacy

1. 'Meet Begum Tabassum Hasan, Who Sailed RLD Boat Against Modi Wave in Kairana.' *India Today*, 31 May 2018, https://www.indiatoday.in/india/story/meet-begum-tabassum-hasan-who-sailed-rld-boat-against-modi-wave-in-kairana-1246791-2018-05-31.
2. 'Tabassum Hasan Is Now the First Muslim MP Elected from UP Since 2014.' *The Indian Express*, 31 May 2018, https://indianexpress.com/article/who-is/who-is-tabassum-hasan-know-about-rld-candidate-for-kairana-bye-poll-5198354/.
3. "Member Details – Hasan, Begum Tabassum." Sansad.in, https://sansad.in/ls/members/biographyM/4261?from=members.
4. Kaif, Aas Mohd. 'Tabassum Hasan: A Mascot of Hindu-Muslim Unity and a United Opposition.' *National Herald*, 1 June 2018, https://www.nationalheraldindia.com/india/tabassum-hasan-a-mascot-of-hindu-muslim-unity-and-a-united-opposition-kairana-bypoll-uttar-pradesh.
5. Javaid, Azaan. 'UP Elections 2017: Friends and Foes – Kairana Divided Between Two Families.' *DNA India*, 4 February 2017, https://www.dnaindia.com/india/report-up-elections-2017-friends-and-foes-kairana-divided-between-two-families-2311601.
6. Kaif, Aas Mohd. 'Tabassum Hasan: A Mascot of Hindu-Muslim Unity and a United Opposition.' *National Herald*, 1 June 2018, https://www.nationalheraldindia.com/india/tabassum-hasan-a-mascot-of-hindu-muslim-unity-and-a-united-opposition-kairana-bypoll-uttar-pradesh.
7. Ibid.
8. Ibid.
9. Ibid.
10. Javaid, Azaan. 'UP Elections 2017: Friends and Foes – Kairana Divided Between Two Families.' *DNA India*, 4 February 2017, https://www.dnaindia.com/india/report-up-elections-2017-friends-and-foes-kairana-divided-between-two-families-2311601.
11. Ibid.
12. 'Meet Begum Tabassum Hasan, Who Sailed RLD Boat Against Modi Wave in Kairana.' *India Today*, 31 May 2018, https://www.indiatoday.in/india/story/meet-begum-tabassum-hasan-who-sailed-rld-boat-against-modi-wave-in-kairana-1246791-2018-05-31.

13. Kaif, Aas Mohd. 'Tabassum Hasan: A Mascot of Hindu-Muslim Unity and a United Opposition.' *National Herald*, 1 June 2018, https://www.nationalheraldindia.com/india/tabassum-hasan-a-mascot-of-hindu-muslim-unity-and-a-united-opposition-kairana-bypoll-uttar-pradesh.
14. 'Tabassum Hasan First Muslim to Enter Lok Sabha from UP Since 2014.' *India Today*, 31 May 2018, https://www.indiatoday.in/india/story/tabassum-hasan-first-muslim-to-enter-lok-sabha-from-up-since-2014-1246767-2018-05-31.
15. 'Kairana Exodus: Hukum Singh Discusses UP's Law and Order with Rajnath Singh.' *The Indian Express*, 29 June 2016, https://indianexpress.com/article/india/india-news-india/kairana-hukum-singh-migration-hindu-uttar-pradesh-law-order-rajnathsingh-2882498/.
16. 'Exodus of Hindu Families from Kairana a Reality, Finds NHRC Probe Report.' *The Times of India*, 22 September 2016, https://timesofindia.indiatimes.com/city/meerut/exodus-of-hindu-families-from-kairana-a-reality-finds-nhrc-probe-report/articleshow/54451892.cms.
17. Kaif, Aas Mohd. 'Tabassum Hasan: A Mascot of Hindu-Muslim Unity and a United Opposition.' *National Herald*, 1 June 2018, https://www.nationalheraldindia.com/india/tabassum-hasan-a-mascot-of-hindu-muslim-unity-and-a-united-opposition-kairana-bypoll-uttar-pradesh.
18. 'Kairana Lok Sabha Election Results 2019 UP: Tabassum Hasan, Who Won Last Year's Bypoll, Loses to BJP's Pradeep Chaudhary.' *DNA India*, 24 May 2019, https://www.dnaindia.com/india/report-kairana-lok-sabha-election-results-2019-up-tabassum-hasan-who-won-last-year-s-bypoll-loses-to-bjp-s-pradeep-chaudhary-2752345.
19. Ara, Ismat. 'Iqra Hasan: Balancing Tradition and Progress.' *Frontline*, 4 June 2024, https://frontline.thehindu.com/politics/profile-of-samajwadi-party-mp-iqra-hasan-lok-sabha-election-2024/article68358344.ece.
20. 'Tabassum Hasan Is Now the First Muslim MP Elected from UP Since 2014.' *The Indian Express*, 31 May 2018, https://indianexpress.com/article/who-is/who-is-tabassum-hasan-know-about-rld-candidate-for-kairana-bye-poll-5198354/.

13. Mausam Benazir Noor: Illustrious Political Legacy, Promising Political Future

1. De Sarkar, Soumya. 'TMC MP Mausam Noor Back Home, Ends Speculations and Worries of Party Leaders and Workers.' *The Telegraph*,

20 March 2024, https://www.telegraphindia.com/west-bengal/tmc-mp-mausam-noor-back-home-ends-speculations-and-worries-of-party-leaders-and-workers/cid/2008042.

2. 'Meet Our MPs: TMC MP Mausam Noor.' *NDTV*, 18 December 2024, https://www.ndtv.com/video/meet-our-mps-tmc-mp-mausam-noor-875060.
3. 'Congress Mourns Loss of Leader Who Filled a Void.' *The Telegraph*, 11 July 2008, https://web.archive.org/web/20080803081742/http://www.telegraphindia.com/1080711/jsp/siliguri/story_9535076.jsp.
4. Lahiri, Ishadrita. 'Malda South: Can Congress Save Ghani Khan's Turf or Will BJP or TMC Breach It?' *The Quint*, 4 May 2024, https://www.thequint.com/elections/malda-south-west-bengal-tmc-bjp-congress-ghani-khan-2024-lok-sabha-elections.
5. 'Riverbank Erosion, Ghani Khan's Legacy Likely Factors in Bengal's Malda Dakshin Lok Sabha Seat.' *Economic Times*, 7 April 2024, https://economictimes.indiatimes.com/news/elections/lok-sabha/west-bengal/riverbank-erosion-ghani-khans-legacy-likely-factors-in-bengals-malda-dakshin-lok-sabha-seat/articleshow/109100594.cms?from=mdr.
6. Roy, Esha. 'Whichever the Party, All Politics in Malda Is Still About Only One Family.' *The Indian Express*, 14 April 2016, https://indianexpress.com/article/india/india-news-india/whichever-the-party-all-politics-in-malda-is-still-about-only-one-family/.
7. Bandopdhyay, Sabyasachi. 'In Malda, It's Still All About Ghani Khan.' *The Indian Express*, 23 April 2024, https://indianexpress.com/article/political-pulse/in-malda-its-still-all-about-ghani-khan/.
8. Chowdhury, Santanu. 'Adhir Fails to Retain Baharampur, Isha Holds Congress' Fort in Malda Dakshin.' *The Indian Express*, 5 June 2024, https://indianexpress.com/article/cities/kolkata/adhir-fails-to-retain-baharampur-isha-holds-congress-fort-in-malda-dakshin-9372845/.
9. '1 Family, 2 Parties, 3 Candidates: The Fight for Bengal's Malda.' *NDTV*, 21 April 2019, https://www.ndtv.com/india-news/lok-sabha-elections-2019-mausam-noor-isha-khan-abu-hashem-choudhary-fight-for-malda-west-bengal-2026410.
10. Ibid.
11. Ibid.
12. Roy, Avijit. 'Mausam Noor Raises Issue of Ganga Erosion in Parliament.' *Millennium Post*, 24 July 2024, https://www.millenniumpost.in/bengal/mausam-noor-raises-issue-of-ganga-erosion-in-parliament-573081.

13. De Sarkar, Soumya. 'Fresh Erosion in Malda.' *The Telegraph*, 4 September 2020, https://www.telegraphindia.com/west-bengal/fresh-erosion-in-malda/cid/1790885.
14. Joy, Shemin. 'Private Members' Bills on AI to Be Tabled in Rajya Sabha.' *Deccan Herald*, 26 July 2024, https://www.deccanherald.com/india/private-members-bills-on-ai-to-be-tabled-in-rajya-sabha-3123018.

14. Kaisar Jahan: A Political Life Shaped by Circumstances

1. Sharda, Shailvee. 'Former BSP MP from Sitapur Joins Congress with Her Husband.' *The Times of India*, 5 March 2019, https://timesofindia.indiatimes.com/city/lucknow/former-bsp-mp-from-sitapur-joins-congress-with-her-husband/articleshow/68264530.cms.
2. Rashid, Omar. "3 Ex-MPs, 5 Ex-MLAs Leave BSP, Congress for Samajwadi Party." *The Hindu*, 9 November 2020, https://www.thehindu.com/news/national/other-states/former-mps-mlas-leave-bsp-congress-for-samajwadi-party/article33058936.ece.

15. Mamtaz Sanghamita: The Good Doctor

1. 'Mamtaz Sanghamita.' Wikipedia, 16 April 2025. https://en.wikipedia.org/wiki/Mamtaz_Sanghamita
2. Roy, Briti. 'Mamtaz Sanghamita.' *Oneindia*, 1 January 2021. https://www.oneindia.com/politicians/mamtaz-sanghamita-36765.html.
3. 'সাংসদের রিপোর্ট কার্ড: মমতাজ সঙ্ঘমিতা' ['MP's Report Card: Mamtaz Sanghamita']. Anandabazar Patrika. https://www.anandabazar.com/west-bengal/lok-sabha-election-2019-report-card-of-mp-mamtaz-sanghamita-1.974343.

16. Sajda Ahmed: Navigating Personal Tragedy and Political Trepidation

1. Ahmed, Zeeshan. 'Parties in Power Play Over Heritage Institute.' *The Telegraph*, 3 March 2012, https://www.telegraphindia.com/west-bengal/parties-in-power-play-over-heritage-institute/cid/1281037.
2. Ibid.
3. Ibid.

4. Ahmed, Sajda. Facebook post. Facebook, 11 January 2018, https://www.facebook.com/sajdaahmedtmc/posts/an-educator-and-social-worker-sajda-ahmed-is-the-wife-of-the-late-sri-sultanahm/153725768612257/.
5. Ibid.
6. Ali, Arshad. 'West Bengal: Late TMC Leader Sultan Ahmed's Son Sharique May Get Ticket for Uluberia Bye-Polls.' DNA India, 26 October 2017, https://www.dnaindia.com/india/report-west-bengal-late-tmc-leader-sultan-ahmed-s-son-sharique-may-get-ticket-for-uluberia-bye-polls-2555573.
7. Aktar, Shabina. 'Interview with Sajda Ahmed.' eNewsroom.in, 2 January 2018, https://enewsroom.in/bjp-tmc-uluberia-sajda-sultan-ahmed/.
8. 'Sultan Ahmed Was Under Stress Due to CBI Interrogation: Mamata Banerjee.' *The Indian Express*, 4 September 2017, https://indianexpress.com/article/india/ahmed-was-under-stress-due-to-cbi-interrogation-mamata-banerjee-4828702/.
9. Aktar, Shabina. 'Interview with Sajda Ahmed.' eNewsroom.in, 2 January 2018, https://enewsroom.in/bjp-tmc-uluberia-sajda-sultan-ahmed/.
10. Ibid.

17. Ranee Narah: Bat, Ball and Politics

1. Himanta Biswa Sarma [@himantabiswa]. 'Congratulation to Smti Rani Narah for Her Induction into Union Council of Ministers.' X (formerly Twitter), 14 February 2023, https://x.com/himantabiswa/status/262449182474903553.
2. Karmakar, Rahul. 'Ex-Cricketer Clean Bowls Dissidence.' *Hindustan Times*, 26 March 2009, https://www.hindustantimes.com/india/ex-cricketer-clean-bowls-dissidence/story-y6wTQHYDJuadV3fONF9IYN.html.
3. 'Ranee Narah.' Wikipedia, https://en.wikipedia.org/wiki/Ranee_Narah.
4. Karmakar, Rahul. 'Ex-Cricketer Clean Bowls Dissidence.' *Hindustan Times*, 26 March 2009, https://www.hindustantimes.com/india/ex-cricketer-clean-bowls-dissidence/story-y6wTQHYDJuadV3fONF9IYN.html.
5. 'Ranee Narah Takes Ball to Sonia Court.' *The Telegraph*, 10 February 2006, https://www.telegraphindia.com/north-east/ranee-narah-takes-ball-to-sonia-court/cid/822371#goog_rewarded.
6. 'Mid-Air Collision Scare over Patna.' *Times of India*, 22 July 2011, https://timesofindia.indiatimes.com/city/guwahati/mid-air-collision-scare-over-patna/articleshow/9315065.cms.

7. 'Congress Leaders Bharat Ranee Narah Grabbed Govt Land to Set up Tea Estate: Lakhimpur MLA Manab Deka.' NewsLiveTV, 16 September 2023, https://newslivetv.com/congress-leaders-bharat-ranee-narah-grabbed-govt-land-to-set-up-tea-estate-lakhimpur-mla-manab-deka/.

18. Nusrat Jahan Ruhi: Being Her Own Woman

1. Anthony, Susan B., and Elizabeth Cady Stanton, editors. *History of Woman Suffrage.* Vol. 1, Chapter 14, Wikisource, https://en.wikisource.org/wiki/History_of_Woman_Suffrage/Volume_1/Chapter_14.
2. Gupta, Poorvi. 'Basirhat MP Nusrat Jahan Rejects "Feminism" Says, "Equality Is Not Feminism"'. Feminism in India, 27 July 2020, https://feminisminindia.com/2020/07/27/basirhat-mp-nusrat-jahan-feminism-equality/#google_vignette.
3. 'Actress Speaks Out on Friend-Turned-Fugitive.' *The Telegraph*, 21 February 2012, https://www.telegraphindia.com/india/actress-speaks-out-onfriend-turned-fugitive/cid/449884.
4. Ganguly, Arnab. 'Nusrat Jahan: The Spotlight Never Leaves Her.' *The Telegraph*, 21 June 2021, https://www.telegraphindia.com/west-bengal/nusrat-jahan-the-spotlight-never-leaves-her/cid/1819585.
5. '"Don't Do Even for CM": TMC MP Nusrat Jahan Loses Temper during Roadshow, Stokes Controversy.' *News18*, 29 March 2021, https://www.news18.com/news/politics/dont-do-even-for-cm-tmc-mp-nusrat-jahan-loses-temper-during-roadshow-stokes-controversy-3586253.html.
6. Dhar, Aniruddha. 'BJP Slams "Part-Time Politician"TMC's Nusrat Jahan for "Beat with Sticks" Remarks.' *Hindustan Times*, 23 May 2023, https://www.hindustantimes.com/india-news/bjp-tmc-mp-nusrat-jahan-for-beat-with-bamboo-sticks-remarks-basirhat-bengal-panchayat-elections-101684855510928.html.
7. 'Nusrat Jahan Ruhi.' PRS Legislative Research, https://prsindia.org/mptrack/17-lok-sabha/nusrat-jahan-ruhi.
8. Ibid.
9. Ibid.
10. Gupta, Poorvi. 'Basirhat MP Nusrat Jahan Rejects "Feminism" Says, "Equality Is Not Feminism"'. Feminism in India, 27 July 2020, https://feminisminindia.com/2020/07/27/basirhat-mp-nusrat-jahan-feminism-equality/#google_vignette.
11. Chakraborty, Saionee. 'For Me, Birthday Is Another Year of Experiences

and Craziness and Being Alive, Says Nusrat.' *Telegraph India*, 7 January 2022, www.telegraphindia.com/my-kolkata/people/for-me-birthday-is-another-year-of-experiences-and-craziness-and-being-alive-says-nusrat-jahan/cid/1846641.

12. Ibid.
13. Ibid.
14. Chakraborty, Snehamoy. 'Nusrat Jahan Ends Silence on Sandeshkhali, Says "Always Followed Party Guidelines".' *Telegraph India*, 25 February 2024, www.telegraphindia.com/west-bengal/nusrat-jahan-endssilence-on-sandeshkhali-says-always-followed-party-guidelines/cid/2002935.
15. Roy, Suryagni. 'Don't Need to Hold Political Post to Do Good Work: Ex-MP Nusrat Jahan.' *India Today*, 16 July 2024, www.indiatoday.in/india/story/nusrat-jahan-former-trinamool-mp-on-political-future-bengal-2567754-2024-07-16.
16. Ibid.
17. Ibid.
18. Ibid.
19. Ibid.

19. Iqra Hasan: A Silver Lining for Progressive Politics

1. Murarka, Shloka. 'Meet Iqra Hasan: SOAS Alum Making History as India's Youngest Female Muslim MP.' SOAS Blogs, 16 July 2024, www.soas.ac.uk/about/blogs/meet-iqra-hasan-soas-alum-making-history-indias-youngest-female-muslim-mp-0.
2. Ara, Ismat. 'Iqra Hasan: Balancing Tradition and Progress.' *Frontline*, 4 June 2024, https://frontline.thehindu.com/politics/profileof-samajwadi-party-mp-iqra-hasan-lok-sabha-election-2024/article68358344.ece.
3. 'Veteran Congress Leader Chaudhary Akhtar Hasan Dies at 82.' *The New Indian Express*, 25 November 2017, www.newindianexpress.com/nation/2017/Nov/25/veteran-congress-leader-chaudhary-akhtar-hasan-dies-at-82-1710788.html.
4. Ara, Ismat. 'Iqra Hasan: Balancing Tradition and Progress.' *Frontline*, 4 June 2024, https://frontline.thehindu.com/politics/profileof-samajwadi-party-mp-iqra-hasan-lok-sabha-election-2024/article68358344.ece.
5. Ibid.
6. Ibid.
7. Ibid.

8. Ibid.
9. Bordia, Radhika. 'In Kairana, BJP Battles SP Candidate Iqra Hasan's Family Legacy and a Simmering EBC Resentment.' *The Wire*, 18 April 2024, https://thewire.in/politics/in-kairana-bjp-battles-sp-candidate-iqra-hasans-family-legacy-and-a-simmering-ebc-resentment.
10. Mishra, Dhiraj. 'Carrying Forward Family Legacy, SP's Kairana Candidate Iqra Hasan Looks to Bridge "Communal Gap".' *The Indian Express*, 19 April 2024, https://indianexpress.com/elections/carrying-forward-family-legacy-sps-kairana-candidate-iqrahasan-looks-to-bridge-communal-gap-9278654/.
11. Ara, Ismat. 'Iqra Hasan: Balancing Tradition and Progress.' *Frontline*, 4 June 2024, https://frontline.thehindu.com/politics/profileof-samajwadi-party-mp-iqra-hasan-lok-sabha-election-2024/article68358344.ece.
12. Dilshad, Mohd. 'Ahead of Polls, Yogi Adityanath Rakes Up Kairana Exodus in UP Assembly.' *Times of India*, 13 February 2019, https://timesofindia.indiatimes.com/india/ahead-of-pollsyogi-adityanath-rakes-up-kairana-exodus-in-up-assembly/articleshow/67968277.cms.
13. Mishra, Dhiraj. 'Carrying Forward Family Legacy, SP's Kairana Candidate Iqra Hasan Looks to Bridge "Communal Gap".' *The Indian Express*, 19 April 2024, https://indianexpress.com/elections/carrying-forward-family-legacy-sps-kairana-candidate-iqra-hasan-looks-to-bridge-communal-gap-9278654/.
14. Bordia, Radhika. 'In Kairana, BJP Battles SP Candidate Iqra Hasan's Family Legacy and a Simmering EBC Resentment.' *The Wire*, 18 April 2024, https://thewire.in/politics/in-kairana-bjp-battles-sp-candidate-iqra-hasans-family-legacy-and-a-simmering-ebc-resentment.
15. Ara, Ismat. 'Iqra Hasan: Balancing Tradition and Progress.' *The Hindu*, 20 April 2024, https://www.thehindu.com/news/national/other-states/iqra-hasan-balancing-tradition-and-progress/article68358344.ece.
16. Mishra, Dhiraj. 'Carrying Forward Family Legacy, SP's Kairana Candidate Iqra Hasan Looks to Bridge "Communal Gap".' *The Indian Express*, 19 April 2024, https://indianexpress.com/elections/carrying-forward-family-legacy-sps-kairana-candidate-iqra-hasan-looks-to-bridge-communal-gap-9278654/.
17. Bordia, Radhika. 'In Kairana, BJP Battles SP Candidate Iqra Hasan's Family Legacy and a Simmering EBC Resentment.' *The Wire*, 18 April 2024, https://thewire.in/politics/in-kairana-bjp-battles-sp-candidate-

iqra-hasans-family-legacy-and-a-simmering-ebc-resentment.

18. Ara, Ismat. 'Iqra Hasan: Balancing Tradition and Progress.' *The Hindu*, 20 April 2024, https://www.thehindu.com/news/national/other-states/iqra-hasan-balancing-tradition-and-progress/article68358344.ece.
19. Ibid.
20. Murarka, Shloka. 'Meet Iqra Hasan: SOAS Alum Making History as India's Youngest Female Muslim MP.' SOAS Blogs, 16 July 2024, www.soas.ac.uk/about/blogs/meet-iqra-hasan-soas-alum-making-history-indias-youngest-female-muslim-mp-0.

Epilogue

1. Rangarajan, R. 'On Political Representation of Women: Explained.' *The Hindu*, 17 July 2024, https://www.thehindu.com/news/national/onpolitical-representation-of-women-explained/article68415532.ece.
2. 'Where Are the Women in Indian Politics?' *Economic and Political Weekly*, 2019, https://www.epw.in/engage/article/where-are-women-indian-politics.
3. Ghosh, Ambar Kumar. 'Women's Representation in India's Parliament: Measuring Progress, Analysing Obstacles.' *ORF Occasional Paper* No. 382, November 2022, https://www.orfonline.org/research/women-srepresentation-in-india-s-parliament-measuring-progress-analysing-obstacles.
4. Tomar, Ajay. 'Representation in the House: South States Have Less Than 10% Women Lawmakers; Andhra Leads.' *South First*, 20 September 2023, https://thesouthfirst.com/andhrapradesh/women-representation-in-thehouse-south-states-have-less-than-10-women-lawmakers-andhra-leads/.
5. Thomas, Rosie. *Bombay Before Bollywood: Film City Fantasies*. London: Orient Blackswan, 2013.
6. Roy, Parama. *Indian Traffic: Identities in Question in Colonial and Postcolonial India*. Berkeley: University of California Press, 1998.
7. 'What Did Sanjay Dutt Say When He Was Questioned and Was He Arrested and Charged?' *Times of India*, 31 March 2016, https://timesofindia.indiatimes.com/deep/bollywoods-original-bad-boy-sunjay-dutt-to-be-free-after-23-years/everything-you-need-to-know/what-did-sanjaydutt-say-when-he-was-questioned-and-was-he-arrested-and-charged/articleshow/50481657.cms.

8. 'Centre Acted Unethically in Bilkis Bano Case, Says Subhashini Ali.' *The Hindu*, 13 February 2024, https://www.thehindu.com/news/cities/Kochi/centre-acted-unethically-in-bilkis-bano-case-says-subhashini-ali/article67839483.ece.
9. Renuka, Methil. 'Former CPI(M) MP from Kanpur Subhashini Ali Plays Shah Rukh Khan's Mother in "Asoka".' *India Today*, 30 July 2001, https://www.indiatoday.in/magazine/eyecatchers/story/20010730-kanpur-subhashini-ali-plays-shah-rukh-khan-mother-in-asoka-773914-2001-07-29.
10. Gupta, Priya. 'Interview with Muzaffar Ali.' *Times of India*, 6 August 2015, https://timesofindia.indiatimes.com/entertainment/hindi/bollywood/news/muzaffar-ali-if-i-could-make-rekha-look-beautiful-i-could-also-make-other-women-look-beautiful/articleshow/48361485.cms.
11. Ali, Subhashini. 'A Life in Service.' *Seminar* 540. https://www.india-seminar.com/2004/540/540%20subhashini%20ali.htm.
12. Ibid.
13. Ibid.
14. 'Out with the Truth on Netaji, Says Subhashini Ali.' *Business Standard*, 6 April 2014, https://www.business-standard.com/article/news-ians/out-with-the-truth-on-netaji-says-subhashini-ali-election-special-114040600276_1.html.
15. Ali, Subhashini. 'A Life in Service.' *Seminar* 540. https://www.india-seminar.com/2004/540/540%20subhashini%20ali.htm.

Bibliography

1. 'About Moinul Hoque Choudhury.' *Moinul Hoque Choudhury Memorial Science College*, mhcmsc.in/about-moinul-hoque-choudhury.
2. 'Actress Speaks Out on Friends-Turned-Fugitive.' *The Telegraph*, 21 February 2012, https://www.telegraphindia.com/india/actress-speaks-out-onfriend-turned-fugitive/cid/449884.
3. 'All India Muslim Women Personal Law Board.' *Shaista Ambar*, https://www.shaistaambar.com/.
4. 'Assembly Election Race in Shrawasti.' *Election Fate*, 2009, https://www.electionfate.in/constituencies/Shrawasti.
5. 'Centre Acted Unethically in Bilkis Bano Case, Says Subhashini Ali.' *The Hindu*, 13 February 2024, https://www.thehindu.com/news/cities/Kochi/centre-acted-unethically-in-bilkis-bano-case-says-subhashini-ali/article67839483.ece.
6. 'Choudhury, Smt Rashida Haque.' *Data Is Info*, https://www.datais.info/loksabha/members/Choudhury+%2C+Smt.+Rashida+Haque/6062472b5a2b87eedf8e30be4b0a7b46/#google_vignette.
7. 'Cong Calm After Ranee Outburst.' *The Telegraph*, 9 February 2006, www.telegraphindia.com/north-east/cong-calm-after-ranee-outburst/cid/821455.
8. 'Congress Leaders Bharat & Ranee Narah Grabbed Govt Land to Set Up Tea Estate: Lakhimpur MLA Manab Deka.' *News Live*, 16 September 2023, https://newslivetv.com/congress-leaders-bharat-ranee-narahgrabbed-govt-land-to-set-up-tea-estate-lakhimpur-mla-manabdeka/.
9. 'Congress Mourns Loss of Leader Who Filled a Void.' *The Telegraph*, 11 July 2008, web.archive.org/web/20080803081742/http://www.telegraphindia.com/1080711/jsp/siliguri/story_9535076.jsp.

10. 'Death Anniversary of Moinul Haque Choudhury.' *The Assam Tribune*, 15 September 2010, assamtribune.com/death-anniversary-of-moinul-haque-choudhury.
11. 'Further Discussion on the Motion of Confidence in the Council of Minister Moved by Dr. Manmohan Singh on the 21st July, 2008 (Concluded).' *Lok Sabha Digital Library*, Parliament of India, https://eparlib.nic.in/bitstream/123456789/732817/1/10243.pdf.
12. 'Granddaughter's Defence: A Lyrical Account of the Personality of Akbar Jehan and Her Role in the Socio-Political Struggle in Kashmir.' *Frontline*, 1 October 2014, frontline.thehindu.com/books/granddaughters-defence/article6464596.ece.
13. 'History of Woman Suffrage/Volume 1/Chapter 14.' *Wikisource*, last modified 9 June 2025, https://en.wikisource.org/w/index.php?title=History_of_Woman_Suffrage/Volume_1/Chapter_14&oldid=10465421.
14. 'HT This Day: Jan 10, 1980 – Cong-I Gets Two-Thirds Majority.' *Hindustan Times*, 9 January 2022, www.hindustantimes.com/india-news/ht-this-day-jan-10-1980-cong-i-gets-two-thirds-majority-101641750140310.html.
15. 'Insider Tears into Muftis and Family Party.' *The Telegraph Online*, 2 March 2016, www.telegraphindia.com/india/insider-tears-into-muftis-and-family-party/cid/1515167.
16. 'J&K on Edge: Omar Abdullah, Mehbooba Mufti Under House Arrest.' *The Quint*, 5 August 2019, https://www.thequint.com/news/india/jammu-and-kashmir-crisis-mehbooba-mufti-omarabdullah-under-house-arrest.
17. 'Kairana Exodus: Hukum Singh Discusses UP's Law and Order with Rajnath Singh.' *The Indian Express*, 29 June 2016, https://indianexpress.com/article/india/india-news-india/kairana-hukum-singh-migration-hindu-uttar-pradesh-law-order-rajnath-singh-2882498/.
18. 'Kairana Lok Sabha Election Results 2019 UP: Tabassum Hasan, Who Won Last Year's Bypoll, Loses to BJP's Pradeep Chaudhary.' *DNA India*, 24 May 2019, https://www.dnaindia.com/india/report-kairana-lok-sabha-election-results-2019-up-tabassumhasan-who-won-last-year-s-bypoll-loses-to-bjp-s-pradeepchaudhary-2752345.
19. 'Mamtaz Sanghamita.' *Wikipedia*, 16 April 2025, en.wikipedia.org/wiki/Mamtaz_Sanghamita.
20. 'Marxist: Theoretical Quarterly of the Communist Party of India (Marxist).' *Marxist*, vol. XXXVIII, no. 4, October–December 2022, https://cpim.org/wp-content/uploads/old/marxist/marxist_oct-_dec_2022.pdf.

21. 'Meet Begum Tabassum Hasan, Who Sailed RLD Boat Against Modi Wave in Kairana.' *India Today*, 31 May 2018, https://www.indiatoday.in/india/story/meet-begum-tabassum-hasan-who-sailed-rldboat-against-modi-wave-in-kairana- 1246791-2018-05-31.
22. 'Mofida Ahmed – First Woman MP of Assam.' *MPositive.in*, 4 December 2018, www.mpositive.in/tag/mofida-ahmed-first-woman-mp-of-assam/.
23. 'Mofida Ahmed.' *Wikipedia*, 22 January 2025, en.wikipedia.org/wiki/Mofida_Ahmed.
24. 'National Herald.' *Parliament Digital Library*, 30 April 1964, https://eparlib.nic.in/handle/123456789/1011153?view_type=browse.
25. 'NC Pays Tributes to Begum Akbar Jahan.' *TwoCircles.net*, 12 July 2007, https://www.twocircles.net/2007jul12/nc_pays_tributes_begum_akbar_jahan.html.
26. 'Noorjehan Safia Niaz: Bharatiya Muslim Mahila Andolan.' *Ashoka*, https://www.ashoka.org/en-us/fellow/noorjehan-safia-niaz.
27. 'Nusrat Jahan Ruhi.' *PRS Legislative*, https://prsindia.org/mptrack/17-lok-sabha/nusrat-jahan-ruhi.
28. 'Out with the Truth on Netaji, Says Subhashini Ali.' *Business Standard*, 6 April 2014, https://www.business-standard.com/article/news-ians/out-with-the-truth-on-netaji-says-subhashini-ali-election-special-114040600276_1.html.
29. 'Parliamentary Consultative Committee Discuss 50 Years of ONGC.' *PIB*, 24 June 2005, https://www.pib.gov.in/newsite/erelcontent.aspx?relid=9840.
30. 'PDP Suffers Worst Electoral Result Since Its Formation 25 Years Back.' *Hindustan Times*, 8 October 2024, https://www.hindustantimes.com/india-news/pdp-suffers-worst-electoral-result-since-itsformation-25-years-back-101728374957059.html.
31. Peerzada, Ashiq. 'PDP Faces a Rout in J&K, Retains Only Three Seats.' *The Hindu*, 8 October 2024, https://www.thehindu.com/elections/jammu-and-kashmir-assembly/pdp-faces-a-rout-in-jk-retainsonly-three-seats/article68733849.ece.
32. 'Profile of Political Leaders: Moinul Haque Choudhury (1923–1976).' *Internet Archive*, 12 December 2014, https://web.archive.org/web/20141224090937/http:/www.unishemay.org/english-pages/geography-content/Profile%20of%20Political%20Leaders.pdf.
33. 'Ranee Deputy Whip of LS.' *The Assam Tribune*, 26 November 2009, archive.ph/20240526083313/www.webcitation.

org/6Bj3pcTjI?url=http://www.assamtribune.com/scripts/details.asp%3Fid=nov2609/at012.

34. 'Ranee Narah Takes Ball to Sonia Court.' *The Telegraph*, 10 February 2006, www.telegraphindia.com/north-east/ranee-narah-takes-ball-to-sonia-court/cid/82237.
35. 'Ranee Narah.' *Wikipedia*, last modified on 23 November 2024, https://en.wikipedia.org/w/index.php?title=Ranee_Narah&oldid=1259079981.
36. 'Rashida Haque Choudhury.' *Hindustan Times*, www.hindustantimes.com/elections/lok-sabha/candidates/rashida-haque-choudhury-GEAS23853.
37. 'Republic of India/Bharat.' *Worldwide Guide to Women in Leadership*, 12 February 2017, www.guide2womenleaders.com/India.htm.
38. 'Rocking at 72: Doordarshan News Anchor Salma Sultan Graces Ramp.' *MPositive.in*, 18 September 2019, www.mpositive.in/tag/salma-sultan/.
39. 'Second Wave Feminism Primary Sources & History | Gale.' *Gale*, n.d., https://www.gale.com/primary-sources/womens-studies/collections/second-wave-feminism#:~:text=The%20second%20wave%20feminism%20movement,spread%20to%20other%20Western%20countries.
40. 'Shrawasti.' *ElectionFate*, www.electionfate.in/constituencies/Shrawasti.
41. 'Tabassum Hasan is Now the First Muslim MP Elected from UP Since 2014.' *The Indian Express*, 31 May 2018, https://indianexpress.com/article/who-is/who-is-tabassum-hasan-knowabout-rld-candidate-for-kairana-bye-poll-5198354/.
42. 'UP Polls: Now Haider Khan Claims Threat to Life, Demands CBI Probe in Grandfather's Death.' *ETV Bharat*, 31 January 2022, https://www.etvbharat.com/english/state/uttar-pradesh/haiderali-khan-claims-threat-to-his-life-from-sp-rival-demands-cbiprobe-into-his-grandfathers-death/na20220131222520062.
43. 'Vajpayee, Advani to Attend Funeral of Begam Akbar Jehan.' *PTI*, 11 July 2000, m.rediff.com/news/2000/jul/11begum.htm.
44. 'Veteran Congress Leader Chaudhary Akhtar Hasan Dies at 82.' *The New Indian Express*, 25 November 2017, https://www.newindianexpress.com/nation/2017/Nov/25/veteran-congressleader-chaudhary-akhtar-hasan-dies-at-82-1710788.html.
45. 'Where Are the Women in Indian Politics?' *Economic and Political Weekly*, 2019, https://www.epw.in/engage/article/where-are-women-indian-politics.
46. 'সাংসদের রিপোর্ট কার্ড: মমতাজ সঙ্ঘমিতা' ['MP's Report Card: Mamtaz

Sanghamita']. *Anandabazar Patrika*, www.anandabazar.com/west-bengal/lok-sabha-election-2019-report-card-of-mp-mamtaz-sanghamita-1.974343.

47. Shairgojri, Aadil Ahmad, and Rashid Manzoor Bhat. 'Muslim Women and Politics of India.' *Multidisciplinary Output Research for Actual and International Issue*, vol. 2, no. 4, January 2023, doi.org/10.54443/morfai.v2i4.647.
48. Kaif, Aas Mohd. 'Tabassum Hasan: A Mascot of the Hindu-Muslim Unity and a United Opposition.' *The National Herald*, 1 June 2018, www.nationalheraldindia.com/india/tabassum-hasan-a-mascot-of-hindu-muslim-unity-and-a-united-opposition-kairana-bypoll-uttar-pradesh.
49. Rolland, Abby M. 'Muslim Women Political Leaders and Electoral Participation in Muslim-Majority Countries.' Student Research Paper, *ANTH 218: Islam and Women*, Gettysburg College, 2015, cupola.gettysburg.edu/islamandwomen/5/.
50. Farooqui, Adnan. 'Political Representation of a Minority: Muslim Representation in Contemporary India.' *India Review*, vol. 19, no. 2, 19 May 2020, pp. 153–75, doi.org/10.1080/14736489.2020.1744996.
51. Tomar, Ajay. 'Representation in the House: South States Have Less Than 10% Women Lawmakers; Andhra Leads.' *South First*, 20 September 2023, https://thesouthfirst.com/andhrapradesh/women-representation-in-the-house-south-states-have-less-than-10-women-lawmakers-andhra-leads/.
52. Ghosh, Ambar Kumar. 'Women's Representation in India's Parliament: Measuring Progress, Analysing Obstacles.' *ORF Occasional Paper*, no. 382, November 2022, https://www.orfonline.org/research/women-s-representation-in-india-s-parliament-measuring-progress-analysing-obstacles.
53. Dhar, Anirudhha. 'BJP Slams "Part-Time Politician" TMC's Nusrat Jahan for "Beat with Sticks" Remarks.' *Hindustan Times*, 23 May 2023, https://www.hindustantimes.com/india-news/bjp-tmc-mpnusrat-jahan-for-beat-with-bamboo-sticks-remarks-basirhatbengal-panchayat-elections-101684855510928.html.
54. Katz, Ariel. 'Margaret Thatcher, Golda Meir, and Indira Gandhi's Actions and Rhetoric Regarding Feminism and Gender During Their Ascent to Power.' Senior thesis, submitted to Professor Hilary Appel and Dean Gregory Hess, Fall 2012, https://scholarship.claremont.edu/cgi/viewcontent.cgi?article=1515&context=cmc_theses.

55. Ganguly, Arnab. 'Nusrat Jahan, the Spotlight Never Leaves Her.' *The Telegraph*, 21 June 2021, https://www.telegraphindia.com/west-bengal/nusrat-jahan-thespotlight-never-leaves-her/cid/1819585.
56. Ali, Arshad. 'West Bengal: Late TMC Leader Sultan Ahmed's Son Sharique May Get Ticket for Uluberia Bye-Polls.' *DNA*, 26 October 2017, www.dnaindia.com/india/report-west-bengal-late-tmc-leader-sultan-ahmed-s-son-sharique-may-get-ticket-for-uluberia-bye-polls-2555573.
57. Hussain, Ashiq. 'PDP Appoints Mehbooba's Daughter Iltija Mufti as Her Media Adviser.' *Hindustan Times*, 31 August 2023, www.hindustantimes.com/cities/chandigarh-news/pdp-appoints-mehbooba-s-daughter-iltija-mufti-as-her-media-adviser-101693421952220.html.
58. Bharadwaj, Ashutosh. 'Why Alliance with Ajmal's AUDF May Not Help Assam Congress Resolve Its "Muslim Dilemma".' *The Wire*, 4 April 2021, thewire.in/politics/why-alliance-with-ajmals-audf-may-not-help-assam-congress-resolve-its-muslim-dilemma.
59. 'Hereditary Politics: Political Families of India.' *India Today*, 12 April 2004, http://indiatoday.intoday.in/story/hereditary-politics-political-families-of-india/1/196747.html.
60. Kohli, Atul, editor. *The Success of India's Democracy*. Cambridge University Press, 2001.
61. Roy, Avijit. 'Mausam Noor Raises Issue of Ganga Erosion in Parliament.' *Millennium Post*, 24 July 2024, https://www.millenniumpost.in/bengal/mausam-noor-raises-issue-of-gangaerosion-in-parliament-573081.
62. Javaid, Azaan. 'UP Elections 2017: Friends and Foes—Kairana Divided Between Two Families.' *DNA*, 4 February 2017, www.dnaindia.com/india/report-up-elections-2017-friends-and-foes-kairana-divided-between-two-families-2311601.
63. Mirza, Azim. 'सपा की पूर्व सांसद रुबाब सईदा का निधन, आज देर रात बहराइच में होगा अंतिम संस्कार'['Death of Former SP MP Rubab Sayeda, the Last Rites to Be Conducted in Bahraich Today Late Night']. *Navbharat Times*, 6 February 2024, navbharattimes.indiatimes.com/state/uttar-pradesh/bahraich/up-news-samajwadi-party-mp-rubab-sayda-death-know-all-about-latest-news-update/articleshow/107452714.cms.
64. Dimitrov, B.E. George, and Noblelyne Nongkynrih. 'A Study on Muslim Women Political Participation in India.' *International Journal of Research*, vol. 4, no. 09, August 2017, pp. 41–54, journals.pen2print.org/index.php/ijr/article/view/8448/8181.
65. Masood, Bashaarat. 'Mehbooba Mufti Re-Elected PDP Chief for Fourth

Time, Blows Bugle for LS Polls.' *The Indian Express*, 26 October 2023, indianexpress.com/article/india/jk-former-cm-mehbooba-mufti-re-elected-pdp-chief-6th-straight-term-9000637/.

66. Masood, Bashaarat. 'Mufti's Son Rise in Kashmir Politics: Dynasty is Destiny?' *The Indian Express*, 20 January 2016, indianexpress.com/article/explained/muftis-son-rise-in-kashmir-politics-dynasty-is-destiny/.
67. Roy, Briti. 'Mamtaz Sanghamita.' *Oneindia*, 1 January 2021, www.oneindia.com/politicians/mamtaz-sanghamita-36765.html.
68. Pateman, Carole. *The Disorder of Women: Democracy, Feminism and Political Theory*. Cambridge: Polity Press, 1990.
69. Jaffrelot, Christophe, et al. 'Understanding Muslim Voter Behaviour.' *Seminar*, no. 602, 2009, www.india-seminar.com/2009/602/602_christophe_et_al.htm.
70. Joly, Danièle, and Khursheed Wadia. *Muslim Women and Power: Political and Civic Engagement in West European Societies*. London: Palgrave Macmillan, 2017.
71. Lahiri, Deepanjali, and Ruha Shadab. 'Muslim Women in India's Workforce: Where Are They?' *India Development Review*, 30 July 2021, idronline.org/article/diversity-inclusion/muslim-women-in-indias-workforce-where-are-they/.
72. Goswami, Dev. 'Tabassum Hasan First Muslim to Enter Lok Sabha from UP Since 2014.' *India Today*, 31 May 2018, www.indiatoday.in/india/story/tabassum-hasan-first-muslim-to-enter-lok-sabha-from-up-since-2014-1246767-2018-05-31.
73. Mishra, Dheeraj. 'Carrying Forward Family Legacy, SP's Kairana Candidate Iqra Hasan Looks to Bridge "Communal Gap".' *The Indian Express*, 19 April 2024, indianexpress.com/elections/carrying-forward-family-legacy-sps-kairana-candidate-iqra-hasan-looks-to-bridge-communal-gap-9278654/.
74. *Digital Sansad*. 'Member Detail.' sansad.in/ls/members/biographyM/4261?from=members.
75. *Digital Sansad*. 'Questions & Answers.' sansad.in/ls/questions/questions-and-answers.
76. *Election Commission of India*. 'List of Successful Candidates.' 10 August 2018, old.eci.gov.in/files/file/2843-list-of-successful-candidates/.
77. Roy, Esha. 'Whichever the Party, All Politics in Malda Is Still About Only One Family.' *The Indian Express*, 14 April 2016, indianexpress.com/article/india/india-news-india/whichever-the-party-all-politics-in-malda-is-still-about-only-one-family/.

78. 'BJP Ends Alliance With PDP: Can't Treat J&K as Enemy Territory, Says Mehbooba After Resigning.' *The Economic Times*, 19 June, economictimes.indiatimes.com/news/politics-and-nation/bjp-ends-alliance-with-pdp-in-jammu-and-kashmir-presidents-rule-likely-in-the-state/articleshow/64646710.cms?from=mdr.
79. McDougall, Gay. 'Meeting the Challenges of Discrimination Against Women from Minority Groups.' *Statement on International Women's Day*, 7 March 2006. *United Nations Human Rights*, www.ohchr.org/en/statements-and-speeches/2009/10/meeting-challenges-discrimination-against-women-minority-groups.
80. Irani, Gustasp, and Jeroo Irani. 'The Begums of Bhopal: A Tale of Royal Women and Their City.' *Outlook Traveller*, 2 November 2024, www.outlooktraveller.com/experiences/heritage/the-begums-of-bhopal-a-tale-of-royal-women-and-their-city.
81. Prakash, Gyan. *Emergency Chronicles: Indira Gandhi and Democracy's Turning Point*. Princeton: Penguin Viking, 2018.
82. Dalwai, Hamid U. *Muslim Politics in India*. Bombay: Nachiketa Publication, 1968.
83. al-Turabi, Hasan. 'The Islamic State.' *Voices of Resurgent Islam*, edited by John Esposito, New York: Oxford University Press, 1983, pp. 244.
84. Coffe, Hilde, and Selin Dilli. 'The Gender Gap in Political Participation in Muslim-Majority Countries.' *International Political Science Review*, vol. 36, no. 5, 12 May 2014, doi.org/10.1177/0192512114528228.
85. Sarma, Himanta Biswa [@himantabiswa]. 'Congratulation to Smti Rani Narah for her Induction into Union Council of Ministers.' *X*, 28 Oct. 2012, x.com/himantabiswa/status/262449182474903553.
86. 'Opportunistic BJP-PDP Alliance Cost India Strategically: Rahul.' *Business Standard*, 19 July 2018, www.business-standard.com/article/news-ians/opportunistic-bjp-pdp-alliance-cost-indiastrategically-rahul-118061900962_1.html.
87. Harun Khan [@iamharunkhan]. *Images and Video on X Handle of Akhilesh Yadav's Visit to Yasar Shah's House After Rubab Sayda's Demise*, x.com/iamharunkhan/status/1761329386924781667.
88. 'Meet Begum Tabassum Hasan, Who Sailed RLD Boat Against Modi Wave in Kairana.' *India Today*, 31 May 2018, www.indiatoday.in/india/story/meet-begum-tabassum-hasan-who-sailed-rld-boat-against-modi-wave-in-kairana-1246791-2018-05-31.
89. 'Assam's First Woman MP Mofida Ahmed.' *India Today*, 8 April 2024,

www.indiatodayne.in/visualstories/webstories/assams-first-woman-mp-mofida-ahmed-124383-08-04-2024.

90. 'India. Parliamentary Debate.' *Rajya Sabha*, 24 August 1983, pp. 202–204 (Maimoona Sultan), www.rsdebate.nic.in/bitstream/123456789/363170/1/PD_127_24081983_21_p204_p206_7.pdf.
91. Indo-Asian News Service. 'Muslim Representation Increases to 27 From its Lowest Margin in Previous Lok Sabha.' *India Today*, 26 May 2019, www.indiatoday.in/elections/lok-sabha-2019/story/muslim-representation-27-lowest-margin-17th-lok-sabha-1534804-2019-05-26.
92. Inter-Parliamentary Union. 'Women in Politics: New Data Shows Growth but Also Setbacks.' *Press Release*, 10 Mar. 2021, www.ipu.org/news/women-in-politics-2021.
93. Lahiri, Ishadhrita. 'Malda South: Can Congress Save Ghani Khan's Turf or Will BJP or TMC Breach It?' *The Quint*, 4 May 2024, www.thequint.com/elections/malda-south-west-bengal-tmc-bjp-congress-ghani-khan-2024-lok-sabha-elections.
94. Ara, Ismat. 'Iqra Hasan: Balancing Tradition and Progress.' *Frontline*, 4 July 2024, frontline.thehindu.com/politics/profile-of-samajwadi-party-mp-iqra-hasan-lok-sabha-election-2024/article68358344.ece.
95. Zenger, Jack, and Joseph Folkman. 'Women Score Higher Than Men in Most Leadership Skills.' *Harvard Business Review*, 25 June 2019, hbr.org/2019/06/research-women-score-higher-than-men-in-most-leadership-skills.
96. Bayes, Jane H., and Nayereh Tohidi, editors. *Globalization, Gender and Religion: The Politics of Women's Rights in Catholic and Muslim Contexts*. New York: Palgrave Macmillan, 2001.
97. Freeman, Jo. *A Room at a Time: How Women Entered Party Politics*. Lanham, MD: Rowman and Littlefield, 2000.
98. Lovenduski, Joni, and Pippa Norris, editors. *Women in Politics*. Oxford and New York: Oxford University Press, 1996.
99. Lovenduski, Joni, and Jill Hills, editors. *The Politics of the Second Electorate: Women and Public Participation; Britain, USA, Canada, Australia, France, Spain, West Germany, Italy, Sweden, Finland, Eastern Europe, USSR, Japan*. Boston: Routledge and Kegan Paul, 1981.
100. Jones, Justin. 'Muslim Feminism as Islamic Modernism: Women's Activism in India Between the Quran and the Constitution.' *Modern Asian Studies* 58, no. 2, 9 October 2024, pp. 421–427, https://www.cambridge.org/core/journals/modern-asian-studies/article/muslim-

feminism-as-islamic-modernism-womensactivism-in-india-between-the-quran-and-the-constitution/34ECABF832630CCAF5582837373 0A34A.

101. Kumari, Khusboo. 'Paying Tribute to Pathbreaking and Forgotten, Muslim Women from the 20th Century.' *The Wire*, 30 May 2018, https://thewire.in/women/paying-tribute-to-pathbreaking-and-forgotten-muslim-women-from-the-20th-century.
102. Calman, Leslie J. *Toward Empowerment: Women and Movement Politics in India*. New York and Abingdon: Routledge, 2018.
103. Beaman, Lori, Esther Duflo, Rohini Pande, and Petia Topalova. 'Political Reservation and Substantive Representation: Evidence from Indian Village Councils.' *India Policy Forum*, 2010–11, https://www.ncaer.org/wp-content/uploads/2022/09/4_Lori-Beaman_Esther-Duflo_Rohini-Pande_Petia-Topalova.pdf.
104. Torregrosa, Luisita Lopez. 'Evaluating Challenges Women Face.' *The New York Times*, 6 March 2012, https://www.nytimes.com/2012/03/07/us/07iht-letter07.html.
105. Erickson, Lynda. 'Making Her Way In: Women, Parties, and Candidates in Canada'. In *Gender and Party Politics*, edited by Joni Lovenduski and Pippa Norris. London: Sage Publications, 1993.
106. Conway, M. Margaret. 'Women and Political Participation.' *Political Science and Politics* 34, no. 2, June 2001, pp. 231–233.
107. *Madhusudan Bag vs Aparupa Poddar (Afrin Ali) And Ors*. Calcutta High Court, 4 July 2014, https://indiankanoon.org/doc/72941143/.
108. Sultan, Maimoona, and Shahbano Begum. *A Trip to Europe*. Translated by G.B. Baksh. Calcutta: Thacker, Spink & Co., 1914, https://archive.org/details/triptoeuropetran00maimuoft/page/6/mode/2up.
109. Mohan, Manasa. 'President Who Took a Tranquiliser After Signing Away India's Democratic Rights to Indira.' *The Print*, 11 February 2019, https://theprint.in/theprint-profile/president-who-took-a-tranquiliserafter-signing-away-indias-democratic-rights-to-indira/190303/.
110. Aiyar, Mani Shankar. 'Mehbooba Was Burdened by Her Father with an Impossible Legacy.' *NDTV*, 22 June 2018, https://www.ndtv.com/opinion/mehbooba-was-burdened-by-her-father-with-an-impossible-legacy-by-mani-shankar-aiyar-1871474.
111. Sawer, Marian, Manon Tremblay, and Linda Trimble. *Representing Women in Parliament: A Comparative Study*. Abingdon: Routledge, 2006.
112. Tadros, Mariz, ed. *Women in Politics: Gender, Power and Development*. London and New York: Zed Books, 2014.

113. Hasan, Masoodul. 'Bahraich SP MLA Quits in Protest.' *Hindustan Times*, 11 February 2007, https://www.hindustantimes.com/india/bahraich-sp-mla-quits-in-protest/story-MXATuPEW4CI8lMdImKGa6L.html.

114. Hasan, Masoodul. 'Women Panel Refutes SP Leader Charges.' *Hindustan Times*, 5 February 2007, https://www.hindustantimes.com/india/women-panel-refutes-sp-leader-charges/story-cV1oaBRxY6cLhhYje4DpoM.html.

115. Noor, Mausam. Interview by Vasudha Venugopal. 'Meet Our MPs: TMC MP Mausam Noor.' *NDTV*, 18 December 2024, https://www.ndtv.com/video/meet-our-mps-tmc-mp-mausam-noor-875060.

116. Renuka, Methil. 'Former CPI(M) MP from Kanpur Subhashini Ali Plays Shah Rukh Khan's Mother in *Asoka*.' *India Today*, 30 July 2001. https://www.indiatoday.in/magazine/eyecatchers/story/20010730-kanpur-subhashini-ali-plays-shah-rukh-khan-mother-in-asoka-773914-2001-07-29.

117. Ministry of Petroleum & Natural Gas. *Parliamentary Consultative Committee Discuss 50 Years of ONGC*. Government of India. https://pib.gov.in/newsite/erelcontent.aspx?relid=9840.

118. Dilshad, Mohd. 'Ahead of Polls, Yogi Adityanath Rakes Up Kairana Exodus in UP Assembly.' *Times of India*, 13 February 2019. https://timesofindia.indiatimes.com/india/ahead-of-pollsyogi-adityanath-rakes-up-kairana-exodus-in-up-assembly/articleshow/67968277.cms.

119. Kidwai, Mohsina, and Rasheed Kidwai. *My Life in Indian Politics*. Gurugram: HarperCollins, 2022.

120. Maulana Abdul Majid Daryabadi. *Tafsir-Ul-Qur'an Vol. IV: Translation and Commentary of the Holy Qur'an*. Karachi: Darul-Ishaat, 1991.

121. Gupta, Monobina. 'Interview: "Post Sachar Report, Condition of Indian Muslims Unchanged".' *The Wire*, 20 February 2019. https://thewire.in/rights/interview-post-sachar-report-condition-of-indian-muslims-unchange.

122. Ahmad, Mudasir. 'Nepotism Row Erupts as Mehbooba Mufti's Cousin Named Executive Officer of Khadi Board.' *The Wire*, 24 February 2018. https://thewire.in/politics/nepotism-row-erupts-as-mehbooba-muftis-cousin-named-executive-officer-of-khadi-board.

123. Falahi, Mumtaz Alam. 'Representation of Muslim Women in Lok Sabha Since Independence.' *TwoCircles.net*, 21 May 2009. https://twocircles.net/2009may21/representation_muslim_women_lok_sabha_independence.html.

124. Urbinati, Nadia. *Representative Democracy: Principles and Genealogy*. Chicago: University of Chicago Press, 2008.
125. Bhandare, Namita. 'Muslim Women Are 6.9% of Population. In Lok Sabha, 0.7%.' *IndiaSpend*, 26 April 2019. https://www.indiaspend.com/muslim-women-are-6-9-of-population-in-lok-sabha-0-/.
126. National Bal Bhavan. 'Overview.' https://nationalbalbhavan.nic.in/aboutus/overview.html.
127. National Bal Bhavan. 'Chairpersons of National Bal Bhavan.' https://nationalbalbhavan.nic.in/aboutus/nbb-chairperson.html.
128. Majumdar, Neera. 'Indira Gandhi's Emergency Era Through Cartoons.' *The Print*, 25 June 2018. https://theprint.in/last-laughs/indira-gandhis-emergency-era-through-cartoons/74536/.
129. Francis, Nikita, and Vignesh Radhakrishnan. 'Data | Eighteenth Lok Sabha Has Lowest Share of Muslim MPs in Six Decades.' *The Hindu*, 18 June 2024. https://www.thehindu.com/data/dataeighteenth-lok-sabha-has-lowest-share-of-muslim-mps-in-sixdecades/article68285104.ece.
130. Hebbar, Nistula. 'Analysis: BJP Didn't Want to Face 2019 Polls as PDP's Ally.' *The Hindu*, 30 September 2023. https://www.thehindu.com/news/national/other-states/analysis-why-the-pdp-bjp-alliance-ended/article61824478.ece.
131. Khandekar, Nivedita. 'British Governor Used to Rest Here Before Boarding Train.' *Hindustan Times*, 15 September 2013. https://www.hindustantimes.com/delhi/british-governor-usedto-rest-here-before-boarding-train/story-iyucfK3vk6Bb0cuW7DLWwJ.html.
132. Khan, Nyla Ali. 'Faith That Moved Mountains.' *The Hindu*, 11 August 2012. www.thehindu.com/opinion/op-ed/faith-that-moved-mountains/article3751106.ece.
133. Khan, Nyla Ali. 'Remembering Begum Akbar Jehan Abdullah.' *Daily Times*, 3 September 2018. https://dailytimes.com.pk/291905/remembering-begum-akbar-jehan-abdullah/.
134. Khan, Nyla Ali. 'Until Lions Have Their Historians, Tales of the Hunt Shall Always Glorify the Hunters: Sheikh Mohammad Abdullah, History Retold.' *Counter Punch*, 22 January 2015. https://www.counterpunch.org/2016/01/22/until-lions-havetheir-historians-tales-of-the-hunt-shall-always-glorify-thehunters-sheikh-mohammad-abdullah-history-retold/.
135. Khan, Nyla Ali. *Sheikh Mohammad Abdullah's Reflections on Kashmir*. London: Palgrave Macmillan, 2018. http://ndl.ethernet.edu.et/bitstream/123456789/61742/1/303.pdf.pdf.

136. Khan, Nyla Ali. *The Life of a Kashmiri Woman: Dialectic of Resistance and Accommodation*. New York: Palgrave Pivot, 2014.
137. OHCHR. 'Meeting the Challenges of Discrimination Against Women From Minority Groups.' n.d. https://www.ohchr.org/en/statements-and-speeches/2009/10/meeting-challenges-discrimination-against-women-minority-groups.
138. Khalidi, Omar. *Indian Muslims Since Independence*. New Delhi: Vikas Publishing House, 1998.
139. Rashid, Omar. '3 ex-MPs, 5 ex-MLAs Leave BSP, Congress for Samajwadi Party.' *The Hindu*, 9 November 2020. https://www.thehindu.com/news/national/other-states/former-mps-mlasleave-bsp-congress-for-samajwadi-party/article33058936.ece.
140. Rajput, Pam, and Usha Thakkar. *Women in State Politics in India: Missing in the Corridors of Power*. Abingdon: Routledge, 2023.
141. Parliament of India, Lok Sabha Digital Library. 'Further Discussion on the Motion of Confidence in the Council of Minister Moved by Dr. Manmohan Singh on the 21st July, 2008 (Concluded).' 22 July 2008. https://eparlib.nic.in/handle/123456789/732817?view_type=browse.
142. Pateman, Carole. *The Disorder of Women: Democracy, Feminism and Political Theory*. Cambridge: Polity Press, 1990.
143. Shrivastava, Piyush. 'SP Paving Way for Rajnath's Victory.' *India Today*, 16 April 2009. www.indiatoday.in/election-news/story/sp-paving-way-for-rajnath-s-victory-44533-2009-04-15.
144. Gupta, Poorvi. 'Basirhat MP Nusrat Jahan Rejects "Feminism" Says, "Equality Is Not Feminism".' *Feminism in India*, 27 July 2020. https://feminisminindia.com/2020/07/27/basirhat-mp-nusrat-jahan-feminism-equality/.
145. *Population Census Data. Census 2011 Data*. www.census2011.co.in/religion.php.
146. Chawla, Prabhu. 'Meerut Burns in Communal Fire Ignited by Squabble for 200 Sq Ft Property.' *India Today*, 31 October 1982. https://www.indiatoday.in/magazine/special-report/story/19821031-meerutburns-in-communal-fire-ignited-by-squabble-for-200-sq-ftproperty-772302-2013-08-26.
147. Press Trust of India. '1 Family, 2 Parties, 3 Candidates: The Fight for Bengal's Malda.' *NDTV*, 21 April 2019. www.ndtv.com/india-news/lok-sabha-elections-2019-mausam-noor-isha-khan-abu-hashem-choudhary-fight-for-malda-west-bengal-2026410.

148. Narayan, Priyanjali. 'How 5 Terrorists Freed for Home Minister's Daughter Set a Benchmark.' *India Today*, 13 September 2024. https://www.indiatoday.in/history-of-it/story/rubaiya-sayeed-muftimohammed-sayeed-ic814-hijack-terrorist-swap-benchmarkomar-abdullah-national-conference-2599163-2024-09-13.
149. Press Trust of India. '"I Don't Do Even for CM": TMC MP Nusrat Jahan Loses Temper During Roadshow, Stokes Controversy.' *News18*, 29 March 2021. https://www.news18.com/news/politics/dont-do-even-for-cmtmc-mp-nusrat-jahan-loses-temper-during-roadshow-stokescontroversy-3586253.html.
150. Press Trust of India. 'BSP's Kaiser Jahan and Jasmir Ansari Join Congress.' *Times of India*, 4 March 2019. https://timesofindia.indiatimes.com/city/lucknow/bsps-kaiser-jahan-and-jasmir-ansari-join-congress/articleshow/68258374.cms.
151. Press Trust of India. 'Former Samajwadi Party MP Rubab Sayeda Passes Away.' *The Print*, February 2024. https://theprint.in/india/former-samajwadi-party-mp-rubab-sayeda-passes-away/1956122.
152. Press Trust of India. 'Mehbooba's Daughter Iltija Mufti Appointed Her Media Advisor.' *The Indian Express*, 30 August 2023. https://indianexpress.com/article/cities/srinagar/mehboobas-daughter-iltija-mufti-appointed-her-media-advisor-8916668/.
153. Press Trust of India. 'Narada Sting Operation Case: TMC MP Aparupa Poddar Moves to Calcutta HC for Quashing CBI FIR.' *The Indian Express*, 22 February 2024. https://indianexpress.com/article/india/narada-sting-operation-case-tmc-mp-aparupa-poddar-moves-to-calcutta-hc-for-quashing-cbi-fir-4627605/.
154. Press Trust of India. 'Riverbank Erosion, Ghani Khan's Legacy Likely Factors in Bengal's Malda Dakshin Lok Sabha Seat.' *The Economic Times*, 7 April 2024. https://economictimes.indiatimes.com/news/elections/lok-sabha/west-bengal/riverbank-erosion-ghani-khans-legacy-likely-factors-in-bengals-malda-dakshin-lok-sabha-seat/articleshow/109100594.cms.
155. Press Trust of India. 'SP MLA in Coma: Guv Sends Plea Seeking His Disqualification To.' *Business Standard*, 24 November 2015. www.business-standard.com/article/pti-stories/sp-mla-in-coma-guv-sends-plea-seeking-his-disqualification-to-115112401421_1.html.
156. Press Trust of India. 'Sportsperson-Turned-Politician Narah Gets Ministerial Berth.' *Zee News*, 28 October 2012. web.archive.org/

web/20180630153208/http://zeenews.india.com/news/nation/sportsperson-turned-politician-narah-gets-minister_808124.html.

157. Press Trust of India. 'Sultan Ahmed Was Under Stress Due to CBI Interrogation: Mamata Banerjee.' *The Indian Express*, 4 September 2017. https://indianexpress.com/article/india/ahmed-was-under-stress-due-to-cbi-interrogation-mamata-banerjee-4828702/.
158. Bordia, Radhika. 'In Kairana, BJP Battles SP Candidate Iqra Hasan's Family Legacy and a Simmering EBC Resentment.' *The Wire*, 18 April 2024. https://thewire.in/politics/in-kairana-bjp-battles-sp-candidate-iqra-hasans-family-legacy-and-a-simmering-ebc-resentment.
158. Chattopadhyay, Raghabendra, and Esther Duflo. 'Women as Policy Makers: Evidence from a Randomized Policy Experiment in India.' *Econometrica* 72, no. 5 (September 2004): 1409–1443. https://doi.org/10.1111/j.1468-0262.2004.00539.x.
159. Karmakar, Rahul. 'Ex-Cricketer Clean Bowls Dissidence.' *Hindustan Times*, 26 March 2009. https://archive.ph/20240526022510/www.webcitation.org/69HmXHb5D?url=http://www.hindustantimes.com/News-Feed/India/Ex-cricketer-clean-bowls-dissidence/Article1-393162.aspx.
160. Vora, Rajendra, and Suhas Palshikar, editors. *Indian Democracy: Meanings and Practices*. New Delhi: Sage Publications, 2003.
161. Guha, Ramachandra. *India After Gandhi: The History of the World's Largest Democracy*. New Delhi: Penguin, 2007.
162. Singh, Ramendra. 'It's BJP vs BSP in Central UP, Bundelkhand Today.' *The Indian Express*, 30 April 2014. https://indianexpress.com/article/political-pulse/its-bjp-vs-bsp-in-central-up-bundelkhand-today/.
163. Ohlan, Ramphul. 'Muslim Women in India: Status of Demographic, Socioeconomic and Health Inequalities.' *Journal of Muslim Minority Affairs* 40, no. 3 (9 September 2020): 429–440.
164. Rangarajan, R. 'On Political Representation of Women: Explained.' *The Hindu*, 17 July 2024. https://www.thehindu.com/news/national/on-political-representation-of-women-explained/article68415532.ece.
165. Kidwai, Rasheed. 'Women's Reservation Bill May Open Pandora's Box.' *India Today*, 20 September 2023. https://www.indiatoday.in/opinion/story/womens-reservation-bill-may-open-pandoras-box-2437970-2023-09-20.
166. Sen, Ronojoy. *House of the People: Parliament and the Making of Indian Democracy*. New Delhi: Cambridge University Press, 2022. https://doi.org/10.1017/9781009180245.

167. Tewari, Ruhi, and Abhishek Mishra. 'Every Second ST, Every Third Dalit & Muslim in India Poor, Not Just Financially: UN Report.' *The Print*, 12 July 2019. https://theprint.in/india/every-secondst-every-third-dalit-muslim-in-india-poor-not-just-financiallyun-report/262270/.
168. Bergeron, Ryan. '"The Seventies": Feminism Makes Waves.' *CNN*, 17 August 2015. https://edition.cnn.com/2015/07/22/living/the-seventies-feminism-womens-lib/index.html.
169. Yunus, Saba, and Manorama Gupta. 'Role of Indian Muslim Women in Politics.' Paper presented at *International Conference on Law, Education, Business and Corporate Social Responsibilities*, Budapest, Hungary, 4–5 September 2017. https://eares.org/siteadmin/upload/6486ED0917024.pdf.
170. Bandhopadhyay, Sabyasachi. 'In Malda, It's Still All About Ghani Khan.' *The Indian Express*, 23 April 2014. https://indianexpress.com/article/political-pulse/in-malda-its-still-all-about-ghani-khan/.
171. Chakraborty, Saionee. 'For Me, Birthday Is Another Year of Experiences and Craziness and Being Alive, Says Nusrat.' *The Telegraph*, 7 January 2022. https://www.telegraphindia.com/my-kolkata/people/for-mebirthday-is-another-year-of-experiences-and-craziness-andbeing-alive-says-nusrat-jahan/cid/1846641.
172. Ahmed, Sajda. 'An Educator and Social Worker, Sajda Ahmed Is the Wife of the Late Sri Sultan Ahmed, a Prominent Parliamentarian Who Represented the Constituency of Uluberia in the 15th and 16th Lok Sabha. For Several Decades, Sajda Ahmed Had an Unwavering Presence and Provided Constant Support to Her Husband.' *Facebook*, 11 January 2018. https://www.facebook.com/sajdaahmedtmc/posts/an-educator-and-social-worker-sajda-ahmed-is-the-wife-of-the-late-sri-sultan-ahm/153725768612257/.
173. Samajwadi Party. 'Condolence Message on the Death of Rubab Sayeda.' *X (formerly Twitter)*, 6 February 2024. https://x.com/samajwadiparty/status/1754754749906252213.
174. Tayyen, Sana. 'From Orientalist Sexual Object to Burkini Terrorist Threat: Muslim Women through Evolving Lens.' *Islamophobia Studies Journal* 4, no. 1 (October 2017): 101–114.
175. Rai, Sandeep. 'Exodus of Hindu Families from Kairana a Reality, Finds NHRC Probe Report.' *Times of India*, 22 September 2016. https://timesofindia.indiatimes.com/city/meerut/exodus-of-hindu-families-from-kairana-a-reality-finds-nhrc-probe-report/articleshow/54451892.cms.

176. Chowdhury, Santanu. 'Adhir Fails to Retain Baharampur, Isha Holds Congress' Fort in Malda Dakshin.' *The Indian Express*, 5 June 2024. https://indianexpress.com/article/cities/kolkata/adhir-fails-to-retain-baharampur-isha-holds-congress-fort-in-malda-dakshin-9372845/.

177. De Sarkar, Saumya. 'TMC MP Mausam Noor Back Home Ends Speculations and Worries of Party Leaders and Workers.' *The Telegraph*, 20 March 2024. https://www.telegraphindia.com/west-bengal/tmc-mp-mausam-noor-back-home-ends-speculations-and-worries-of-party-leaders-and-workers/cid/2008042.

178. Akhtar, Shabina. 'BJP Will Play Communal Card but We Will Stick to Development Agenda: TMC's Uluberia Candidate.' *E News Room*, 2 January 2018. https://enewsroom.in/bjp-tmc-uluberia-sajda-sultan-ahmed/.

179. Aktar, Shabina. 'Interview with Sajda Ahmed.' *E News Room*, 2 January 2018. https://enewsroom.in/bjp-tmc-uluberia-sajdasultan-ahmed/.

180. Sharda, Shailvee. 'Former BSP MP from Sitapur Joins Congress with Her Husband.' *Times of India*. https://timesofindia.indiatimes.com/city/lucknow/formerbsp-mp-from-sitapur-joins-congress-with-her-husband/articleshow/68264530.cms.

181. Sharda, Shailvee. 'Mohd Jasmeer Ansari: Once a Tea-Seller, Now an MLA.' *Times of India*, 17 February 2017. https://timesofindia.indiatimes.com/elections/assembly-elections/uttar-pradesh/news/mohd-jasmeer-ansari-once-a-tea-seller-now-an-mla/articleshow/57211910.cms.

182. Arnimesh, Shanker. 'New Election, Old Rivalry: Jailed Azam Khan & Son Make It "People vs Nawabs" in Rampur & Suar.' *The Print*, 7 February 2022. https://theprint.in/india/new-election-old-rivalry-jailed-azamkhan-son-make-it-people-vs-nawabs-in-rampur-suar/821653/.

183. Singh, Shashi Kumar. 'Immortal Saga of Courage and Struggle: Indira Gandhi.' *Indian National Congress*, 7 November 2024. https://inc.in/congress-sandesh/tribute/immortal-saga-of-courage-andstruggle-indira-gandhi.

184. Shukla, Shashi. 'Political Participation of Muslim Women.' *The Indian Journal of Political Science* 57, no. 1/4 (1996): 1–13. https://www.jstor.org/stable/41855734.

185. Abdullah, Sheikh Mohammad. *The Blazing Chinar*. Kashmir: Gulshan Books, 2023.

185. Joy, Shemin. 'Private Members' Bills on AI to Be Tabled in Rajya Sabha.' *Deccan Herald*, 26 July 2024. www.deccanherald.com/india/private-members-bills-on-ai-to-be-tabled-in-rajya-sabha-3123018.

186. Murarka, Shloka. 'Meet Iqra Hasan: SOAS Alum Making History as India's Youngest Female Muslim MP.' *SOAS University of London*, 16 July 2024. https://www.soas.ac.uk/about/blogs/meetiqra-hasan-soas-alum-making-history-indias-youngest-femalemuslim-mp-0.
187. Bose, Shohini. 'BJP Lists 5 Reasons for Dumping the PDP in Jammu & Kashmir.' *The Quint*, 20 June 2018. www.thequint.com/videos/news-videos/bjp-lists-5-reasons-for-dumping-the-pdp-in-jandk#read-more.
188. Chakraborty, Snehamoy. 'Nusrat Jahan Ends Silence on Sandeshkhali, Says "Always Followed Party Guidelines".' *The Telegraph*, 26 February 2024. https://www.telegraphindia.com/west-bengal/nusrat-jahan-endssilence-on-sandeshkhali-says-always-followed-party-guidelines/cid/2002935.
189. Nandi, Soumitra. 'Won't Allow Outsiders to Capture Bengal.' *Millennium Post*, 28 February 2025. www.millenniumpost.in/big-stories/wont-allow-outsiders-to-capture-bengal-600543.
190. De Sarkar, Soumya. 'Fresh Erosion in Malda.' *The Telegraph*, 4 September 2020. www.telegraphindia.com/west-bengal/fresh-erosion-in-malda/cid/1790885.
191. Ali, Subhashini. 'A Life in Service.' *Seminar* 540 (August 2004). www.india-seminar.com/2004/540/540%20subhashini%20ali.htm.
192. Rinehart, Sue Tolleson. *Gender Consciousness and Politics*. New York: Routledge, 1992.
193. Roy, Suryagni. 'Don't Need to Hold Political Post to Do Good Work: Ex-MP Nusrat Jahan.' *India Today*, 16 July 2024. https://www.indiatoday.in/india/story/nusrat-jahan-formertrinamool-mp-on-political-future-bengal-2567754-2024-07-16.
194. Bourque, Susan C., and Jean Grossholtz. 'Politics an Unnatural Practice: Political Science Looks at Female Participation.' *Politics and Society* 4, no. 2 (June 1994): 225–266. https://doi.org/10.1177/003232927400400205.
195. Wright, Theodore P., Jr. 'Muslims and the 1977 Indian Elections: A Watershed?' *Asian Survey* 17, no. 12 (December 1977): 1207–1220.
196. TNN. 'President Fakhruddin Resented Indira, Sanjay's Family Planning Policy: WikiLeaks.' *The Times of India*, 10 April 2013. https://timesofindia.indiatimes.com/india/president-fakruddinahmed-resented-indira-sanjays-family-planning-policywikileaks/articleshow/19468622.cms.
197. TNN. 'Mid-Air "Collision" Scare over Patna.' *Times of India*, 22 July 2011. https://timesofindia.indiatimes.com/city/guwahati/mid-air-collision-scare-over-patna/articleshow/9315065.cms.

198. Chamorro-Premuzic, Tomas. 'If Women Are Better Leaders, Then Why Are They Not in Charge?' *Forbes*, 7 March 2021. www.forbes.com/sites/tomaspremuzic/2021/03/07/if-women-are-better-leaders-then-why-are-they-not-in-charge/.
199. Rashid, Toufiq. 'Why the Kashmir Protests in 2010 and 2016 Are Different.' *Hindustan Times*, 18 August 2016. www.hindustantimes.com/india-news/kashmir-s-summers-of-discontent-why-the-protests-in-2010-and-2016-are-different/story-xy9w5KiPO7VGSehQcwJ2bM.html.
200. Tribune News Service. 'Vajpayee Invites CM for Talks: Farooq's Mother Laid to Rest.' *The Tribune*, 11 July 2000. www.tribuneindia.com/2000/20000712/main1.htm.
201. TwoCircles.net Staff Reporter. 'NC Pays Tributes to Begum Akbar Jahan.' *TwoCircles.net*, 12 July 2007. www.twocircles.net/2007jul12/nc_pays_tributes_begum_akbar_jahan.html.
202. UN Women – Asia-Pacific. 'Political Participation of Women.' n.d. https://asiapacific.unwomen.org/en/focus-areas/governance/political-participation-of-women.
203. Randall, Vicky. *Women and Politics: An International Perspective*. 2nd ed. Basingstoke: Palgrave Macmillan, 1987.
204. Singh, Vijaita. 'Women's Reservation Bill Will Only Be Implemented Only After 2029: Amit Shah.' *The Hindu*, 20 September 2023. https://www.thehindu.com/news/national/womens-reservationbill-will-be-implemented-only-after-2029-amit-shah/article67327038.ece.
205. Jawed, Zeeshan. 'Parties in Power Play over Heritage Institute.' *The Telegraph*, 3 March 2012. www.telegraphindia.com/west-bengal/parties-in-power-play-over-heritage-institute/cid/1281037.
206. Zenger, Jack, and Joseph Folkman. 'Research: Women Score Higher Than Men in Most Leadership Skills.' *Harvard Business Review*, 25 June 2019. https://hbr.org/2019/06/research-women-score-higher-than-men-in-most-leadership-skills.
207. Majid, Zulfikar. 'Mehbooba Mufti Unanimously Re-Elected PDP Chief.' *Deccan Herald*, 26 October 2023. www.deccanherald.com/india/jammu-and-kashmir/mehbooba-mufti-unanimously-re-elected-pdp-chief-2742668.

Acknowledgements

This book would not have been possible without the active support and prodding by Swati Chopra, editorial director of Juggernaut Books. At every stage of writing and editing, Swati remained a part of us, giving valuable and fitting advice. We would also like to thank Jyotsna Raman and Rhea Gupta for their editorial support, and Gunjan Ahlawat for the cover design.

Among friends and associates, we would like to name Sheela Bhatt, Alim Bazmi, Ananda Sen, Sumit Dasgupta and his ALLCAPS team, Arnab Ganguly, Anup Dutta, Naghma Sahar, Priya Sahgal, Nistula Hebbar, Nirmal Pathak, Sunetra Choudhury, Ketan Trivedi, Ibad Ur Rahman, Dr Haneef and Mahant Rajendranand Giri, for their inputs, help, assistance and support in providing deeper insight into many of the characters in the book. Without their cooperation, the book may not have materialized. Thus, it is our privilege to acknowledge our debt and gratitude to them. As authors, we bear all responsibility for the views expressed and for all its shortcomings. A special word of appreciation to Dr Farah Kidwai for her patience with my constant traveling during the many months when this work was in progress. Grateful to Dr Rahul V Karad, executive president of MIT-WPU, Pune for his guidance and support. MIT-WPU generously offered it's resources and useful research material.

– Rasheed Kidwai

I wholeheartedly share and endorse Mr Kidwai's acknowledgements provided above. I would like to make few more additions to this inexhaustive list. I express my sincere gratitude to a number of experts, academics, journalists, working professionals, party leaders and workers who have shared their valuable insights which have been instrumental for the completion of this book. My special gratitude goes to many friends and acquaintances whom we came across during the fieldtrips for this project, who extended relentless and unconditional help for us to connect with the relevant respondents to make this endeavour a success. Fellow friends from the academia, Dr Udayan Das and Mr Abhinav Borbora have been extremely encouraging in supporting me to write this book. I want to extend my sincere thanks to my loved one, my parents and all my friends who remained not only patient and considerate towards me but have also been supportive enough to give me the motivation to finish this project. Importantly, I want to mention a special word of appreciation for my life partner Debosmita whose support, encouragement, valuable feedback and constant presence throughout this period helped me to overcome all odds for ensuring that I could give my best to this project. Lastly, I want to extend my heartfelt affection and gratitude to my co-author, Mr Kidwai, for trusting me with this challenging project, for giving me a fascinating learning opportunity, and for showing his eternal patience and kindness that helped us to work as a great team to make this happen. Also, it is absolutely essential to reiterate that Swati and the entire editorial team of Juggernaut Books has been indispensable in taking this project towards its meticulous and fulfilling completion.

– Ambar Kumar Ghosh

We would both also like to thank Sujit Kumar Ghosh and Saktidas Roy at ABP Pvt. Ltd. for providing us with the photos we've included in the book.

A Note on the Authors

Rasheed Kidwai is a journalist, author, columnist and a political analyst. A former associate editor of *The Telegraph*, Kidwai tracks government, politics, community affairs and Hindi cinema. Kidwai is the author of *Sonia: A Biography*; *24 Akbar Road: A Short History of the People behind the Fall and Rise of the Congress*; *Ballot: Ten Episodes That Have Shaped India's Democracy*; *Neta Abhineta: Bollywood Star Power in Indian Politics*; *Bharat Ke Pradhanmantri: Desh, Dasha, Disha*; and *The House of Scindias: A Saga of Power, Politics and Intrigue*. He is co-author of *The Scam That Shook a Nation: The Nagarwala Scandal* with Prakash Patra, *My Life in Indian Politics* with Mohsina Kidwai, and *Five Decades in Politics* with Sushil Kumar Shinde. A graduate from St. Stephen's College, New Delhi, Kidwai holds a master's degree in mass communication from the University of Leicester, United Kingdom. He also contributes as a political analyst to numerous television news channels.

Ambar Kumar Ghosh is a political scientist who works on diverse areas, including political leadership and institutions, welfare politics, constitutionalism, women and youth political participation, governance, and electoral politics in India. He is a Young Researchers' Network (YRN) Fellow with the Youth Democracy Cohort, European Partnership for Democracy, Brussels. He recently completed his PhD from the Department of International Relations, Jadavpur University, Kolkata. He was a member of the Tokyo Youth Democracy Forum 2024. He has authored a number of research papers and book chapters on issues concerning domestic politics and democratic governance. He has also participated in a number of international workshops, conferences, and panel discussions. He regularly contributes commentaries and opinion pieces to newspaper columns and digital platforms.